The Complete Guide to Acquisitions Management

Library and Information Sciences Text Series

The Academic Library: Its Context, Its Purpose, and Its Operation.
By John M. Budd.

Information Sources in Science and Technology. 3rd ed. By C. D. Hurt.

The School Library Media Center. 5th ed. By Emanuel T. Prostano and Joyce S. Prostano.

The School Library Media Manager. 2nd ed. By Blanche Woolls.

Introduction to Library Public Services. 6th ed. By G. Edward Evans, Anthony J. Amodeo, and Thomas L. Carter.

A Guide to the Library of Congress Classification. 5th ed. By Lois Mai Chan.

The Organization of Information. By Arlene G. Taylor.

Developing Library and Information Center Collections. 4th ed. By G. Edward Evans, with the assistance of Margaret R. Zarnosky.

The Humanities: A Selective Guide to Information Sources. 5th ed. By Ron Blazek and Elizabeth Aversa.

Wynar's Introduction to Cataloging and Classification. 9th ed. By Arlene G. Taylor.

Systems Analysis for Librarians and Information Professionals. 2nd ed. By Larry N. Osborne and Margaret Nakamura.

The Economics of Information: A Guide to Economic and Cost-Benefit Analysis for Information Professionals. 2nd ed. By Bruce R. Kingma.

Reference and Information Services: An Introduction. 3rd ed. Richard E. Bopp and Linda C. Smith, General Editors.

The Collection Program in Schools: Concepts, Practices, and Information Sources. 3rd ed. By Phyllis Van Orden and Kay Bishop, with the assistance of Patricia Pawelak-Kort.

Libraries in the Information Age: An Introduction and Career Exploration. By Denise K. Fourie and David R. Dowell.

The Social Sciences: A Cross-Disciplinary Guide to Selected Sources. 3rd ed. Nancy L. Herron, General Editor.

Introduction to Technical Services. 7th ed. By G. Edward Evans, Sheila S. Intner, and Jean Weihs.

Library Information Systems: From Library Automation to Distributed Information Access Solutions. By Thomas R. Kochtanek and Joseph R. Matthews.

United States Government Information: Policies and Sources. By Peter Hernon, Harold C. Relyea, Robert E. Dugan, and Joan F. Cheverie.

Library and Information Center Management. 6th ed. By Robert D. Stueart and Barbara B. Moran.

THE COMPLETE GUIDE TO ACQUISITIONS MANAGEMENT

Library and Information Sciences Text Series

Frances C. Wilkinson

Associate Dean of Library Services
The University of New Mexico
Albuquerque, New Mexico

Linda K. Lewis

Director of Collection Management and
Resource Acquisitions
The University of New Mexico
Albuquerque, New Mexico

A Member of the Greenwood Publishing Group

Westport, Connecticut • London

Library of Congress Cataloging-in-Publication Data

Wilkinson, Frances C.
   The complete guide to acquisitions management / Frances C. Wilkinson and Linda K. Lewis.
      p.   cm.—(Library and information sciences text series)
   Includes index.
   ISBN 1-56308-890-8 (alk. paper)—ISBN 1-56308-892-4 (pbk. : alk. paper)
   1. Acquisitions (Libraries)—United States. I. Lewis, Linda K. II. Title. III. Series.

Z689.5.U6W54   2003
025.2—dc21   2003053880

British Library Cataloguing in Publication Data is available.

Library of Congress Card Catalog Number: 2003053880
ISBN: 1-56308-890-8
         1-56308-892-4 (pbk.)

First published in 2003

Libraries Unlimited, 88 Post Road West, Westport, CT 06881
A Member of the Greenwood Publishing Group, Inc.
www.lu.com

Printed in the United States of America

(∞)™

The paper used in this book complies with the Permanent Paper Standard issued by the National Information Standards Organization (Z39.48-1984).

10   9   8   7   6   5   4   3   2   1

Copyright Acknowledgments

Extracts from *American Library Association Code of Ethics* (http://www.ala.org/alaorg/oif/ethics.html); *Library Bill of Rights* (http://www.ala.org/work/freedom/lbr.html); American Library Association, "Librarianship: Core Values" (http://www.ala.org/congress/corevalues/draft.html); American Library Association, ALCTS, *Guidelines for ALCTS Members to Supplement the American Library Association Code of Ethics* (http://www.ala.org/alcts/publicatons/ethics/ethics.html); and American Library Association, ALCTS, Acquisitions Section, *Statement on Principles and Standards of Acquisitions Practice* (http://www.ala.org/alcts/publications/ethics/aesthics.html) reprinted with permission.

Excerpts from Frances C. Wilkinson and Connie Capers Thorson, *The RFP Process: Effective Management of the Acquisition of Library Materials* (Englewood, CO: Libraries Unlimited, 1998) reprinted with permission.

To my acquisitions and serials colleagues, especially those at the University of New Mexico General Library and the North American Serials Interest Group. I value what you have taught me and I treasure the friends that I have made.

—Fran

To my mother, Elva Page Lewis.

—Linda

Contents

Acknowledgments

Fran and Linda gratefully acknowledge many of our colleagues, friends, and relatives for their assistance and support as we wrote this book. Our special thanks go to the members of the University of New Mexico General Library Collections and Technology Services division for their advice, encouragement, and support. Also special thanks to Sue Awe, Dan Barkley, Donna Cromer, and Kate Luger for their reference assistance; Rita Critchfield for her assistance with human resources issues—she is also the best mediator in the business; Nancy Dennis for her guidance on information technology and for reviewing every IT term in the glossary; Rasma Goldfeder for her assistance with fiscal processes, her ability to always have just the right descriptive word, and her role as a human thesaurus; Brenda Maler for her incredible knowledge of Microsoft Word and its many "features" as well as her incredible patience; and Randy Moorhead and his team for their speedy delivery of hard-to-find materials via interlibrary loan.

Our unending gratitude goes to Roberta Innan and Gail Lane, who read and edited every word of this book before we submitted it to Libraries Unlimited. We could say that the book would not have been as understandable and organized without their assistance, but in reality we doubt that we could have done it at all without them. Fran credits Gail for more than ten years of guiding her to write in a clearer, stronger fashion. Special thanks also go to Jonathan Haus, our "midnight" editor.

And finally, we thank Fran's at-home office staff, Bosco (the Himalayan), Wrarebit de Azul "Bitsy" (the Russian Blue), and Tomisita Olivia "Toon" (the red tiger tabby), for keeping our spirits up, entertaining us, and serving as paperweights for whichever chapters we were trying to work on at the time.

Introduction

Several years ago, the authors of this book were looking for a single, up-to-date text on acquisitions for training staff new to the field. Various books on either technical services or collection management contained chapters on the subject but did not treat it comprehensively. In *Technical Services Today and Tomorrow* (Michael Gorman, ed., Libraries Unlimited, 1998), Karen A. Schmidt states that "this activity [acquisitions work] was once well described, comprehensively and in detail in *Melcher on Acquisitions* and Ford's *The Acquisition of Library Materials*, published in 1971 and 1973 respectively. Though Melcher and Ford have not aged well as guides to acquisitions practices today, no one has attempted to supersede them with an up-to-date standard guide to acquisitions work and issues."

The authors wondered if others saw the same need for an up-to-date book on acquisitions. In the summer of 1999, they conducted the "Survey of ALA Accredited M.L.S. Programs: Teaching of Acquisitions in M.L.S. Courses." The survey was sent to all American Library Association–accredited library schools in the United States and Canada and consisted of five questions: Does your library and information science program offer a course in acquisitions? If not, do any of your courses include a component about acquisitions? If they do include a component, approximately what percentage of the course involves acquisitions? Do you use a textbook for this course or course component? Would a new textbook concerning acquisitions be useful to you? Slightly more than 64 percent of the schools responded to the survey. The authors found that while only 13.9 percent of library schools teach a course solely on acquisitions, 93.5 percent include a component on acquisitions in one or more of their courses. When asked if a new textbook concerning acquisitions would be useful to them, 79.3 percent said that it would be.

The authors intend this text to provide the reader with both procedural and philosophical approaches to acquisitions. They discuss how acquisitions departments are organized; explain what to look for when selecting an acquisitions system and how they work; provide insights into the publishing industry; advise how to select and evaluate book and serials vendors; describe how to acquire books, media, serials, electronic resources, out-of-print materials, and gifts and exchange programs as well as bindery operations; examine outsourcing acquisitions; and explore some thoughts about professional ethics.

The field of acquisitions is constantly changing. As these words are being written, new technologies are transforming library acquisitions. Librarians must stay ever vigilant, flexible, and current on new trends in the industry. To aid in this endeavor and supplement library literature, the authors provide an appendix with numerous Internet sites and print resources on topics related to acquisitions, including automated acquisitions systems, conferences and seminars, vendor sites, electronic discussion lists, journals, and organizations. A comprehensive glossary is also provided.

Chapter 1

Organization of Acquisitions Departments

WHAT IS ACQUISITIONS?

Acquisitions is the process of locating and acquiring all types of library materials after they have been selected for a library's collection. Others have defined acquisitions as follows:

- Acquisitions is "the process of identifying what the library ought to acquire, determining how and from whom it can be obtained, and actually getting it" (Magrill and Corbin 1989, vii).

- "Acquisitions work involves locating and acquiring the items identified as appropriate for the collection" (Evans 2000, 313).

- "The term *acquisitions* refers to the process of obtaining library materials after they have been selected....Acquisitions includes all the tasks related to obtaining all kinds of library materials" (Heitshu 1991, 101–2).

- "Acquisitions is the process of acquiring library materials.... Acquisitions includes *all* tasks related to obtaining *all* library materials" (Diedrichs and Schmidt 1999, 1).

Acquisitions departments are generally located in technical services divisions. Technical services operations provide access to information in all its many forms and formats. Functions in technical services divisions may include

- identifying and selecting materials for the library's collection;
- preorder searching to identify duplicate orders and to verify correct author and title as well as availability and price;
- ordering materials from vendors or publishers;
- negotiating licensing agreements and contracts for electronic resources;
- claiming materials not delivered within the expected time frame;
- receiving materials;
- approving invoices for payment;
- physical processing such as ownership identification, security taping, and call number marking;
- binding; and
- preserving materials as needed.

In some libraries, acquisitions staff may also perform copy cataloging and may interact directly with the public through a service window or desk or via email.

Staff in public services divisions work more directly with the public. Public services operations help library patrons locate and use appropriate materials to meet their needs. Public services divisions may include information, reference, government documents, circulation, reserves, interlibrary loan, and instruction (either individual or group instruction).

Organizational structures in libraries may vary significantly from library to library. Collection management, which handles the identification and selection of materials for the library's collection, may be located in either technical or public services divisions. The same variations hold true for library information technology operations, which are an integral part of all aspects of the modern library.

Regardless of the library's organizational structure, all acquisitions departments have the same core functions. "The fundamental aspects of acquisitions work—financial management, acquisitions of material regardless of its disposition, negotiation of contracts, service-oriented activities, and personnel management, for example—continue to be critical to the fulfillment of the goal of libraries' work that reflects the very best principles of service and stewardship" (Diedrichs and Schmidt 1999, 10).

The mission and goals of the acquisitions operation evolve from the library's mission and goals, just as the library's mission and goals evolve from the parent institution's mission and goals. The acquisitions staff must be committed to attaining these goals. The work of the acquisitions department should never be seen as an end in itself. Rather, the staff must understand that the context of the acquisitions operation within the library, regardless of its type or size, is to best serve its external and internal customers.

A typical mission statement for acquisitions might read thus: "The mission of the Acquisitions Department is to support the mission of the parent institution by acquiring, processing, and providing access to materials for the collection in an efficient, cost-effective, timely, accurate, and courteous manner."

Although goals will be specific to each operation and will typically vary from year to year, goals of an acquisitions department might include establishing performance standards and average turnaround times for tasks, analyzing and streamlining a departmental procedure, implementing new software, or evaluating vendor performance.

Acquisitions departments are service units to both collection management and cataloging and serve as a conduit between the two. Acquisitions departments work with these departments in both an independent and coordinated way. For example, the ordering process is an independent operation in the acquisitions department, in that the process has a distinct beginning and end. However, the ordering process is also a coordinated process that is part of the entire selection and cataloging workflow and must be coordinated with those departments. The role of the acquisitions department is "to serve, to accommodate, and to adjust" (Hewitt 1989, 111).

The core functions of acquisitions operations remain the same regardless of the type of library or number of its staff. "No matter how much the work is automated or what portion of it is placed in the hands of an outside agency, acquisitions staffs are still needed to make certain that the library secures the materials needed by its clientele, that these materials are appropriately entered into the library's files, and that they are purchased within the constraints of the library's budget" (Magrill and Corbin 1989, 76–77).

Types of Libraries

Academic and research libraries, providing for the information needs of students, faculty, and scholars, often have large acquisitions departments. Public libraries endeavor to support the information needs of the communities they serve and may range in size from one-person libraries to very large multilibrary systems, with their acquisitions operations varying in size accordingly. School libraries provide for the information needs of students and teachers. The acquisitions processing for public school systems is frequently centralized through the school system, while private schools often either handle their acquisitions on-site or outsource them. Special libraries provide for the information needs of a defined group such as an association, a corporation or company, or a government agency. They range in size from one-person operations to very large ones, and their in-house acquisitions operations vary accordingly; however, they frequently outsource their acquisitions functions.

Types of Customers

External customers of the library, often interchangeably referred to as patrons, users, or clients, are generally well known. Usually the acquisitions staff does not deal directly with this group of external customers, but their goal is to meet the information needs of the customer by acquiring library materials. Their external contacts include publishers and vendors. These external customers of acquisitions departments may include companies or individuals that produce or supply the materials being acquired for the library.

Their internal customers are coworkers, supervisors, and subordinates in the department, library, and parent institution. Internal customers within the parent institution that acquisitions staff may deal with include purchasing and legal departments for negotiations of contracts and site licenses for electronic materials, human resources departments for personnel management issues and training, and financial and accounting departments.

HOW ARE ACQUISITIONS DEPARTMENTS ORGANIZED?

Acquisitions departments are organized to perform a variety of functions and to obtain materials in a variety of forms. In small libraries, one or several persons may share all library tasks with acquisitions processes playing a small role in their overall job. In larger libraries, especially academic libraries, but also in large public libraries or in centralized technical processing units for public library systems or school library systems, acquisitions departments may be much larger, with numerous staff positions and areas of responsibility.

To better understand why an acquisitions department is organized the way it is in a given institution, one needs to consider the philosophical underpinnings of the technical services operation. An initial and informative question is "Are its departments divided by form or by function?"

Some libraries have separate departments that acquire only selected formats. These libraries are organized by form. For example, a library may have an acquisitions department that acquires nonrecurring materials such as books and a separate serials department that acquires materials issued in successive parts and intended to continue indefinitely, such as magazines, journals, newspapers, and yearbooks.

At the same time, the acquisition of specialized materials may be handled in departments other than acquisitions departments, where such specialized materials are acquired as a small part of the departments' overall mission. These departments may perform both technical services and public services functions. For example, government documents may be acquired in a separate government documents department, and rare books may be acquired in a special collections department. When specialized materials are acquired outside the acquisitions department, the department acquiring the material should coordinate policies and procedures with the acquisitions department to minimize confusion.

Other libraries that are organized by function may have separate departments that order materials, receive materials, or authorize payment for materials, or a combination thereof, or perhaps they will have a single acquisitions department that acquires materials in all formats—print, electronic, microform, and so on—and in all forms—books, serials, media, and so on.

Whether technical services divisions organize their departments by form or function has received considerable attention in the library literature. Acquisitions departments and serials departments have experienced considerable turmoil and evolution over time.

Serials first appeared on the publishing scene in the seventeenth century, but centralized serials departments did not begin to appear, at least in American libraries, prior to the 1930s (Potter 1981, 85). Around that time, staff in acquisitions departments began to specialize in serials and were later moved into newly created serials departments that handled all serials operations from ordering to cataloging. Since those early days, libraries have vacillated between serials functions being performed centrally in acquisitions departments and being accomplished in separate serials departments. For example, in a 1987 survey of Association of Research Libraries (ARL) members, Schmidt (1987, 37) found that 57 percent of libraries had separate monographic and serials acquisitions departments. By 1994, Wilson (1994, 51) reported that the most frequently mentioned change at an Association of Library Collections and Technical Services (ALCTS) Creative Ideas in Technical Services Discussion Group involved serials units being absorbed into acquisitions departments. In a 1997 survey of ARL members, Wilkinson and Bordeianu (2000, 6) found that serials management most frequently occurs in a combined acquisitions and serials department. Recent trends in reorganization in technical services have involved combining acquisitions and serials functions with collection management, with interlibrary loan and document delivery, and with copy cataloging. No one model is superior because organizational structures develop and grow to meet the needs of each institution.

In addition to organization by form or function, methods of acquisition may play a role in how acquisitions departments are organized. In addition to purchasing materials, acquisitions departments can acquire materials as gifts from donors, through library exchange programs with other libraries or organizations, through leasing and license agreements, and by borrowing them for a specified time from other libraries through interlibrary loan programs.

STAFFING AND MANAGING ACQUISITIONS UNITS

Acquisitions personnel order, receive, and pay for materials of all types, in all formats, from all sources. They may use online ordering systems or purchase materials from people at street fairs. Many acquisitions personnel review electronic contracts and select online ordering systems. To accomplish these functions, acquisitions personnel need a variety of skills. Technical knowledge of acquisitions work and systems is very important; however, some personal characteristics are perhaps even more valuable. Acquisitions personnel—indeed all library personnel—should be adaptable and flexible. Libraries are continually changing, and personnel must be able to deal with the evolution of technology in the world of publishing. Personnel should be able to analyze situations, apply common sense, and resolve problems. They must be able to communicate with others in the department and the organization.

The staff need increasingly well-developed technical skills. Most libraries use some automated systems; large libraries frequently have integrated library systems in which system modules work together to perform functions such as ordering, cataloging, and circulation and to serve as the library's online public catalog. Acquisitions personnel must be able to use online systems developed by libraries and vendors, as well as be able to search the Internet effectively. "In order to adjust successfully to patron needs, budget pressures, and networked information complexities, libraries need staff who understand how to relate their expertise to other library functions and services" (Ray 1998, 80).

Managers and heads of acquisitions units or departments need additional skills. Managers must be able to supervise personnel, develop and evaluate procedures, and define and implement priorities. "An acquisitions department is unlike most other departments in the library, except perhaps circulation. In acquisitions, there are generally few professional librarians and a larger support staff. . . . This high concentration of paraprofessional and clerical staff requires that the acquisitions librarian possess excellent managerial skills" (German 1998, 347). Typically, large academic or major public library acquisitions departments have one or two professional librarians and several paraprofessional and clerical staff members. Smaller libraries may have one or two staff who make up a technical services unit, which includes acquisitions and cataloging functions.

In addition to personnel management, acquisitions managers are responsible for a wide range of duties including working with vendors, maintaining accurate financial records, and cooperating with other library departments. "As the bridge between the profit and not-for-profit worlds, the average acquisitions librarian has to have—among other things—a strong set of financial skills; understand the publishing industry in all its formats, old and new; be able to deal with a wide variety of librarians and sales people; have good bibliographic skills; be a skilled negotiator; understand the nature of serials; and be able to select, implement, and manage an automated system" (German and Schmidt 2000, 139).

Acquisitions librarians deal with negotiations and contracts for electronic resources, and often they must teach their institutions what the contracts involve for libraries. They must deal with consortium agreements in which a number of libraries join together to produce more advantageous pricing arrangements and other negotiated items. Acquisitions personnel must work more closely than ever before with systems, cataloging, and public services departments. In an analysis of advertisements for acquisitions librarians, Fisher (2001, 182) discovered that the most frequently desired qualifications included acquisitions experience, employee supervision, communication skills, systems knowledge, and interpersonal skills.

The American Library Association provides resources for personnel at all levels. The Library Administration and Management Association provides information, sponsors institutes, and publishes a journal; see http://www.ala.org (accessed June 1, 2003) for more information. The American Library Association has a group for paraprofessionals, the Library Support Staff Interests Round Table; see http://www.ala.org (accessed June 1, 2003) for more information and resources. In addition, many library groups offer workshops at regional locations or on the Internet. The American Library Association has offered short tutorials in which lessons were sent by email. Regional bibliographic utilities such as AMIGOS frequently give workshops on a variety of topics. State libraries may host workshops broadcast over satellites. State and regional library groups often give workshops and conferences. Colleges and universities may have employee training programs that offer courses in personal computers or management skills.

FUNCTIONS OF ACQUISITIONS UNITS

The basic function of acquisitions is to obtain materials for library users. That process has many steps, and they continue to develop with the growth of electronic resources. The tools used in acquisitions work have changed dramatically in recent years. Online bookstores such as Amazon.

com and the information about titles in stock at warehouses one finds in R. R. Bowker's *Books in Print* give acquisitions personnel information that would have astonished previous generations of acquisitions librarians.

The acquisitions process begins with a decision to acquire specific materials. In large libraries, that decision is usually made in a collection development department. In smaller libraries, all personnel may recommend purchases. Many libraries ask for suggestions from their patrons as well. Once the desired items have been identified, the acquisitions process begins.

The functions of the acquisitions process remain largely the same regardless of the size of the library. In small libraries one person may perform all the functions, while in large academic, research, public, or school-system libraries each function may be performed by several people who specialize in only that function.

In 1989, Magrill and Corbin (1989, 78–80) composed the following list of the functions of an acquisitions unit:

- Obtaining information about materials
- Initiating the purchasing process
- Maintaining records for materials ordered
- Receiving and checking materials
- Authorizing payment for materials
- Clearing order records
- Claiming and canceling orders
- Handling materials that need special treatment
- Dealing with special situations
- Developing and analyzing performance statistics

While many things have changed in acquisitions since 1989, these core activities remain the basic functions of an acquisitions unit. The major changes have been in the way the functions are carried out and in the addition of the task of acquiring electronic resources. In some libraries, acquisitions personnel may also perform copy cataloging, which is a process of cataloging materials by taking the existing records for a title from resources such as WorldCat and using them in the library's catalog with minimal changes to the records.

The way acquisitions functions are performed has changed largely due to the advent and proliferation of the electronic capabilities of the Internet and integrated library systems. Acquisitions functions once performed using paper-based tools are now usually accomplished using computer-based tools. Materials once identified in the print format of *Books in Print* or in paper catalogs from publishers or vendors are now identified through online tools. Integrated library systems in many larger libraries and database software used by many smaller libraries have made it possible to track materials throughout the acquisitions process, replacing the multitude of paper files previously kept.

When books and serials are purchased in paper format, they are processed and shelved and will theoretically be available in perpetuity (unless they are lost, stolen, or withdrawn or they physically deteriorate). Some electronic resources may be acquired with the intent that the library will own them and make them available in perpetuity. Others are leased for a given time and may be renewed. If the library chooses not to renew them, all access to them ceases. Still other electronic resources may be purchased as individual articles for patrons without intending to add the items to the permanent collection of the library. Even in these cases, acquisitions personnel are responsible for identifying, acquiring, and arranging for payment for the materials. For detailed information about the acquisitions process, see chapter 5, "Acquiring Books and Media"; chapter 6, "Acquiring Serials"; chapter 7, "Acquiring Electronic Resources"; chapter 8, "Acquiring Out-of-Print and Antiquarian Materials"; and chapter 9, "Gifts and Exchange Programs."

CONCLUSION

Acquisitions departments are responsible for getting the materials needed by the libraries' users, in the most appropriate format and in the most efficient manner. Formats and methods change, but the responsibility and the functions of acquiring library materials remain at the core of the acquisitions department.

REFERENCES

Diedrichs, Carol Pitts, and Karen A. Schmidt. 1999. Acquisitions, the organization, and the future. In *Understanding the business of library acquisitions*. 2nd ed. Edited by Karen A. Schmidt. Chicago: American Library Association.

Evans, G. Edward. 2000. *Developing library and information center collections*. 4th ed. Englewood, CO: Libraries Unlimited.

Fisher, William. 2001. Core competencies for the acquisitions librarian. *Library Collections, Acquisitions, and Technical Services* 25: 179–90.

German, Lisa. 1998. Serials acquisitions: Trends and prospects. In *Technical services today and tomorrow*, edited by Michael Gorman. Englewood, CO: Libraries Unlimited.

German, Lisa, and Karen A. Schmidt. 2000. Acquisitions. *Advances in Librarianship* 24: 139–55.

Heitshu, Sara C. 1991. Acquisitions. In *Library technical services: Operations and management*. 2nd ed. Edited by Irene P. Godden. San Diego: Academic Press.

Hewitt, Joe A. 1989. On the nature of acquisitions. *Library Resources and Technical Services* 33: 105–22.

Magrill, Rose Mary, and John Corbin. 1989. *Acquisitions management and collection development in libraries*. 2nd ed. Chicago: American Library Association.

Potter, William Gray. 1981. Form or function? An analysis of the serials department in the modern academic library. *Serials Librarian* 6: 85–96.

Ray, Ron. 1998. Where is the future of acquisitions written in the future of libraries? *Journal of Academic Librarianship* 24: 80–82.

Schmidt, Karen A. 1987. The acquisitions process in research libraries: A survey of ARL libraries' acquisitions departments. *Library Acquisitions: Practice and Theory* 11: 35–44.

Wilkinson, Frances C., and Sever Bordeianu. 2000. Using serials vendors in academic libraries, revisited: An ARL survey. *Advances in Serials Management* 7: 1–29.

Wilson, Karen A. 1994. Reorganization of technical services staff in the 90s: A report of the ALCTS Creative Ideas in Technical Services Discussion Group. Midwinter meeting of the American Library Association, February 1994, Los Angeles. *Technical Services Quarterly* 12: 50–55.

Chapter 2

Acquisitions Systems

Automated acquisitions systems range from systems that use software such as Microsoft Access on personal computers in very small public, special, or school libraries to specialized modules that are part of large integrated library systems (ILSs) in large academic or public libraries. Medium-sized libraries may use stand-alone acquisitions systems, which may be independent programs or may be modules that are part of an ILS. Integrated library systems consist of components or modules that work together to perform library functions such as acquisitions, serials, fund accounting, cataloging, circulation, reserve, online public access catalog functions, and access to the World Wide Web and databases. They provide on-site as well as remote use to patrons and library staff. "Thus 'automating the library' no longer refers only to computerizing operations in a discrete, physical place. It has assumed a wider frame of reference—namely that of enabling the library user to reach beyond what is 'merely' local to an information and knowledge base that is truly global and interconnected" (Cohn, Kelsey, and Fiels 2001, xv).

All areas within a library can share the records in an ILS; data entered when items are ordered by acquisitions can become the core of cataloging records. The integrated nature of such systems can lead to increased cooperation among library departments because each department shares and builds upon the information provided by other areas. "Automated acquisitions and serials control make it easier to monitor library materials expenditures, handle receiving and claiming of materials, pass descriptive and holdings information along to the catalog and the circulation system, collect useful management statistics and generally manage the business of buying and processing materials for the collection. Savings in staff time generally accrue as a result" (Beiser 1999, 127).

Even small automated systems that run on a personal computer can reduce paper files, improve the ability to track orders, and improve the ability to create reports. "With some of the free programs and a personal computer or two, any library can order books so much more efficiently and economically than it can with even the leanest staff doing it all manually that it is almost criminal *not* to take advantage of the technology" (Eaglen 2000, 119).

This chapter discusses the types of automated systems available for acquisitions and the factors to consider when selecting and implementing the systems.

HISTORY OF AUTOMATED SYSTEMS

Libraries began experimenting with automation in the 1930s when the University of Texas began using a punch-card serials system (Gardner 1986/87, 72–73). Serious efforts at developing computerized automated systems began in the 1950s and 1960s and became widespread in the 1970s (Boykin 1991, 10). Punched cards were replaced by computers that produced serials and book catalogs. As technology improved, librarians began using online, interactive computers in all areas of the library. These first attempts at library automation began with small, stand-alone modules, such as acquisitions, circulation, and online catalogs. Librarians wanted systems that would integrate all functions, but the technology required to do that was inadequate for many years. With the rapid improvement in computer technology, both vendors and libraries began to develop successful integrated systems in the late twentieth century.

Library systems have evolved through several generations, with each successive generation representing significant improvement over its predecessor. The first-generation systems, which consisted of stand-alone modules devoted to a specific function, were soon replaced by more powerful systems supporting Boolean logic. Third-generation systems began to appear in the late 1980s. These systems included free-text capabilities and tailored displays as well as online catalog links to multiple databases such as dictionaries, encyclopedias, and online indexes and bibliographies (Millsap 1996, 87). Fourth-generation systems began to realize true integration of modules so that acquisitions, serials, circulation, and the online catalog could all run from one single bibliographic record. By the late 1990s, most systems offered Web interfaces to their catalogs. As the Internet expanded, ILS vendors began providing the ability to link from their systems to Internet resources such as full-text databases.

QUESTIONS TO ASK BEFORE AUTOMATING OR MIGRATING

Whether a library is selecting a large integrated system or a software program that can track orders and expenditures, the process begins with some basic questions. Among the more important initial questions a library should ask are these: How does the institution select automation programs and equipment? What does the library want? What does the library need? What can the library afford?

Institutional Planning for Automation

Some organizations have technology plans that describe how technological growth will be carried out. Other institutions have purchasing preferences that include the types of computers or brands of software that will be acquired. Some state-funded libraries may be required to comply with state purchasing guidelines. Librarians considering automation projects must work closely with systems personnel and the purchasing officer within the library or the parent organization.

What Does the Library Want?

Libraries beginning to plan an automation project must define the specific goals of the project. Is the purpose to create or improve an online catalog? Or is the goal to improve the financial accounting and control of expenditures? Any automation project must contribute toward improving the library's ability to meet the institutional mission; a project that does not fulfill that goal should be abandoned.

What Does the Library Need?

Automation projects are nearly always costly, devouring money and personnel time. Libraries must decide what their basic needs are, as well as identify what additional functions they would like to have. Some ILS vendors offer products that are very strong in one area but only adequate in other areas. Libraries must identify the functions most important to their operations and concentrate on finding the best system that fills those needs.

What Can the Library Afford?

Large automation systems may require not only the initial purchase of the system but also annual maintenance charges, fees for later system upgrades, and money to implement the system. Libraries may need to purchase additional hardware, software, workstations, or telecommunications. Libraries must identify the money required for the initial purchase, the maintenance, and the upgrades. Some vendors may be willing to negotiate the total price; libraries should not hesitate to ask. Libraries may also be able to schedule payments to vendors over a few years if their institutions allow such arrangements.

TYPES OF AUTOMATED LIBRARY SYSTEMS

Automated library systems come in a wide range of types and sizes; some systems are appropriate for smaller special or public libraries, and some larger systems are designed for huge library systems and multilibrary consortia. Smaller systems may support only a few functions such as ordering or circulation. Larger integrated systems may provide a combination of functions ranging from ordering to online public access catalogs. Systems may be modular, allowing libraries to purchase specific functions separately and to add functions as the libraries' resources permit.

Automated library systems vary widely in the level of technical support the library must provide. Smaller libraries can adapt commercial software used on personal computers to create a local program to track orders, create financial reports, or function as an online catalog. Such independent programs require very little technical support from the software companies. Large libraries with extensive technology departments may develop "in-house" systems, essentially creating their own systems. Other libraries may select "turnkey" systems that are created by companies; these systems are designed to be ready to operate without major time or maintenance needed from the libraries. Libraries must decide whether they have the personnel necessary to develop and maintain systems created in-house or whether they have the financial resources to purchase a turnkey system. "The first integrated library systems were created for large libraries and groups of libraries. With every passing year, these large systems are evolving into even more elaborate, powerful and multifaceted products. Yet systems aimed at and priced for much smaller libraries are sprouting components and features that by name and general function directly correspond to their counterparts at the high end of the library automation marketplace" (Beiser 1999, 122). Libraries can find systems that will fill most of their needs if they analyze the systems carefully.

FUNCTIONS OF INTEGRATED LIBRARY SYSTEMS

Although all integrated library systems perform the same basic functions in all modules of the system, each system will have unique characteristics. Libraries must decide which functions are critically needed and which are desirable but not required for their operations.

Searching

Personnel should be able to retrieve the bibliographic records in an ILS by searching fields that include the author, title, subject, keywords, call numbers, and International Standard Serial Number (ISSN) or International Standard Book Number (ISBN). Other desirable search fields are the library's item record numbers, content notes, and the names of publishers and vendors. The system should allow search results to be combined or limited by factors such as publication date or format. Personnel in library systems with multiple locations should be able to limit searches to items held in specific libraries.

Library Control

Many vendors provide standard methods of displaying records and creating lists. Libraries should be able to adapt such vendor-supplied tools to create displays customized to meet their needs. Libraries should be able to decide how fields are to be displayed; for example, should an index of words in the bibliographic record include the name of the publisher? Libraries should be able to create the appearance of the display screens and the content of the help screens.

Access

Users will access the system from multiple buildings and locations. Personnel must be able to search the database, add new records, and alter existing records from any library location or from their homes when off-site work arrangements are permitted. Patrons should be able to search the online catalog and use the library's databases from their personal computers using any Internet service provider. For security reasons, this level of access may require that patrons and staff be issued passwords for some functions, or it may require that the library use a proxy server that identifies authorized users. The ILS should provide options allowing libraries to customize their chosen system.

Functionality

The ILS should support both textual and graphic presentations. While graphic formats are now dominant, the transition is not complete, and the system should still support both methods.

ILSs provide a number of fields that are assigned codes to identify factors such as format, language, order type, number of copies ordered, vendor, and so on. When libraries begin using a system, they should determine which codes are needed. Although new codes can be added later as libraries discover that something new is needed, it is best to add them when the system is initially configured. Using these codes, libraries can create lists and statistical reports quickly and easily. They should be able to create specialized reports in addition to the standard management reports the vendors create. Personnel should be able to print, download, and email reports.

The ILS should be reliable, with minimal interruptions in service. The system should have both basic and advanced search capabilities; should respond to searches quickly; and should be easy to learn, use, upgrade, and maintain. The documentation and help screens should be clear. Data in the ILS must be backed up regularly, at intervals determined by the library. If files are damaged or destroyed, libraries should be able to recover or recreate the information readily.

Libraries should be able to code selected records to mask them from patrons. For example, libraries may need to maintain records for items that could not be delivered or for items that are not available to the public such as books or journals library staff require in the performance of their jobs. Libraries frequently create levels of access to their databases, allowing only selected persons to alter the structure of or enter data in the database.

Libraries should be able to add internal notes that are not restricted to a specific MARC (machine-readable cataloging record) format in both order records and item records. The systems should allow notes that are masked from the public as well as notes that may be viewed by patrons. Vendors should follow library standards, such as MARC or ANSI (American National Standards Institute), and use standard programming languages that allow information from vendors to be imported and exported easily. "Following the MARC standard, though, is like following the Yellow Brick Road. You stray from it at your peril, substantially risking your chances of getting to the Emerald City—that is, to a successful automation project—without expensive, sometimes fatal, encounters with the Wicked Witch of Bibliographic Incompatibility" (Cohn, Kelsey, and Fields 2001, 175).

The ILSs must be able to link to Internet resources such as serials subscription vendor databases and full-text resources. New systems must be compatible with standard computing equipment such as personal computers, printers, and bar code readers. Nearly all systems are compatible with current computing equipment, but libraries with older computers should ask vendors whether their existing equipment will work with the newer systems. Some software programs that have extensive graphical features require personal computers with large amounts of memory in order to function effectively.

Vendors must provide customer support, supplying technical assistance and advice on the best methods to use the system. In addition to providing training and documentation, vendors should have personnel available to help libraries with problems. Many vendors have Internet sites or electronic discussion lists that are additional resources for users of their system.

TYPES OF ACQUISITIONS AND SERIALS SYSTEMS OR MODULES

Three general types of automated acquisitions systems are available from vendors. First, libraries may use a system in which an Internet password or software loaded on personal computers provides access to the database of a vendor. These programs allow libraries to order materials and monitor the status of their shipments. Most such programs are available from vendors who sell books or media to libraries; these systems provide information only about the library's orders with the specific vendor and cannot provide comprehensive financial reports. Second, libraries may purchase individual modules that perform functions such as ordering or serials check-in. These stand-alone modules do not connect with other modules in the library. Some of them are less complex and less expensive than integrated library systems, but they offer fewer functions and may require more local maintenance for problem solving and upgrades. Third, libraries may purchase complete integrated library systems that link all records from all library functions from the beginning of the ordering process through the circulation of the cataloged materials.

FUNCTIONS OF ACQUISITIONS MODULES

Acquisitions systems, whether stand-alone modules or components of integrated library systems, facilitate and manage the purchase of all types of library materials. In addition to the functions of ILSs discussed previously in this chapter, all acquisitions systems should have several functions specifically designed for the operations of ordering, claiming, receiving, and paying for materials.

Order Records

When an item is identified and is ready to be ordered, personnel must create an order record in the system. They may key the information into a standard format or download the information from another database. All systems will include fields for the basic information: author, title, bibliographic description, estimated price, date the item was ordered, the starting volume for serials, ISBN or ISSN, and vendor. More advanced systems will include fields for various information such as fund, number of copies, location, language, or format. Adding information to a record, such as responses from vendors concerning the status of orders, should be simple.

Claiming

If libraries do not receive items within a reasonable time as defined by the library, they must claim the items by asking the vendor to investigate the order. Libraries can program the acquisitions system to create these notices after a specified time period. Systems should also allow claims to be created whenever personnel identify problems with specific items. Often problems with delayed or missed serials are identified when staff observe when checking in a new issue that the previous issue was not received. A patron may request a book that is on order causing an expedited claim to be generated.

Financial Functions

Acquisitions modules must be able to perform fund-accounting functions such as allocating specific dollar amounts into one or a series of "funds" and tracking library expenditures. Some systems have a separate module for fund accounting, while others combine it with the acquisitions module.

Libraries allocate their materials budgets by creating funds with specific amounts that are designated for materials based either on format, such as serials, or on subject, such as science. While some libraries will have only one general fund, most will have many funds for specific subjects and locations. The responsibility for the allocation of the materials budget varies by library; in some libraries this function is done by collection management, in others by the library director, and in a few by the acquisitions librarian. Regardless of who makes the allocation decisions, acquisitions personnel are generally responsible for entering the allocations into the system.

Libraries must regularly monitor their expenditures against their allocations to effectively expend their materials budget. When an order is placed, the system must encumber the money in the proper category or fund.

Libraries should also be able to assign multiple funds to one item, such as a multidisciplinary title, and to track those expenditures appropriately. When items are received, the system must be able to show that the library has accepted the items, subtract the encumbrances, and record the money as expended. The system must allow libraries to cancel items easily and must then remove the encumbrances. Systems should have a mechanism to notify personnel when individual funds have been overspent. The systems should allow personnel to view the status of all funds online. Personnel should be able to create financial and statistical reports as needed.

Integrated systems should allow libraries to receive electronic invoices from vendors, enabling libraries to process large invoices automatically, thus saving the time and expense of reentering all the data manually.

Some institutional financial records management systems may be able to link to the library's ILS. Libraries should investigate this option with their vendors and fiscal services personnel.

FUNCTIONS OF SERIALS MODULES

Serials modules, whether stand-alone modules or components of ILSs, are designed for serials control. In addition to the general functions of ILSs and of acquisitions modules discussed previously in this chapter, serials modules will have several functions specifically designed to check in, route, and bind serials.

Check-In Records

Serials modules include functions that allow libraries to check in issues of serials. Personnel can enter the frequency of a title into the system, prompting the module to create a display that shows which issues have been received and when the next issues are expected. The system should allow personnel to change these patterns when serials change frequency. The check-in record should also allow personnel to record the arrival of special issues, supplements, and indexes. Serials modules can produce notices of issues that are late in arriving, based on the data entered in the check-in records, allowing personnel to claim issues from their subscription agents.

Many larger libraries assign classification numbers to their serials; the serials modules should be able to produce labels with the call number of the issues that are received. Libraries should be able to print labels with information such as the name of the journal, the name of the library, and the date the issue was received.

Routing

Most serials modules allow libraries to identify selected serials titles to be routed to one or more individuals on a routing list. Serials can be routed to selected library staff. They can also be routed to selected patrons. For example, in academic libraries a math journal may be routed to several faculty in the mathematics department, and in special libraries journals may be routed to researchers in the organization.

Binding Records

Some serials modules allow libraries to record what has been sent to the binder and how the serials volumes are to be bound each year. Some serials modules can interface with the computer systems used by some larger binders. This can reduce rekeying and improve the library's ability to process shipments being sent to binderies.

SELECTING AN AUTOMATED SYSTEM

Selecting an automated system must be done carefully; large systems are very expensive, and new systems change how all personnel work and how patrons use the library. Librarians must analyze their needs and the potential products thoroughly. Libraries must decide what they need, what they can afford, and what is available. In 1990, Basch and McQueen wrote, "When defining a library's serials acquisitions needs, there is no substitute for plain old-fashioned thinking" (99). More than a decade later, this opinion is still true for libraries selecting any type of automated system.

Librarians must learn whether their organization has procedures and regulations that apply to the purchase of an automated system. Some organizations require a request for proposal (RFP) for any purchase over a specified amount, such as $10,000. Please see chapter 4, "Domestic and Foreign Vendor Selection and Evaluation," for information about an RFP process that can be adapted to automated systems. Other institutions may have technology departments that approve all computer purchases.

First, the library must decide what type of system it needs. A small library that needs a basic accounting system may find that a commercial software program operating on a personal computer is adequate. In such cases, the librarians should ask whether their institution prefers a specific program. Large libraries and consortia may need to investigate integrated library systems with modules for all major library functions. "What processes within the library, present and future, do you want to automate?

What benefits do you expect to receive from doing so?...It is important to think these questions through ahead of time and be able to answer succinctly and convincingly" (Beiser 1999, 126).

Second, the library must decide what it can afford. Large ILSs require a major initial purchase fee. In addition to the initial costs, vendors may charge an annual maintenance fee. Libraries must also consider the costs required to install or upgrade equipment, telecommunications, and electrical wiring.

Before talking with vendors, libraries must compile data describing their organization. The needed information will include the nature of the library: its location, the number of buildings, the parent institution, and its mission. The vendor will also need to know the size of the library: the number of patrons, the number of volumes, the number of items circulated, the number of serials checked in, and the number of employees. Libraries must also identify their existing computer equipment, wiring, and telecommunications. The detailed analysis is vital; vendors need the information to provide accurate proposals.

When libraries have decided what they want and what they can afford and have gathered information describing themselves, they are ready to identify potential vendors. Libraries can consult several resources to identify possible vendors. Among the useful Internet sites are Library Technology Guides (http://www.librarytechnology.org, accessed June 1, 2003), AcqWeb (http://acqweb.library.vanderbilt.edu, accessed June 1, 2003), and Biblio Tech Review (http://www.biblio-tech.com, accessed June 1, 2003). Automation vendors exhibit at major library conferences; librarians can compare systems, meet with sales representatives, and request information. Some state libraries have technology consultants who can advise libraries.

Who Decides Which System to Purchase?

Because large integrated systems are expensive and affect nearly all library functions, many libraries create a committee to review the library's needs and recommend which systems should be purchased. The committee should include both managers and personnel who will work directly with the system; both views are crucially important. The committee should include representatives from the systems department who can evaluate the technical capabilities and requirements of the system. "Who should be involved? That varies from library to library. In some settings, the librarian and library staff can do the legwork and present their recommendations to the library's funding authority with little more than an occasional interim notice to that body that an effort is under way in this direction. In other environments, representation from a governing or administrative body in whatever planning and review process is undertaken is called for. In still others, the person in charge of computer and telecommunications technology, or perhaps someone with the title of Chief Information Officer, is the key player who should be involved to some degree from the start if the necessary approvals are to be forthcoming later on" (Beiser 1999, 125).

The committee must keep everyone informed of its progress. While the specific details of the negotiations must usually remain confidential, the committee should let everyone know which stages of the process are happening, notifying them when there are unanticipated delays.

Librarians should ask for opinions from library users. As patrons have become more experienced computer users, their expectations of library catalogs have increased. Patrons frequently want more flexibility and functionality than traditional catalogs provide. Libraries can gather information from surveys and focus groups. Even though meeting certain desires may not be possible, the opinions can help librarians identify priorities. Community awareness of and participation in the project can result in good public relations and perhaps even increased financial support.

Evaluating a System

After libraries have identified a few systems that appear to meet their needs, they must compare those systems carefully. Libraries should ask the vendors to provide demonstrations, to give the libraries access to trial versions of the systems, and to provide lists of libraries using the systems.

Libraries should schedule demonstrations when the selection committee and representative library personnel can attend. Any interested personnel should be able to attend; people who will work directly with the system should be required to attend. The selection committee should verify what equipment and telecommunications will be needed for the demonstrations. Personnel should be encouraged to ask questions and to use the trial databases. Any questions that the vendors' representatives cannot answer should be referred to their support personnel. The selection committee should persevere to obtain the answers.

Libraries must ask vendors for references from libraries that are similar to their size and mission. A system that functions well for a small special library may not perform as well for a large consortium. Members of the selection committee should agree on a list of basic questions to ask the references, such as the following: What are the best and worst features of this system? Is the customer service good? Is the system easy to use? If possible, libraries should test some of these systems as well as the vendors' trial databases in order to learn how the systems function in the actual working environment.

Libraries should investigate the vendors as well as their systems. Most companies will provide financial statements. In addition, libraries should review the financial information available about publicly owned companies. Libraries may also want to consider the reputation, management, and size of the companies. Libraries need to consider whether vendors have the resources to handle the library's database and to provide the level of service needed.

The selection committee can develop a checklist or evaluation sheet to document the rankings of each system. Such a sheet should list all factors being used to evaluate the products, such as the ease of ordering, the ability to import and export records, or the display of financial information. Each item can be assigned a range of points, with the most important items being assigned a higher percentage. This process of ranking factors can clarify the committee's decisions and provide documentation when composing recommendations.

Once a committee has reached its decision, it must present it to the administration. The recommendation must remain confidential until the process is complete; nothing is final until the contract has been negotiated and signed by the institutions.

SIGNING THE CONTRACT

Most agreements to purchase and maintain automated systems are legal contracts. Librarians must read the proposed agreement very carefully and clarify any portions that are unclear. The agreement should protect both library and vendor; therefore, the contract should be specific and understandable. It will have sections that define the parties, the material being purchased or leased, the costs, and the ways the contract can be terminated. The contract requires the signatures of individuals authorized to sign on behalf of the organization.

Definitions

Most contracts begin by identifying the parties involved in the agreement. If the library consists of multiple sites or if the agreement involves a consortium, the contract should indicate which institutions are participating.

The contract must identify what is being purchased. If a system has several versions or modules, the contract should specify which portion of the system the agreement covers. Many ILS vendors offer annual maintenance agreements and regular upgrades of the software; the contract should state whether such items are included. If the vendor has features in development and promises delivery within a stated time period, the contract should include a description of the features and the timeline.

Costs

The contract should state the purchase price and the timetable for payments. If the library is going to pay the vendor in multiple payments, the contract should include the amounts and the time periods. The contract should include any penalties that the library will owe if the payments are late. The contract should also include provisions for the library to withhold payments if the system does not perform satisfactorily. Some institutions may wish to put a portion of the payment in escrow until the new system is operating successfully.

Termination

Termination clauses define when and how the agreement can be ended. Reasons for terminating an agreement may include the failure of the library to pay the vendor on time or the failure of the vendor to deliver a working system. The contract should state how failure will be determined, what notice of termination is required, and how the disagreement will be resolved. Although libraries and vendors rarely need such legal guarantees, contracts are occasionally terminated; librarians should include this protection in the contract.

Legal Signatures

Most institutions have procedures for reviewing and signing contracts. Some organizations require that their lawyers or purchasing departments sign all contracts. Librarians must learn who can sign the agreements and work closely with them. The individuals authorized to sign agreements may not be familiar with the operations of libraries; therefore, librarians must be able to explain what their library needs and work with the lawyers to make certain the contract meets the needs of the institution.

IMPLEMENTING THE SYSTEM

Once a library has purchased an acquisitions or serials system, the system must be installed, the data entered, and the personnel trained before the library makes the system available to its users. This implementation may progress very smoothly or may be very difficult. Librarians must plan the implementation carefully, adapt to changes, and remain flexible.

Communication

The first and most important thing to do while implementing a new system is to communicate regularly with everyone the new system affects. Email and library newsletters are excellent methods of informing everyone of plans and progress. Librarians should offer demonstrations and meet with all departments to show how the system will work. Inadequate communication can result in confusion and resentment. Personnel who do not understand a new system can become frustrated and their work can suffer. Sharing information about the new system is vital to a successful implementation project. Some backlogs are inevitable during a major implementation project; personnel must communicate their progress toward eliminating such backlogs once the project has been completed.

Managing Change

While some people will embrace change and be enthusiastic about working with a new system, others will feel threatened, perhaps fearing their jobs will be radically changed or eliminated. Managers must respect both attitudes and work closely with personnel to resolve any conflict.

Implementing new systems will result in changes in the library operations, and personnel must participate in the planning. Librarians must encourage the personnel and the institution to remain flexible. Some functions of the new system will affect the existing workflow in unanticipated ways. Personnel must be ready to adapt the processing of materials as the system is installed.

Libraries must establish a timeline for installing and testing the new system. While unanticipated delays may happen, librarians must continue to work toward a completed installation as quickly as possible. Any delays must always be explained rapidly.

As the new system is installed, librarians must test it thoroughly. Personnel must adjust the workflow, adapting processes to make the best use of the capabilities of the new system. The process of testing, adapting, and revising the workflow is an ongoing sequence; as personnel become more familiar with the system, they will discover new ways to use it.

Infrastructure

As soon as a system has been selected, personnel must identify what hardware, software, wiring, telecommunications, and ergonomic furniture will be needed. Some of this information will be included in the contract or the documentation from the vendor. Other needs will be discovered as the system is actually installed.

Systems with many modules and graphical features require computers with large amounts of memory. Printers that are networked together must have the proper software installed. New systems usually require the newest generations of software; some computers may need to be upgraded. If specific forms are needed for printed purchase orders or labels for serials, libraries must order those. Existing wiring may need to be upgraded or relocated. Acquisitions personnel must work closely with their systems departments, electricians, and telecommunications personnel to ensure that the infrastructure supports the new system.

ENTERING DATA INTO AN AUTOMATED SYSTEM

Libraries may have their acquisitions and serials records in an existing automated system or in a manual file. These records need to be transferred into the new system. Depending upon the system and the library, the data may include records for outstanding orders for monographs and serials, serials check-in records, vendor records, and financial-accounting records. Before libraries enter data into a new system, personnel should clean up as much of the data as possible, closing records for canceled orders and resolving problems.

The process of entering the data into the new system is crucial; the records form the core of the library's catalog. If the information is incomplete or inaccurate, users cannot find the materials they need. If a library has its records in manual files, all the information must be entered into the new system. If the library's records are already in machine-readable format, the data must be transferred into the new system. "The most time-consuming and perhaps most expensive activity that you will undertake to automate your library is converting your manual files to machine-readable ones.... This means that you must convert your files using a standard that can be read and used by most library automation systems so that your bibliographic database will be transportable when you decide to trade in your existing system for a new one....Those libraries with bibliographic databases in full MARC formats have a relatively easy time extracting their records from the old system and loading them into the new one. This is not the case for libraries with bibliographic records that do not conform to the MARC format. For these libraries, it often costs thousands of dollars to reformat their records and sometimes they are faced with yet another retrospective conversion project" (Cohn, Kelsey, and Fiels 2001, 173). Libraries may be able to create a test database to determine whether their records can be successfully transferred before having the entire database migrated.

If libraries must input their manual records into an automated system, they must plan for the staff time that will be required to enter the data.

Personnel will have to be reassigned from their other responsibilities, or additional staff will need to be hired. If libraries have machine-readable records that cannot be loaded into the new system, they may hire vendors to clean up their records, converting them into the format accepted by the new system. The costs for conversion will depend on the number and types of records. Items such as media or materials in non-Roman alphabets may be more expensive to convert.

TRAINING

Vendors of large integrated systems usually provide training for their systems. Libraries should schedule as many sessions as possible. Not all corporate trainers are equally knowledgeable; personnel should ask questions and follow up to resolve any questions that remain unanswered during the initial training. People working directly with the system should receive the most extensive training, of course, but all personnel should be given training on the basic features of the system.

Libraries should identify a few individuals who will be the local experts and train their coworkers on the system; these people may also be the primary contacts with the vendor. These local trainers should attend user group meetings, discuss questions with vendor representatives, read the company documentation, and monitor electronic discussion lists devoted to the system. Learning about new systems and the constant upgrades must be an ongoing process, and the local trainers must be responsible for informing their colleagues about new developments. Some large libraries may consider establishing an internal electronic discussion list to share information and questions about the new system.

Training can be a beneficial public relations tool. If the new system includes a new online catalog, libraries can have sessions for their patrons in which library personnel promote the new system as part of a program of improved services. Some local media may be willing to cover the new system and help promote the library.

Trainers must remain flexible and adaptable. Personnel will ask unanticipated questions, and the system will produce unexpected results; surprises are inevitable. When there are questions that cannot be resolved during the training sessions, the trainers should consult with the vendor or other colleagues rapidly and answer those questions as soon as possible.

Learning styles vary widely. Some people learn best when provided with written documentation; others prefer visual demonstrations. Trainers must prepare themselves to work with personnel in the manner that best meets the needs of the individuals.

EVALUATION

Before the library makes the final payment for a new system, personnel must test all functions to determine whether everything promised in the contract has been delivered. If the library believes that the contract has not been satisfactorily fulfilled, it must discuss the concerns with the vendor. As a last resort, when librarians believe that the company is not in compliance with the contract, they must discuss the problems with the institutional lawyers.

Systems should be informally evaluated continually. Personnel should make notes of their questions as they begin to use a new system. Some of the questions will be answered as personnel learn more about the system; remaining problems should be discussed with the vendor. Some vendors have annual meetings of their users; others have meetings at the various annual library conferences. Some systems have electronic discussion lists that allow users to exchange information and advice about them.

Libraries must evaluate the impact of the new system on the library's workflow. The system should simplify work and make it easier for everyone to locate items being ordered and processed. After the installation and implementation, libraries should determine whether the new system meets those goals; if the system does not improve the library's services, librarians should identify the problems and attempt to resolve them.

WHEN TO UPGRADE

After a major automation project involving large amounts of time and money, libraries are reluctant to consider more major changes. The rapid changes in automation and libraries make continued projects inevitable, however. Libraries may need to upgrade or change systems, a process known as "migration," for a number of reasons. Vendors may offer an expanded version of a system that is very different from the original edition. Companies may stop supporting the original system completely. The vendor may go out of business or be purchased by another firm. Libraries that purchased only one module of a system may decide to add other portions of the product. The library's collections or patron database may grow so large that the initial system can no longer support the level of activities needed.

Migration projects are generally as complicated as initial automation projects. "'Migration' is certainly a term that gives no clue about the monumentality of the project ahead. One envisions herds of majestic animals or flights of graceful birds, not the brain-wrenching planning and worry that we have seen so far in this project. The huge job of developing the RFP (request for proposal) is behind us, so now we have the ability to relax and be picky!... Regardless of the package you choose and the implementation plan, keep in mind that change of this magnitude is very upsetting for all involved" (Simpson 1999, 49). Migration projects should not be undertaken casually, but they are inevitable. Libraries should maintain an archival copy of their existing data until they have successfully implemented the new system.

CONSORTIA

A library consortium is a group of libraries working together for a common purpose. The consortium may share an integrated library system including all functions from acquisitions through an online catalog, or it may share only a single module such as its online catalog. Consortium catalogs may be large statewide systems or may include only a few libraries in the same geographic area.

Consortium catalogs allow members to share information about their resources. Patrons can see what materials are available at several libraries without searching each individual catalog. Many consortium libraries give priority to interlibrary loan requests from other consortium members. Consortium purchases of online systems frequently offer individual libraries the opportunity to acquire catalogs with far more functions than they otherwise could afford; pooling resources allows the members to increase their purchasing power.

Libraries considering creating a consortium need to develop operating guidelines and policies. Some consortia are created and governed by formal agreements that require the signatures of those individuals who are legally authorized to sign contracts for their organization. Other consortium arrangements may be much more informal. All consortia should define what is expected of the members, what fees are involved, and how the relationship can be terminated.

Expectations of Consortium Members

Libraries must decide which library will be the primary institution responsible for maintaining the hardware, communication with the vendor, and coordination of system maintenance and upgrades.

Libraries sharing systems must decide what types of records will be shared. Multiple libraries may be able to add their order or item records to a single, shared bibliographic record, but adding multiple serials check-in records to one bibliographic record may not be desirable. The patron records of each library should remain separate to protect patrons' privacy.

Libraries must decide how the results of searches are retrieved and displayed. Systems may be able to present the results arranged by the individual locations, allowing patrons to view the records of their local library before viewing records of other consortium members.

Consortium members must realize that the individual libraries give up some amount of local control in exchange for the expanded features and shared resources the consortium provides. The group may determine cataloging policies and the structure of the database; individual members may not be able to adapt the system extensively. The requirement that members share control may meet some resistance, and negotiations may require careful diplomacy.

Costs of Consortia

Most consortia divide operating costs among the members. Libraries may decide that fees should be based on a number of factors such as the relative size of the individual libraries' budgets, the number of patrons the libraries serve, or the percentage of records included in the online catalog. The libraries must agree upon the method by which fees are assessed and upon what the fees cover. Consortium costs may include annual maintenance fees, personnel costs, or the cost of system upgrades.

NEW AND FUTURE DEVELOPMENTS

By the time this book is published, new systems, new technology, and new companies may have appeared, while other companies will have vanished. The only certainty is that technology is constantly changing and that "long-term technological stability is a chimera" (Abram 2000, 43). Among the major current factors influencing integrated systems are the nature of the business of library vendors and the impact of the Internet.

Many automated systems were developed by small companies or by libraries; these automated systems were the companies' primary products. Now large companies whose principal business has been providing materials to libraries own some systems, and large multinational publishers own other systems. Whether the smaller companies can remain competitive is unclear. The mergers and consolidations that have dominated the worlds of publishing, approval vendors, and serials subscription services may spread to the world of systems vendors.

The Internet continues to have a profound impact on automated systems, just as it has had in all other areas of libraries. Systems originally created in computer text languages were upgraded to Windows-compatible versions; now they must work with Web browsers. Patrons expect online catalogs to function like Web browsers, retrieving citations and full-text resources from a wide range of sources in all formats and languages. Since many commercial sites have programs that rank results by their probable relevance, offer corrections to misspellings, and include supplemental information such as reviews and related information, patrons believe that library systems should provide the same extensive information. Patrons believe that an ideal system should allow them to enter their search terms once; the system should then search all possible databases including the Internet. If patrons find items that are not held in their local library, the system should offer the choice of requesting the items on interlibrary loan, asking the library to purchase the items, or allowing the patrons to purchase them. The entire process should be seamless; patrons should not have to leave one system and enter another.

Librarians are also asking for increased technical developments. The systems should support new computer encoding languages, a wide variety of alphabets and languages, and new standards such as the Dublin Core as well as MARC. Patrons should be able to search the systems and download information using their wireless laptops or PDAs (personal digital assistants).

Many systems can support some of these functions, although few can provide most of them in a seamless presentation that is easy for patrons to use. As vendors continue to develop new products, users will also continue to expect more features. Librarians must talk with their users, colleagues, and vendors, attend library and online conferences, read the relevant literature, and monitor electronic discussion lists to keep abreast of the latest developments in the field.

CONCLUSION

Libraries, technology, and systems are changing rapidly, but librarians cannot stop and wait for the perfect system. Librarians must analyze their needs and plan the selection and implementation of a system that supports the mission and priorities of the institution. Both the selection and implementation processes require thorough planning in order to obtain a system that helps the library acquire materials more efficiently and improves service to patrons.

REFERENCES

Abram, Stephen. 2000. Shift happens: Ten key trends in our profession and ten strategies for success. *Serials Librarian* 38 (1/2): 41–59.

Basch, N. Bernard, and Judy McQueen. 1990. *Buying serials: A how-to-do-it manual for librarians.* New York: Neal-Schuman.

Beiser, Karl A. 1999. Integrated library system software for smaller libraries. Part 1. *Library Technology Reports* 35: 119–261.

Boykin, Joseph F., Jr. 1991. Library automation 1970–1990: From the few to the many. *Library Administration and Management* 5: 10–15.

Cohn, John M., Ann L. Kelsey, and Keith Michael Fiels. 2001. *Planning for integrated library systems and technologies: A how-to-do-it manual for librarians.* New York: Neal-Schuman.

Eaglen, Audrey. 2000. *Buying books: A how-to-do-it manual for librarians.* New York: Neal-Schuman.

Gardner, Ronald A. 1986/87. The evolution of automated serials control. *Serials Librarian* 11 (3/4): 71–83.

Millsap, Larry. 1996. A history of the online catalog in North America. In *Technical services management, 1965–1990: A quarter century of change and a look to the future,* edited by Linda C. Smith and Ruth C. Carter. New York: Haworth Press.

Simpson, Carol. 1999. Migration, a moving experience. *Book Report* 18 (1): 49–51.

Chapter 3

The Publishing Industry

The publishing industry is the source of most materials acquired by libraries. It is a business that sells billions of dollars of books and serials annually, created by companies ranging from huge multinational conglomerates to one-person operations. It produces hundreds of thousands of items that include everything from handmade books to electronic articles with multimedia attachments. It is a diverse industry undergoing dramatic changes as a result of technological developments and economic pressures, and it must deal with complex challenges.

In the last few decades, the publishing industry and libraries have faced a number of controversial issues. The number of publishers has declined as a result of many mergers, purchases, and closures. Some people fear this consolidation of publishers will result in less diversity in what is published. Others believe that the change will generate more pressure to produce items that make large profits, which may therefore result in lower quality in the content of the materials that are published. These same critics believe that publishers may abandon a traditional role of many publishers: to educate readers rather than only entertaining them. The huge increases in the cost of scholarly journals have led libraries and scholars to seek alternative methods of distributing scholarly information, including ways that exclude the publishing industry. The demand for electronic journals and books has forced publishers and libraries to spend large amounts of money to develop infrastructures that support these rapidly changing technologies.

Publishers vary widely in their size, scope, and purpose. They may be huge international corporations, scholarly associations, government agencies, universities, museums, small companies, or individuals. They may publish scholarly or popular serials or books; they may publish the materials in print, electronic, or media formats. They may be nonprofit organizations, societies, or private companies with international stockholders. Regardless of these differences, they share a common function: to prepare information for dissemination.

This chapter looks at the types of publishers; the economics of the publishing industry; the characteristics of the publishers that specialize in serials, books, and electronic materials; and the crisis in scholarly publishing.

FUNCTIONS OF PUBLISHERS

All publishers carry out some core functions regardless of the types of materials involved. Publishers identify the materials that they want to publish; edit the materials; organize and design their presentation; distribute and promote the product; and track the legal contracts, sales, and any profits or losses. The first step is to find materials to publish. Publishers may receive manuscripts from hopeful authors or may solicit materials directly from authors. Most publishers receive far more manuscripts than they could possibly publish; they reject a large percentage of materials that are submitted to them. Publishers evaluate the proposals and manuscripts to determine whether they wish to publish the titles.

Scholarly publishers frequently send manuscripts to experts in the appropriate subject areas for their review. These peer reviewers may suggest revisions that need to be made before the manuscripts are published, or they may recommend that the manuscripts not be published at all. Whether the manuscript is to be published in print or electronic format, the peer-review process "assures that the information made available meets the content standards for any particular discipline" (Grycz 1997, 9).

All publishers negotiate the contracts signed with their authors, which include specific information about what payments will be made and who owns the copyright to the materials. Contracts signed before the manuscript is complete have clauses that allow the final product to be rejected if it does not meet the publisher's standards.

Publishers may have an editorial staff who work closely with authors to improve their manuscripts. Others may not do any editing; they may require that their authors submit the manuscripts ready to be published, generally referred to as camera-ready condition. Once the edited manuscripts are submitted, the publishers arrange for the actual publication of the materials; this process varies between book publishers and serials publishers and is discussed later in this chapter.

Publishers track the sales and determine whether the items make a profit. Most trade book and magazine publishers pay authors for their materials; few scholarly serials publishers do so. Vanity publishers of books charge the authors to produce the books.

TYPES OF PUBLISHERS

Publishers may be described in many ways—by their size, their intended audiences, or the types of materials they publish. Three broad categories that describe both the size and the intended audiences are trade publishers, scholarly publishers, and small presses. Trade publishers are companies whose main sales are to bookstores; these are frequently large corporations that print 10,000 or more copies of their titles. Scholarly publishers include university presses and departments, societies, and associations whose main sales are to libraries and researchers; they often print between 500 and 5,000 copies of their books. Small presses usually specialize in specific subjects and may print only a few hundred copies of each book. Some serials publishers may issue hundreds of titles; others may issue only one journal.

Another method used within the publishing industry to describe publishers is by the types of materials they publish. The largest category of publishers is trade publishers, which issue materials about all subjects in all formats. These companies frequently publish both fiction and nonfiction in hardcover, paperback, and audio formats. Other categories of publishers include those that publish textbooks and classroom materials; those that publish religious books; publishers of business, law, and technical professional books; book clubs; and university presses (Greco 1997, 22–23). Government agencies are also publishers; the U.S. government is one of the world's largest publishers.

Publishers may be active in multiple categories, and the distinctions between the types of publishers are becoming less clear. For example, scholarly and trade publishers may join to copublish books, such as exhibition catalogs jointly published by museums and trade publishers. Many university presses are publishing materials such as regional history or scholarly works similar to those that had previously been published by trade presses. Most publishers of books do not also publish serials as well, although the larger scholarly associations, such as the American Chemical Society, often publish books, serials, and conference proceedings in their areas of interest.

Some publishers specialize in a subject area, such as geology, or a format, such as maps. Some may publish their materials only in print while others have begun publishing only in electronic formats; many issue materials in both print and in electronic formats. Many fiction books are published in both print and audio formats.

The majority of materials purchased by libraries are published by either scholarly or trade publishers. Because these types of publishers are so important to libraries, they are examined in more detail in the following sections.

Scholarly and Nonprofit Publishers

Scholarly publishers include societies, schools, universities, museums, associations, and charities. These presses may issue a couple of titles a year or may have a very large publishing operation. Their main purpose may be publishing, or the publishing process may be a minor part of their operation. They may rely on the profits from their publishing to support the other activities of the organization, or they may subsidize the publishing operation with funds from their other activities. The purpose of their publications is to share information related to their organizational focus. "A learned society raises the level of knowledge and understanding of the subject matter in which the society specializes" (Morris 2001, 163).

The Association of American University Presses represents more than 120 university presses, scholarly societies, research institutions, and museums that publish books and journals in all areas. They are a small but significant portion of the publishing industry, accounting for slightly less than 2 percent of U.S. publishing revenues (Greco 2001, 97). For many years, universities supported their presses financially; recently many have begun demanding that their presses become self-supporting (Schiffrin 2000, 138). University presses are also dealing with reduced purchases by academic libraries. "Library budget cuts mean editors of university presses can now count on selling only half the number of monographs that they did 20 years ago" (Swain 1999, 22). The combination of declining monograph purchases and increasing pressure to become self-supporting has led many university presses to search for new ways of increasing their revenues. Some presses have merged with others in their geographic region. Others have increased their publication of regional materials such as photography books or cookbooks that sell more copies than most of the scholarly nonfiction that many university presses publish. Some university presses are publishing general nonfiction works that previously would have been the midlist titles of trade publishers—general scholarly works that are aimed at educated lay readers (Baker 2001, 10).

Trade Publishers

Trade publishers form the largest portion of the publishing industry; they publish all types of materials, in all subject areas, in all formats. In the late twentieth century, many trade publishing companies merged with or were purchased by larger companies. Many communications and media companies that were seeking content for their online and media divisions purchased book and magazine publishers. Some of the large European publishers purchased U.S. companies. These mergers and purchases led to considerable debate in the information industry about the purpose and future of publishing.

Some experts say that publishing has always been a business and that the mergers are merely another step in the growth of the industry. Consolidation and efficient management are necessary for publishers to survive. Just as independent grocery stores and bookstores have struggled to compete with large national chains, small publishers must change in order to compete with larger companies. Given factors that include the rise of chain stores, small profit margins, the need to update technological infrastructures, and huge advances to prominent authors, many companies might have collapsed without the money flowing in from the media companies and international conglomerates (Greco 1997, x).

Other commentators are concerned that the consolidation of the companies is approaching a monopoly in some areas. "Today the top twenty-five firms alone own 45 percent of all newspapers and control 64 percent of all newspaper circulation" (Picard and Brody 1997, 56). From 1960 to 1990, nearly 600 mergers and purchases occurred in the U.S. publishing industry (Greco 1997, 45). At the beginning of the twenty-first century, five companies have 80 percent of American book sales, and most of these five are multimedia conglomerates; they are AOL/Time Warner, Disney, Viacom, Bertelsmann, and News Corporation (Schiffrin 2000, 2). Similar concerns in the area of scientific, technical, and medical serials resulted in a U.S. government investigation of a proposed merger of two major publishers (McCabe 1999, 1).

Schiffrin (2000, 5) expresses a different concern: "Publishers have always prided themselves on their ability to balance the imperative of making money with that of issuing worthwhile books. . . . It is now increasingly the case that the owner's *only* interest is in making money and as much of it as possible." He maintains that the emphasis on high profits means that books without the potential to earn profits will no longer be published, a change from the past practice when many publishers accepted that some individual titles would be supported by others that would be more profitable (103–4). He fears that books appealing to a smaller audience and works with new and possibly unpopular views will no longer be published because the conglomerates care only for their profits.

ECONOMICS OF PUBLISHING

Publishing is a business. Almost all publishers need to make a profit to remain in business. Some economic factors involved in the publishing process are the same regardless of the size of the publisher or the format of the materials; some of the unique factors involved in publishing serials, books, and electronic materials are discussed later in this chapter.

Discounts

Many publishers sell books to libraries and booksellers at a price lower than that charged to the consumer. This discount varies with the type of publisher and the purchaser. Large trade publishers may offer national chain bookstores discounts of as much as 50 percent, while societies and associations may not offer any kind of discount to anyone except members of their organizations. Libraries generally receive smaller discounts than those given to bookstores; they frequently receive discounts of 10 to 20 percent, while large bookstore chains may receive discounts of more than 50 percent.

Serials publishers almost never give discounts to libraries. A few serials publishers give discounts to serials vendors, but this practice is declining swiftly.

The Library Market

When looking at the numbers of items sold, many publishers see a pyramid with the huge numbers of commercial sales as the foundation of their sales. The next smaller levels are the educational market, which includes textbooks, and the professional books, covering the technical, law, and medical materials. At the peak of the pyramid with the fewest sales are the scholarly research materials, frequently written about narrow topics of interest for a relatively small audience (Hunter 2000, 26). For most commercial publishers and textbook publishers, library orders account for a very small part of their sales. For publishers of scholarly and research materials, the library market is extremely important. While the library market for books represents approximately 10 percent of overall publishers' revenues, it can account for 50 to 90 percent of the sales of nonfiction, poetry, children's books, and reference books (Schuman and Harmon 1999, 25). Some publishers of scholarly journals also rely on libraries for the majority of their sales.

In the late twentieth century, research libraries, dealing with relatively stable budgets, higher serials prices, and new electronic resources, reduced their purchases of books. In a report for the British publishing industry concerning libraries and scholarly publishing, Watkinson (2001, 28) wrote, "The American library market is crucial to all monographic publishers. For most other areas of the publishing industry, libraries are a nice supplemental market, but are not a major factor in the corporate profits."

While libraries depend on publishers to provide materials, and many scholarly publishers depend on libraries for their profits, some antagonism has developed between libraries and publishers, especially in the United States. Many research librarians believe that some publishers have increased their prices, especially of serials, at unreasonable rates, are repackaging content in order to sell the same information in multiple ways, and are demanding that libraries sign highly restrictive licensing agreements for access to electronic resources. Publishers are faced with declining purchases of books, cancellations of serials, increasing interlibrary loans, and demands for expanded electronic access. For additional information on this antagonism, see the section on scholarly publishing later in this chapter.

BOOK PUBLISHING

The Association of American Publishers, the major trade association of the industry, has more than 2,500 members. Thousands of other companies and organizations also publish materials. In 2000, R. R. Bowker estimated there were more than 66,000 publishers of books and multimedia materials in the United States (R. R. Bowker 2000, vi). When the international publishers and distributors are considered, the total number of companies involved in publishing and distributing materials may well exceed 100,000. In 1998, more than 2.5 billion books were sold in the United States, earning more than $23 billion (Schiffrin 2000, 7). Sales have increased steadily in recent years, growing 6.3 percent in 1999 and 3 percent in 2000 (Milliot 2001, 12). The publishing and media industries are huge, employing thousands of people and playing a major role in the U.S. economy and society. Profits vary widely among companies, influenced by factors that include sales, advances to authors, infrastructure expenses, and corporate acquisitions or mergers. In 1999, John Wiley & Sons reported a profit of 15 percent, and Simon and Schuster reported a profit of 8.9 percent (Milliot 2000, 11).

In 1999, about 120,000 books were published in the United States, approximately the same number published in 1998. The largest subject category was the combined area of sociology and economics, followed by fiction, children's books, history, and technology. In 1999, mass-market paperback output increased by almost 20 percent, while output of hardcover books and trade paperbacks declined about 2 percent (Ink and Grabois 2001, 485–86).

While all publishers hope to find the next best-seller, those titles are comparatively rare. Most publishers do extensive analysis to determine whether proposed titles will make any profit. Some of the larger trade publishers will not publish items that may not sell 20,000 copies (Schiffrin 2000, 105–6). Books that do not sell the anticipated number of copies are rapidly declared out of print (Schiffrin 2000, 118). Scholarly publishers print far fewer copies. Watkinson (2001, 24) reports that the average print run for scholarly books is approximately 1,000 in the United States and 800 in the United Kingdom. The combination of the reluctance to publish titles that may not sell a large number of copies, the short time before items are declared out of print, and the decline in the number of copies printed results in books disappearing from the market before many libraries can obtain them.

Publication Process for Books

The publication process for books begins with the concept for the book. Manuscripts may be solicited or unsolicited. Publishers may ask authors to write books on desired topics, soliciting the manuscripts, or authors may send their manuscripts to publishers, submitting unsolicited manuscripts. Most publishers receive far more manuscripts than they could ever possibly publish. Many unsolicited manuscripts are rejected after an initial reading because they are poorly written. Others are rejected because they are sent to the wrong type of publisher; for example, most scholarly publishers will reject a manuscript of a poetry book written for children.

A manuscript that passes the initial review goes through an extensive editorial review by most large publishers. The first questions that publishers ask are whether the manuscript is well written and whether a need exists for the proposed book. The publisher will look at the potential market and the books already available on the subject to determine if the proposed book adds new information to the subject area. If the answer is yes, then the publisher will decide whether the manuscript covers the topic adequately and whether extensive changes are needed. Finally, the publisher will analyze the costs to produce the book and the potential profits (Schuman and Harmon 1999, 19).

After the publisher decides to publish a book, the legal and technical portions of the process begin. The author and publisher sign a contract describing the nature of the book, the deadline for completion, the royalties or payments, and the legal rights and obligations of both parties. The manuscript is reviewed, edited, and revised as needed. If it contains graphic materials, the publisher adds them, and selects the appropriate typeface, paper, and physical design. The semifinal version is created and proofed. Depending on the type of book, it may be indexed. The book is printed and bound. The publisher sets the price and distributes, advertises, and sells the book (Schuman and Harmon 1999, 21). If the book is being issued as an electronic file, the item is created in the desired electronic format rather than printed and bound. The publisher maintains the financial records and pays royalties as stated in the original contract.

Economics of Publishing Books

The profit margin for most books is relatively small. According to Schuman and Harmon (1999, 17), here are the basic factors that make up the expenses of publishing books:

+ Design, typesetting, and returns: 20 percent
+ Royalties: 10 to 15 percent
+ Marketing: 10 to 15 percent
+ Discounts: 0 to 60 percent
+ Fulfillment (storage, shipping, billing): 10 percent
+ Damaged or returned books: 5 to 40 percent
+ Overhead: 25 to 30 percent
+ Profit: 0 to 15 percent

Most trade book publishers pay authors for their manuscripts, usually paying royalties after the books are published, and sometimes paying the authors advances before the books are published. Some publishers, known as vanity presses, charge authors to publish their books. Libraries rarely purchase materials from vanity presses unless the items are in subject areas in which the libraries collect comprehensively.

As economic pressures have increased, publishers have begun seeking additional methods to improve their profits. Publishers have used automation to streamline the physical production of materials, have reduced print runs to reduce costs and to lower the number of copies that remain unsold, and have laid off employees. While these steps have helped some publishers, many continue to look for sources of additional support. Some have obtained subsidies from foundations and organizations to support the publication of titles in mutual areas of interest. Small publishers have worked together to copublish titles, sharing the expenses and profits.

A more controversial development is the payment by a jewelry company to a publisher in order to have the jewelry company mentioned a specific number of times in a novel. For many years, companies have paid movie and television companies to have their products appear in shows. The literary version of product placement is new to the publishing industry. It has been praised as "fantastic" and also condemned because "it erodes reader confidence in the authenticity of the narrative" (Reid 2001, 17). Whether product placement in novels continues, publishers will continue to explore ways to deal with financial uncertainty.

Paperback Books

Until relatively recently, libraries in the United States purchased mainly hardback books. Libraries bought paperback books only if no other edition was available. Paperback books began to appear in the British and American markets in the early twentieth century. In the 1940s they became more popular and were published in all subject areas. Most paperback books are mass-market paperbacks, produced in large numbers, and not designed to last for many years. The paper is inexpensive, and the books are lightly glued together. Since frequently read paperbacks will disintegrate within a few years, many libraries purchase them only when the items are not available in a better format or when the library is building a temporary collection that will not be needed after a few years. Some libraries purchase and bind paperbacks, which increases their life somewhat but does not address the problem of the fragile, often more acidic, paper, which will quickly tear and turn yellow.

In the late twentieth century, some publishers began to issue a new type of paperback. Unlike the common mass-market paperbacks, these new trade paperbacks were the same size and printed on the same type of paper as the clothbound hardback editions. The only differences were in the binding and the price. The hardback editions have a cloth or hard cover while the trade paperbacks have a stiff paper cover. Trade paperbacks frequently cost a third or a half less than the hardbacks. Some libraries prefer to purchase the trade paperbacks instead of the hardback editions. Even when the libraries decide to have some of the trade paperbacks re-bound, the cost is less than purchasing the hardback versions.

SERIALS PUBLISHING

Scientific journals began to appear in the seventeenth century as a means of sharing the results of research done by members of scientific academies. Almanacs, magazines, and newspapers began in the late seventeenth and early eighteenth centuries. Cultural and literary reviews became common in the mid-nineteenth century (Nisonger 1998, 18–20).

Serials formats may be print, electronic, or multimedia. Types of serials include newspapers, magazines, scholarly journals, annual publications, conference proceedings, series, and government publications. Magazines and newspapers may have local or international audiences. Publishers may be individuals, societies, or commercial corporations. The audience may be a few hundred people or hundreds of thousands of readers. The publishers may issue one serial title or hundreds. Titles may be free or cost thousands of dollars each year. Some serials may be distributed only within an organization; others have worldwide readership.

Given the wide variety of serials, it is understandable why statistics describing the number of serials that are published each year vary widely. According to *Ulrich's Periodicals Directory,* more than 164,000 serials exist (R.R. Bowker 2002, vii). Other sources state that approximately 22,000 consumer and business magazines are published in the United States, but only about 160 have a readership of more than 500,000 copies and revenues of more than $1 million (Daly, Henry, and Ryder 1997, 22).

Publication Process for Serials

The publication process for serials is similar to the process for publishing books; however, the entire process is done each day in the case of newspapers or weekly for many magazines. All publishers identify materials to be published; edit and organize the materials; produce, distribute, and promote their product; and handle all related legal and financial activities. In addition to these general procedures, the editorial steps in producing serials include obtaining the articles; reviewing, editing, and revising the articles; adding graphics; designing the appearance of the articles and of the entire issue; verifying the facts and editing the product; and finally, reviewing the finished issue. The issue is printed or created in the final electronic version and then distributed to subscribers and newsstands (Daly, Henry, and Ryder 1997, 68). Then the entire process starts over from the beginning.

Economics of Publishing Serials

Magazines and newspapers rely on two major sources of revenue: purchases of the issues and advertising. For a small group of consumer magazines, sales accounted for 54 percent of their revenue and advertising accounted for 45 percent (Johnson and Prijatel 2000, 137). While the ratio may vary for other types of serials, most general trade serials such as *Time* or *Fortune* depend heavily on advertising revenues. Other sources of revenue may include the sale of subscription lists and data, reprints and collections of articles, and licensing fees paid by online or media companies for information. Some scholarly serials published by societies receive subsidies from their parent organizations; however, other organizations expect that their serials will make money to support the societies' activities. Some scientific journals charge authors a page charge, a fee for each published page.

Expenses include the costs of production, editorial review, distribution, and administrative operations. The majority of costs are in the initial publication process. As in most areas of publishing, a few serials are very profitable while most titles make only a small profit. While profits for many general magazines are relatively small, some publishers of scientific and research journals make big profits. Discussing the profits of some of these companies, Lawal (2001, 138) writes, "Tables of publicly available data show that the profit margin was higher than that of 491 companies in the Standard & Poor 500 Index for 1997." The money spent on research in the late twentieth century grew dramatically, as did the related publishing industry. "It is estimated that the international research journal publishing business is worth about $2.5 billion. As such it represents about 2% of worldwide research expenditures" (Bolman 1996, 154).

The growth of full-text electronic access to serials has led to additional expenses for publishers, who must create the infrastructure required to support this format. It has also led to additional revenue from the companies that create the electronic databases; these companies pay to license the content from the publishers. Revenue also comes from readers purchasing individual articles online. Most libraries and publishers are maintaining the print versions while adding the electronic formats. Publishers must invest in the hardware, software, and personnel required to create the electronic versions while still producing and distributing the print versions. Publishers who drop the print versions of their journals and issue only electronic serials no longer have to pay for printing, mailing, and storing the physical copies; however, they do have the costs of housing the electronic versions.

In the past few decades, annual costs paid by libraries for serials have increased dramatically. This increase in serials prices, especially for the scientific and research journals, combined with the need to acquire expensive electronic resources, has created major problems for libraries that are facing stable or declining budgets. For more information on this situation, see the section on scholarly publishing later in this chapter.

ELECTRONIC PUBLISHING

The ability of the Internet to provide rapid distribution of information has a dramatic impact on publishing. As is frequently true, technological capabilities outrun the abilities of society and the law to deal with the implications of the rapid changes. In the academic world, scholars debate whether materials in electronic format are as valuable in tenure and promotion reviews as materials published in print. Libraries and publishers debate who should be responsible for permanent archiving of the materials. Some geographic areas and groups of people have minimal access to the Internet, leading to discussions about methods of correcting this access inequity.

Electronic publications can be produced more rapidly and updated more frequently than most print materials. They can include links to related information, such as multimedia resources, and can even include feedback from readers. Such additional material must be created, the links must be verified, and the data must be maintained; this all requires considerable infrastructure. Staff must produce the materials, and adequate technology must be acquired to create and house the information. The data must be archived in accessible files, and the users must have the technical ability to find and use the information.

Electronic publications include serials, books, and databases, which may include a variety of resources.

Electronic Serials

The growth of the Internet has led to the development of electronic journals whose full content is available online. The first electronic journals appeared in the 1980s, and they became common in the 1990s (Nisonger 1998, 26–27). Now *Ulrich's Periodicals Directory* lists almost 30,000 online serials (R. R. Bowker 2002, vii). "If a journal publisher today is publishing only on paper, with no plans to migrate to electronic distribution, it must be either extremely specialized and in close contact with its readers (such as a small society) or be prepared to go out of existence within 5 years. Electronic distribution is no longer optional for the long term—it is essential" (Hunter 2000, 37).

Initially, publishing an electronic serial meant that the text of the print serial was made available electronically. While that is still a major part of the process, electronic serials now frequently include supplemental materials such as the statistical data used in the research, audio and video materials, links to articles cited in the bibliography, or commentary about the article. An electronic serial may include far more information than was available in the print version if the authors and publisher have the capabilities to produce the expanded version. An increasing number of electronic journals are created as electronic publications without ever having existed in print versions. These new journals include scholarly peer-reviewed journals and newsletters. Some of these titles are free, whereas others charge subscription fees.

Traditionally print journals were available by subscription; libraries or individuals paid for a year of the title. Publishers of electronic serials have developed a wide variety of pricing models. The electronic journal may be available free with a print subscription. If a library wants only the electronic version, that option may be available at a lower cost than purchasing the print edition. Libraries wanting both the print and electronic versions may pay the cost for a print subscription plus a supplemental fee for access to the electronic version. In addition, libraries may subscribe to online databases that include full-text journals from a large number of publishers. If libraries or users do not subscribe to a journal, they can purchase individual articles from the publisher or database producer. No standard model dominates the market; nor is one likely to emerge in the near future. Libraries frequently find that they prefer one model for one subject area or serial title, while an entirely different method is better suited for a different area.

Publishing electronic serials remains an unsettled area; publishers, librarians, and scholars continue to discuss many questions about the future of publishing in this format. Issues about the legal right to include articles in databases seem to have been resolved by court decisions requiring the database publishers to obtain permission from authors to include their articles in these databases. Other questions such as whether electronic journals will replace print versions and who will maintain perpetual archives of the materials are still undecided. Publishers, librarians, vendors, and aggregators are working together to resolve such concerns.

Electronic Books

Electronic books have been slower to develop than electronic journals for a number of reasons, most of which involve the current technology. Electronic books are available in three ways: books that can be read on a personal computer screen, books that can be read on PDAs (personal digital assistants), and those that must be read on handheld devices designed only for reading electronic books. Most people do not enjoy reading long texts on computer screens, frequently printing longer documents to read in a printed format. The handheld readers designed to read electronic books are somewhat expensive, and the different brands are incompatible. These electronic readers and books are described as "dead on arrival" and "unwieldy and unreadable" (Lichtenberg 2001, 21). Print books, especially mass-market paperbacks, are convenient and reasonably priced; electronic versions are unlikely to replace them in the near future.

Other types of electronic books are more successful. Reference books such as encyclopedias are very well suited for electronic formats. They can be updated frequently and are designed for quick checking of facts rather than for extensive reading. Technical manuals, handbooks, indexes, dictionaries, and other reference tools are also very successful in electronic formats. Nonfiction works and supplemental readings for college and university courses are gaining acceptance in electronic formats. The Internet also allows individuals to create electronic books tailored to their specific needs; a tourist could carry one electronic book that contained a personal guidebook consisting of dictionaries, maps, histories, novels, and shopping guides about the region.

Authors, publishers, and libraries are all working on ways to handle electronic books. Some authors sell their works in electronic formats directly to their readers. A few publishers, such as the National Academy Press, make the full text of their books available electronically for free and have found that this option actually improves sales of the print versions. Some research and academic libraries provide electronic books through companies that sell permanent or temporary access to books from a large number of publishers. A few public libraries are beginning to lend hand-held readers and electronic books.

The future of electronic books remains more uncertain than the future of electronic journals. The legal and technical issues may be resolved, but the issue of acceptance of this format by readers remains less clear. The electronic book industry has been described as "complex, undisciplined, in a state of flux, and plagued by premature announcements" (Peters 2001, 212–13). Given that uncertainty, many libraries are proceeding with caution when dealing with electronic books.

Electronic Databases

Electronic databases are files of materials compiled by either publishers or aggregators, companies that gather materials from a number of publishers. Some databases are created by commercial companies while others are produced by nonprofit groups. Some databases are very expensive; others are free.

Any type of electronic publication may be included in a database. Databases such as EBSCOhost's Academic Search Elite contain references to articles as well as the full text of some articles. JSTOR provides access to the complete contents of academic journals. Early English Books Online contains the complete text of books published in Britain before 1700. The arXiv database contains research and preliminary reports about physics. CogNet has the full text of books and articles, citations to resources, and links to Internet sources about cognitive and brain sciences. These electronic databases can bring together resources about specific topics and provide rapid access to information. As with most electronic resources, questions about permanent archiving and costs continue to be debated by librarians, scholars, and publishers.

Electronic publications are developing very quickly. Many librarians believe that the costs required to provide electronic resources contribute to the scholarly publication crisis. Others believe that electronic publications may be the solution to this crisis.

SCHOLARLY PUBLISHING CRISIS

In the 1980s research and academic libraries began to face a combination of factors that included stable or declining university and institutional budgets; stable or declining library budgets; the development of the Internet and electronic resources; and rapidly increasing prices for research journals in the areas of science, technology, and medicine. Although librarians had been concerned about the inflationary increases in serials pricing as early as the 1920s, librarians in the late twentieth century were outraged at the price increases (Works 1927, 40).

As the funding for research grew in the middle of the twentieth century, funding for most research libraries also increased. This growth slowed in the latter part of the century, resulting in stable or declining funding for libraries. "Library materials budgets, which have increased over the past decade at almost seven percent a year, have not been able to keep pace with the 12-percent annual increase in the average price of science journals" (SPARC and chemists 1998, 1).

Publishers cite a number of reasons for the dramatic annual increases in the costs of scientific, technical, and medical serials. First, publishers planning to use the Internet as a means of distributing their publications faced infrastructure costs for equipment, software, and staffing as they developed a new type of publishing. Second, both commercial and non-profit publishers became increasingly concerned with making greater profits as attitudes changed within the publishing industry due to the numerous mergers and purchases of companies. Third, many journal publishers received an increasing number of articles as a result of the growth in research and the pressures on university scholars to publish more articles, and the publishers increased the number of issues or pages in their serials in order to publish the additional articles. This growth also contributed to the increases in the costs of the journals.

Scholars and researchers became concerned that the results of their research projects were being seen by fewer people as a result of declining subscriptions. As libraries continued to cancel journals, the readership of journals naturally declined. Researchers also began to use email and the Internet to distribute reports of their research. These electronic methods allowed researchers to share information rapidly and avoid the long delays that occurred between the submission of articles and their final publication.

Libraries were faced with stable budgets, rapid increases in journal costs, and the new demands to provide electronic resources. Most responded by canceling journals and purchasing fewer books in order to shift money into electronic resources. "Both the high prices and steep annual increases have forced libraries to cancel thousands of journal subscriptions, prompting publishers to raise prices even higher to make up for the loss" (SPARC and chemists 1998, 1). Some publishers responded by publishing fewer titles and printing fewer copies of the books they did publish; others continued to increase the prices of their books and journals. The cycle of price increases and subsequent cancellations became a spiral without an end in sight. The relationship between research libraries in the United States and publishers became antagonistic as libraries blamed a few large commercial publishers and society publishers for price increases that libraries considered outrageous and unjustified. As Guédon (2001, 1) states, the responsibilities for the serials pricing crisis "are now clearly identified: they rest squarely on the shoulders of commercial publishers." Libraries, researchers, and societies began to search for solutions to the situation many described as a crisis.

RESEARCH LIBRARIES RESPOND TO THE SERIALS CRISIS

In 1997, representatives from universities, scholarly societies, and university presses met to discuss the challenges in maintaining access to research information. The Association of American Universities, the Association of Research Libraries, and the Pew Higher Education Roundtable sponsored the meeting. The participants recommended that

- "promotion and tenure committees disentangle the notions of quality and quantity in the work of faculty;
- libraries leverage their resources by creating a more coherent market for scholarly publications;
- universities, led by their national associations, help faculty understand the implications of signing away their intellectual property rights;
- universities and scholarly societies invest in electronic forms of peer-reviewed scholarly communication; and
- universities and scholarly societies decouple publications and faculty peer-reviewed evaluations of the merit of scholarly work" (Case 1998, 5).

Scholarly Publishing and Academic Resources Coalition

SPARC, the Scholarly Publishing and Academic Resources Coalition, was created in 1998 as a result of the discussions about the future of scholarly publishing. It is one response to rising journal prices and to the declining role of scholars in the future of scholarly communication (Stoffle 2001, 34). An alliance of libraries and societies, SPARC's purpose is to create a more competitive marketplace; reduce the prices of journals; ensure fair use; ensure educational and library uses of electronic resources; and apply new technologies to improve the process of scholarly communication and to reduce the costs of production and distribution of scholarly materials (SPARC 1998, 3).

SPARC works with scholarly societies and scholars to create new journals that will compete with established journals in areas where "prices are highest and competition is needed most—primarily in the science, technical, and medical areas" (SPARC 1998, 3). As of 2003, SPARC had established partnerships with several societies, including the American Chemical Society, and sponsored several journals. The SPARC-sponsored journals are frequently 50 to 100 percent less expensive than the commercial journals with which they are competing. Editorial boards of some journals published by commercial publishers have resigned as a group to work with SPARC to create new journals that compete with their former journals. SPARC has convinced publishers, both directly and indirectly, to reduce some prices and keep others stable (Stoffle 2001, 36–38). "By exploring the possibility of helping learned societies to retain control over their journal whenever they are facing financial difficulties, by helping editors to negotiate better deals with their publishers when they are in the hands of a commercial publisher, by educating research colleagues about the economic realities of scientific publishing, SPARC works toward creating stronger alliances between libraries and at least that category of gatekeepers which refuses to give in too willingly to the big publishers" (Guédon 2001, 19). SPARC also provides information to scholars about the future of scholarly communication and helps libraries and societies develop new products. SPARC has proposed that academic institutions create online collections of the publications of their faculty. These "institutional repositories" could be factors in efforts to reform scholarly communication as well as tangible evidence of the institutions' research activities (Crow 2002, 4). For more information about SPARC, see http://www.arl.org/sparc/ (accessed June 1, 2003).

Open Archives

Open archives are electronic databases of research information that are available free of charge. These archives may contain articles that have been published in scholarly journals or preprints, which are preliminary reports about research projects. One of the first archives was arXiv (http://arxiv.org, accessed June 1, 2003), which "revolutionized communication among physicists" by making new research results available rapidly on the Internet (Feder 2001, 26). Other archives have been created in areas such as economics and computer science. These archives allow scholars to exchange information about their research quickly and easily. New ideas can be shared with researchers, and colleagues can validate or correct concepts immediately. The long delays resulting from publication and letters can be replaced by an instantaneous exchange of information.

PubMed Central, an archive of peer-reviewed research in the life sciences, provides free and unrestricted access to full-text electronic journal literature. It is designed to allow easy searching of the literature and to provide a stable archive (see http://www.pubmedcentral.nih.gov/, accessed June 1, 2003).

Open archives and preprint services are seen by some publishers as threats; other publishers seek ways to adapt the concepts of open archives to their corporate activities. These projects are developing rapidly, and librarians must be involved in their growth.

Consortia

Library consortia are groups of libraries working together for agreed-upon purposes. Libraries have formed consortia for many purposes including to catalog materials cooperatively, to purchase materials jointly, and to provide preferential services such as interlibrary loan. Many consortia have negotiated with publishers to provide electronic resources to the consortia members. The goals are either lowering costs to members or increasing access to materials; occasionally both goals can be achieved. Statewide consortia such as OhioLINK have licensed electronic collections for all their libraries, providing their libraries with greatly increased resources.

Consortia have successfully negotiated agreements with publishers that create programs to provide greatly increased access to materials, extending access to libraries that could never afford to acquire the resources independently. There are some disadvantages, of course. Larger libraries may actually see their costs increase. The additional titles that are included in the expanded package may not be relevant to the libraries' collections. The responsibility for selecting materials for the libraries is shifted from the selectors to the publishers. The most crucial disadvantage is that the libraries pay increasing amounts of money to these publishers; they cannot cancel portions of the package when the next budget crisis arrives.

Consortia are another response to the scholarly publishing crisis; they have been successful in developing some alternative approaches to providing access to resources. Neither they, nor SPARC, nor the open archives projects are the sole solution to the crisis; it calls for multiple approaches and continuing efforts to find successful answers.

CONCLUSION

The publishing industry is in a state of rapid, revolutionary change. Many publishers that had been operating for many decades have gone out of business, while media companies have purchased many others. Technology has transformed the physical process of publishing. Serials prices have increased dramatically, causing libraries to respond by canceling serials and buying fewer books. The serials pricing crisis became the scholarly publishing crisis as electronic publishing revolutionized research, publishing, and libraries. Librarians and scholars have begun searching for alternatives to the traditional methods of scholarly publishing. Publishers strive to remain profitable while they adapt to the new electronic publishing developments. New types of documents, such as electronic articles that are accompanied by statistical files and multimedia supplements, are being created.

Predicting the future of publishing is easy; predicting it correctly is far more difficult. Print books and electronic books have both been declared doomed frequently, and equally inaccurately so far. As the changes in publishing continue to transform the world of publishing and of libraries, librarians must strive to stay aware of the developments that will determine the future of both publishing and libraries.

REFERENCES

Baker, John F. 2001. University presses urged to expand their reach. *Publishers Weekly* 248 (28): 10–11.

Bolman, Pieter S. H. 1996. Journals face the electronic frontier. In *The book in the United States today,* edited by W. Gordon Graham and Richard Abel. New Brunswick, NJ: Transaction.

Case, Mary M. 1998. Academic community sets agenda to reclaim scholarly publishing. *ARL: A Bimonthly Report* 198: 5.

Crow, Raym. 2002. *The case for institutional repositories: A SPARC position paper.* Washington, DC: Scholarly Publishing and Academic Resources Coalition.

Daly, Charles P., Patrick Henry, and Ellen Ryder. 1997. *The magazine publishing industry.* Boston: Allyn and Bacon.

Feder, Toni. 2001. Ginsparg takes electronic preprint archive to Cornell. *Physics Today* 54 (9): 26.

Greco, Albert N. 1997. *The book publishing industry.* Boston: Allyn and Bacon.

———. 2001. The market for university press books in the United States: 1985–1999. *Learned Publishing* 14: 97–105.

Grycz, Czeslaw Jan. 1997. *Professional and scholarly publishing in the digital age.* New York: Association of American Publishers.

Guédon, Jean-Claude. 2001. In Oldenburg's long shadow: Librarians, research scientists, publishers, and the control of publishing. In *Association of Research Libraries proceedings of the 138th annual meeting.* <http://www.arl.org/arl/proceedings/138/guedon.html> (accessed June 1, 2003).

Hunter, Karen. 2000. Publishing in 2000. *Advances in Librarianship* 24: 25–49.

Ink, Gary, and Andrew Grabois. 2001. Book title output and average prices: 1999 final and 2000 preliminary figures. In *The Bowker annual: Library and book trade almanac*. 46th ed. 485–89. New Providence, NJ: R. R. Bowker.

Johnson, Sammye, and Patricia Prijatel. 2000. *Magazine publishing*. Lincolnwood, IL: NTC/Contemporary Publishing Group.

Lawal, Ibironke. 2001. Scholarly communication at the turn of the millennium: A bibliographic essay. *Journal of Scholarly Publishing* 32: 136–54.

Lichtenberg, James. 2001. Libraries look for niche in electronic publishing world. *Publishers Weekly* 248 (39): 21–23.

McCabe, Mark J. 1999. The impact of publishing mergers on journal prices: An update. *ARL: A Bimonthly Report* 207: 1–5.

Milliot, Jim. 2000. Publishers' profits had solid gains in 1999. *Publishers Weekly* 247 (36): 11.

———. 2001. Industry sales rose 3% in 2000, to $25.3 billion. *Publishers Weekly* 248 (10): 12.

Morris, Sally. 2001. Guest editorial. *Learned Publishing* 19: 163–65.

Nisonger, Thomas E. 1998. *Management of serials in libraries*. Englewood, CO: Libraries Unlimited.

Peters, Thomas A. 2001. A year of growing pains for the electronic publishing movement. In *The Bowker annual: Library and book trade almanac*. 46th ed. 201–17. New Providence, NJ: R. R. Bowker.

Picard, Robert G., and Jeffrey H. Brody. 1997. *The newspaper publishing industry*. Boston: Allyn and Bacon.

R. R. Bowker. 2000. Preface to *Books in print, 2000–2001*. Vol. 1. New Providence, NJ: R. R. Bowker.

R. R. Bowker. 2002. Preface to *Ulrich's periodicals directory, 2002*. 40th ed. Vol. 1. New Providence, NJ: R. R. Bowker.

Reid, Calvin. 2001. Weldon's Bulgari product placement raises eyebrows. *Publishers Weekly* 248 (37): 17.

Schiffrin, André. 2000. *The business of books: How international conglomerates took over publishing and changed the way we read*. London: Verso.

Schuman, Patricia Glass, and Charles Harmon. 1999. The business of book publishing. In *Understanding the business of library acquisitions*. 2nd ed. Edited by Karen A. Schmidt. Chicago: American Library Association.

SPARC and chemists to collaborate on new reduced-cost journals. 1998. *ARL: A Bimonthly Report* 199: 1–2.

SPARC: The Scholarly Publishing and Academic Resources Coalition. 1998. *ARL: A Bimonthly Report* 199: 3–4.

Stoffle, Carla. 2001. A library view of the SPARC initiative. *Against the Grain* 13 (2): 34–38.

Swain, Harriet. 1999. Rumours of a death that may be true. *Times Higher Education Supplement* 1414: 22–23.

Watkinson, Anthony. 2001. *Electronic solutions to the problems of monographic publishing*. London: Resource: The Council for Museums, Archives, and Libraries.

Works, George Alan. 1927. *College and university library problems*. Chicago: American Library Association.

Chapter ▶ 4

Domestic and Foreign Vendor Selection and Evaluation

A library vendor, sometimes called an agent, dealer, supplier, bookseller, or jobber, is a seller of materials in one or more formats or languages. Most libraries, regardless of type or size, use vendors to acquire their books, serials, and media rather than order library materials directly from dozens or, depending on the library's size, hundreds of individual publishers. Vendors serve in a partnership with the library as an extension of the library's staff. Libraries rely on vendors for library materials and services, while vendors rely on libraries for their continued existence.

Vendors have been around for many years. Through a complex series of mergers and buyouts, and through extremely creative and intricate means, some can trace their lineage back to the 1800s. The relationship between libraries and vendors has changed over the past fifty years when libraries began entering the information age; however, many similarities endure. The late 1950s witnessed a great outpouring of state and federal funding to encourage education and technological development. Demand for materials increased, requiring new ways to create, reproduce, and disseminate them. The partnership between libraries and vendors mainly involved vendors supplying libraries with books and serials in printed format.

By the mid-1970s, runaway inflation and eroding buying power, combined with a continued increase in the number of materials being produced, altered the purchasing patterns of libraries. Vendors affected by all the events that influenced the library and publishing industries were caught in the middle (Fisher 1993, 61–69).

In the 1980s, two major events changed the library-vendor relationship forever: the escalating cost of serial publications and the introduction of

55

automation into all aspects of library operations. Libraries began to expect the vendors to advocate on their behalf against price increases and to be forerunners in automation (Presley 1993, 55–56).

The 1990s introduced a new consumerism, further altering the library-vendor partnership. Librarians were canceling serials in record numbers and conducting tougher price negotiations, as well as beginning to shift information access to new formats (Shirk 1993, 145). These trends continue in the twenty-first century with even tighter library budgets and increasing reliance on electronic formats. Further, many libraries are members of consortia, working with other libraries to procure more advantageous pricing arrangements for electronic packages of journals, usually directly with publishers, eliminating the use of vendors altogether.

WHY LIBRARIES USE VENDORS

Libraries form relationships, partnerships, with vendors to benefit from the expertise of the vendor's staff. Their staff have established connections with publishers and they place orders, claim missed materials, and provide simplified invoicing to the library as well as payment to the publisher for materials on behalf of the library. Vendors save the library time and staff because they provide a single point of service rather than requiring the library to deal with dozens or hundreds of individual publishers.

Vendors provide a full array of service and technological options to libraries. They provide databases to libraries with bibliographic information such as author, title, ISBN or ISSN, publisher, price, and so on. They also provide recent and projected pricing trends. In addition, they may provide cataloging services, shelf-ready books, and serials check-in.

TYPES OF VENDORS

Library vendors range from broad based to highly specialized. Some vendors sell books and approval plans in paper, referred to in the industry as print, while others offer electronic books. Some vendors specialize in serials. These vendors provide serials in both print and electronic formats. Still other vendors specialize in media formats such as music CDs, videos, or DVDs, while others specialize in material types such as art exhibition catalogs or music scores. Some vendors sell both domestic and foreign library materials, while others differentiate themselves by offering foreign materials either from a single country, such as Brazil, or from a region, such as continental Europe.

AcqWeb lists more than 260 library vendors selling library materials to the U.S. market (http://acqweb.library.vanderbilt.edu/acqweb/pubr/vendor. html, accessed June 1, 2003).

IDENTIFYING VENDORS

Vendors can be identified in several ways. A number of directories provide information about vendors. Acquisitions staff may consult readily available general directories such as *Literary Marketplace* and *International Literary Marketplace* or specialized directories such as *Book and Serial Vendors for Africa and the Middle East, Book and Serial Vendors for Asia and the Pacific,* and *Book and Serial Vendors for Eastern Europe and the Former Soviet Union.* Visiting vendor websites is another way to locate information about vendors and their services (see "Corporate and Vendor Internet Sites" in the appendix).

Talking with other librarians about their experiences with various vendors can be informative. Participation in electronic discussion lists such as ACQNET and SERIALST also provides valuable insights (see "Electronic Discussion Lists" and their URLs in the appendix). In addition, visiting vendor exhibits at conferences affords librarians the opportunity to talk with vendors and to see demonstrations of their electronic databases. Finally, the library's parent institution's purchasing office may have a list of vendors.

SELECTING VENDORS

The method used by the library to select its vendor, or vendors, will vary by library type and size and the requirements of the parent institution. Some libraries are required to do business only with vendors designated by state or parent institution agreements resulting from a formal bid process. Such libraries have no input into the criteria by which the vendor was selected. Other libraries may be able to use an informal selection process consisting of little more than reading literature provided by the vendor and conversations with vendor representatives, selecting the vendor that the librarian likes best. Most libraries use a process that falls somewhere between these two extremes.

Increasingly, libraries are using some form of competitive procurement process, affording vendors an equal opportunity to submit proposals or bids stating their ability to supply goods and services to the requesting body.

Which Process to Use

The competitive procurement process is most often accomplished via the request for proposal (RFP). The request for quotation (RFQ) and the request for information (RFI) are also methods of vendor selection used by libraries, but they have limitations.

The RFQ, sometimes referred to as a "request for quote" or the "bid process," bases vendor awards of the library's account on the lowest-price bid. The bid process works well when purchasing a specified good such as printer ribbons where there is little variance, but it does not work well when contracting for a service. While price—either service charge for serials or discount for books and media—is an important part of the decision, its value pales when service is poor. With the RFQ, all factors other than price are ignored, so services to libraries are often limited or unreliable, or both.

The RFI simply asks the vendor for information about its services and generally does not ask for firm price quotations as does the RFQ. RFIs can be a valuable tool for libraries to use in the planning phase, when they are deciding which elements to include prior to writing an RFP. "The less formal nature of the RFI allows vendors to present information about themselves without investing an inordinate amount of time in the preparation of the document" (Wilkinson and Bordeianu 1997, 38). The RFI may prove especially useful when the library is not planning for on-site vendor visits as part of its decision-making process.

The RFP "represents a formalized process for documenting, justifying, and authorizing a procurement; allows for evaluating different solutions; and provides a means for establishing, monitoring, and controlling the performance of the winning vendor" (Porter-Roth 1991, 26). In the RFP document, the library's required and desired elements are clearly stated, along with the steps that vendors must follow if they wish to submit a proposal for the library's account. The RFP provides a clear, reasonably objective method for a library to evaluate vendor proposals, justify the contract award, and monitor vendor performance and compliance, avoiding decisions made on emotional reactions either for or against a particular vendor. Though time consuming, the RFP is often the best method for the library to use because it considers vendor service as well as price. The library awards its account to the vendor for its ability to provide materials as ordered, on time, and to resolve the problem when a breakdown occurs at any stage of the process, as well as to deliver the materials at the agreed-upon price.

Both opponents and proponents of the RFP process abound. The process is both time consuming and labor intensive. Numerous authors have warned librarians against its use, while others have sung its praises. Regardless of its shortcomings, no more thorough, objective method is available. Because it is generally the preferred method for most libraries, this chapter concentrates on the RFP as the method for domestic and foreign vendor selection for books, serials, and other materials, regardless of format.

Planning the RFP Process

Whether the RFP process is voluntarily embarked upon by the library or mandated by a governing body, a plan will clearly outline the process and keep it on track. The planning elements this chapter describes are easily applied to larger academic libraries and can readily be adapted to fit the needs of consortia (groups of libraries that work together to procure more advantageous pricing arrangements or other negotiated items) as well as public, school, and special libraries. Although the RFP process described in this chapter concentrates on book and serials vendors, the process outlined herein can be adapted to fit RFPs for integrated library systems, the outsourcing of materials processing, or commercial binders.

The RFP plan described below clearly outlines the steps to take and specifies the timeline to be used throughout the RFP process. It affords the librarian the opportunity to gain increased knowledge of options in vendor services and systems currently available in the marketplace.

The first step is to determine who should be involved in the RFP process. Planning is hard work, time consuming, and requires well-considered input. One person can conduct the process, but in larger libraries or consortia a committee or task force is often better at providing balanced input to the process. "The library has to decide who should, or must, contribute to it" (Schatz and Graves 1996, 422). Depending on the type of proposal, the library task force may include experienced personnel, knowledgeable in acquisitions, serials, and collection management. Usually someone from one of these areas will chair the task force. In addition to these staff, someone from systems and public services areas may be involved, as well as either the dean or director or a designate, depending on the institutional culture.

Once the task force has been formed and the chair selected, the group will need to define the role of each member and who is responsible for what in the process. The group needs to be clear on how their feedback will be gathered and evaluated and understand clearly who will make the award based on the group's evaluation—will it be the library dean or director or the institution's purchasing officer? "It is imperative that committee members understand clearly why they were appointed to the committee, what their role is within the committee, what the committee's role is in the award process, and the time frame in which they are expected to accomplish the tasks associated with that role" (Wilkinson and Thorson 1998, 8).

Next the task force must identify which materials the library is interested in procuring: what part of the library's materials will be acquired in this cycle? For example, is the library looking for a vendor to provide books through an approval plan (where books are supplied based on a preapproved profile of subjects desired by the library) or with which to place firm orders for a specific title? (See chapter 5, "Acquiring Books and Media," for more information.) Or is the library looking for a vendor to handle its domestic or foreign, or both, serial subscriptions? (See chapter 6, "Acquiring Serials," for more information.) Or perhaps the library is looking for a vendor that specializes in art exhibition catalogs or music scores?

To avoid having to do an RFP for all types of materials collected by the library at the same time, the library may alternate which years certain types of materials are up for proposal. If, for example, a library uses a four-year vendor contract, it may choose to undertake the RFP process for approval books in 2004 and serial subscriptions in 2006, repeating the process for approval books again in 2008 and so forth.

The library will need to decide if it will write the RFP to allow only one vendor to receive the award for a given category or material or if it will allow the award to be divided among two or more vendors. Generally, dividing an approval plan award makes little sense for domestic titles (e.g., separating out trade from university press titles or dividing by subject areas). This type of separation creates a strong probability of receiving duplicate titles, especially in interdisciplinary subjects, and the library is likely to receive a reduced discount corresponding to the lower number of books purchased from each vendor. Contracts for books ordered on a title-by-title selection basis, called firm orders, are often awarded to the vendor handling the library's approval plan. However, a library may desire to have one vendor for its domestic approval plan and a separate vendor for an approval plan specializing in area studies such as Latin America. Also, in some cases the library may want to divide a serial subscription account. It may choose to award its domestic serials to one vendor and its foreign serials to another vendor. Some librarians think that a vendor can provide serials in its country of origin better than a U.S. vendor with offices abroad can. Other librarians are just not comfortable "putting all their eggs in one basket" because of concerns over vendor mergers or possible failure of the company. Still others believe that the advantages of having all serial titles consolidated with one vendor, such as unified management reports on all titles and generally a lower service charge, outweigh these concerns.

Another decision the library must make is whether to place its standing orders (where the vendor regularly supplies a nonperiodical serial such as a yearbook or series) on its approval plan or serial vendor's RFP. Although they are generally viewed as serials, placing them with the approval plan vendor can reduce the risk of receiving duplicate copies and often provide a discounted price.

Once the library determines what categories of materials it is requesting a vendor proposal for (e.g., serial subscriptions) and whether the proposal covers all or part of these materials (e.g., only U.S., only European, only African, only Latin American, only Asian, or all), it is ready for the next step in the planning process: the timeline. The timeline is a document displaying the projected activities involved in the RFP process, in order of their occurrence, with corresponding dates during which those activities will be accomplished. The RFP task force should prepare a timeline as one of its first actions. It should be a dynamic document, open to modification as needed, especially during initial meetings with the purchasing officer.

The timeline must clearly describe each stage of the process, allowing enough time to complete each step. This planning not only should ensure a successful outcome but will contribute to the sanity of the task force as well. When possible start the timeline nine months to a year before the contract will begin. This generous time frame will allow for the unexpected delays with some part of the process that will inevitably occur.

Phase 1 of the timeline is the preparation of the RFP, which may include meeting with the institution's purchasing officer, selecting vendors to receive the RFP, arranging for them to visit the library (or gathering information by sending an RFI to vendors), writing the RFP document, and sending it to the purchasing officer or library staff or both for preliminary review. Careful attention should be paid to phase 1 of the process because the quality of work at this stage sets the tone for the rest of the process. Mistakes made now will create serious problems later especially in the evaluation phase. If the process is regulated by the state, a single overlooked regulation may invalidate the entire RFP, wasting time and causing considerable frustration.

Phase 2 of the timeline involves receipt of the vendor proposals, evaluation of these proposals, recommendation by the RFP task force to the dean or director and purchasing officer, and awarding the contract or contracts.

Meeting with the institution's purchasing officer early in the planning process can avoid delays later. The meeting not only provides an opportunity to begin building rapport between the parties, it provides the library with the boilerplate requirements of the purchasing office. "Typical requirements include a description of the library and its parent organization, the type of materials the contract covers, the dollar amount per annum of expenditure with a vendor for which a contract is required, the terms for shipping, the beginning and end dates for the contract, the number of years the contract will cover, and the evaluation criteria" (Wilkinson and Thorson 1998, 9). In addition, most organizations require all contracts to include a disclaimer stating that the dollar amount per annum is intended to provide the vendor with an estimated contract value but should not be considered a commitment to purchase that amount if the library's budget changes.

The criteria that the library will use when evaluating the proposals must be agreed upon in advance by the purchasing officer. Usually some amount of negotiation between the library and the purchasing department is needed regarding criteria for evaluating responses and making contract awards. The purchasing department will be chiefly concerned about lowest cost, but it is critical that the library define the set of minimum acceptable standards that must be met before any consideration of lowest cost can take place. Only the library is qualified to do this (Dowd 1991, 66).

Once a list of vendors has been identified to receive the RFP (through directories, discussion lists, the institution's purchasing office, or other means), the library may wish to learn more about what vendor services are available before it writes the RFP document. This can be accomplished either through the RFI process or through site visits. In an on-site visit, a vendor representative gives a presentation to a library's staff at its location or site. Although this is generally done in the planning phase, the top vendors may be invited to do it during the final negotiation stage. Advantages to vendor visits include the opportunity for the library to meet with vendor representatives and through this personal contact get a sense of the vendor's way of conducting business, as well as to give the task force additional ideas of what elements it wants to include as either required or desired elements of the RFP. These visits also give the vendor a clearer perspective of the library to aid in its proposal or to help in its decision not to respond to the RFP.

Writing the RFP

Writing a clear, thorough, well-thought-out RFP document is the most important element in the process. All parts of the document must be written using nonprejudicial language—language that is unbiased, impartial, and nondiscriminatory. The RFP task force must ensure that the RFP document, reference questions, and evaluation forms are free from prejudicial language that unfairly favors one vendor over another.

The library's RFP task force will work with its purchasing officer to determine which vendors should receive the RFP, based on the vendor's ability to provide materials in the RFP category. Obviously an RFP for an approval plan should not be sent to a vendor that handles only serials subscriptions. If the task force is not familiar with a given vendor, care needs to be taken to research what types of materials each vendor can and cannot provide as well as the vendor's specialization. For example, can the vendor provide materials in all subjects, in all formats (e.g., print, electronic, AV, microform, newspaper, etc.), from all country or geographic origins (e.g., United States, Continental Europe, Eastern Europe, Africa, Asia, Latin America, etc.), and from all publishers (e.g., trade, small presses, associations, societies, government agencies, etc.)? What categories of materials does it provide—for example, domestic approval plans, specialized approval plans, firm orders for books and media, standing orders for nonperiodical serials, and serials subscriptions? Does the vendor handle license agreements for electronic books, serials, or both?

The RFP document provides vendors the information they need to prepare their response. Because contacts are awarded for several years, when writing the request, libraries must consider not just what they want today, but what they may want tomorrow. The task force should review developing technology and consider any anticipated changes in staffing and any other known factors such as plans to change its integrated library system during the contract period.

Major categories of RFPs include domestic approval plans, specialized approval plans, firm order books or media, standing order nonperiodical serials, and serial subscriptions. The RFP will consist of several parts including the boilerplate "instructions to vendors" section, the library's requirements, its desired elements, and the evaluation criteria.

Boilerplate Instructions to Vendors

Boilerplate instructions to vendors are provided jointly by the library task force and the parent institution's purchasing office and communicate details about pragmatic matters to the vendors responding to the RFP. The standard information and instructions include the proposal number; purchasing and library contact information; the due date and time by which vendors must submit their proposal; the number of copies that must be received; any format requirements for the proposal; instructions pertaining to alternative offers, cancellations, clarifications, failure to respond, late submissions, modifications, period of offer acceptance, public information, rejection of offers, telegraphic offers, taxes (materials versus services), and withdrawal of offers; equal opportunity or affirmative action statements; a detailed statement of conflict of interest and debarment; and other information as determined by individual institutions.

The vendor should be instructed to provide a minimum of three references. Ask that these references be libraries comparable in size and type to your library. Ask that one of these references be a library that recently transferred its account to the vendor. Contacting this reference will give the library some indication of how well the vendor handles the account transfer process. Also, ask that one of the references use the same integrated library system as your library. This will give the library insight about how well the vendors' systems interface with the library's system.

In addition, background information about the library may be included in this section. This background information could include a description of the library's parent organization (university, community, school, or agency) or consortium, including its clientele, programs, and size and strength of collections; operating budget; staff size and other appropriate information pertaining to the library such as the bibliographic utility it uses; and information about its integrated library system or in-house system, or in the case of small libraries, that it has no automated system.

Required and Desired Elements

Required elements are nonnegotiable. The vendor either can and will provide each and every one of them or its proposal is invalid. The library's RFP task force should take great care in determining which elements it requires versus which ones it desires. The library's statement of requirements is usually relatively small, containing only those elements that the vendor must provide or be eliminated from consideration. The library's list of desired elements can be as long as needed to reflect its desires. However, the list should not be unrealistically detailed. Remember that the vendor has to respond to all questions on the RFP, and then the task force has to evaluate all of them to be able to justify its decision to its administration.

Vendor Management   Some required elements vary by RFP type (approval plans versus serials), while some are consistent across RFP categories. One such consistent element involves vendor management. The library will require some company data and information about the financial condition of the vendor. Company data include the history of the vendor, locations of its offices, number of libraries similar to yours that the vendor serves, and what distinguishes the vendor from other vendors of its kind. The financial condition of the vendor or its parent company documents its financial state, indicating whether it is financially sound and stable. To ensure the vendor's financial solvency, the RFP will often require the respondent to supply a statement of the financial health of the company such as an internal auditor's report. This type of auditor's report is carried out by the vendor itself on a continuous basis, ensuring the accuracy and reliability of the vendor's accounting records. The vendor can supply such reports as part of its proposal to demonstrate its financial stability and solvency. The library may prefer an external auditor's report, carried out by an accounting firm hired by the vendor as opposed to internal auditors that work directly for the vendor. In addition to or instead of an auditor's report, the library may require a statement of financial solvency or a letter of credit from the vendor's bank, or both.

The library will pose a series of questions to vendors to elicit information about vendor management issues. The questions will vary by the type of library and the issues of greatest concern to it. Some of the instructions and statements will be about requirements and must be labeled as such, while others will be designed to elicit information about how the vendor addresses desired elements. Sample questions follow (adapted from Wilkinson and Thorson 1998, 138–39):

+ How many years has the vendor been in business?
+ What distinguishes this vendor from others of its kind?
+ What are the vendor's mission and vision statement, corporate goals, and annual report?
+ How long has the vendor offered [specify: approval plans, serial subscriptions, etc.] to libraries?

- How many offices does the vendor have, where are they located, and which one would handle the library's account?
- How many libraries does the vendor serve in each category: academic (specify the number that are Association of Research Libraries members), public, school, special, government, and other categories of libraries?
- What is the vendor's total staff size?
- What are the qualifications and training of the vendor's staff who would be working with the library's account? [Note: this is especially important information for the library to have for individuals who select, buy, and profile titles for approval plans.]
- What is the financial condition of the vendor?

Customer Service   Another required element that cuts across all types of RFPs is customer service. Customer service is of great importance to the library; its value should not be underestimated. Good customer service creates satisfaction and loyalty, whereas poor customer service will eventually cost the vendor the library's account.

The library will have the most frequent contact with a vendor account representative, who is usually based on-site at the vendor's home or branch office. Although vendors have tried various models—from "account team approaches" to "ask any representative that is available"—most libraries prefer a designated account representative for their account. Libraries want knowledgeable, service-oriented vendor staff, who are readily available by email, phone, or fax and who resolve problems promptly. Nothing is more frustrating than an account representative who does not return phone calls promptly, does not resolve problems satisfactorily, or cannot answer questions readily.

In addition to the account representative, the vendor will provide a sales representative. This person, usually based out of his or her home somewhere in the region of the library, visits the library at least annually and more often as needed. He or she can also be reached by email, phone, or fax. This person keeps the library informed regarding new vendor products and services, trends in the market, and improvements in the vendor's electronic systems and has often been said to share industry gossip. When the library experiences problems with its account representative, often the sales representative can amicably resolve them or arrange for the library to have a different and more responsive account representative.

Customer service is the core of the vendor-library relationship. The library may wish to require that the vendor designate an account representative to service its account, or it may require performance standards such as specifying within how many minutes or hours the vendor will respond to the library's email or phone calls. Because of the importance of quality customer service, the library will want to craft its desired elements carefully to get the best understanding possible of how the vendor views its customer service role. Some sample questions to consider follow (adapted from Wilkinson and Thorson 1998, 139–40):

- How quickly (average minutes or hours) will an account representative respond to a problem or question from the library?
- How many accounts does each account representative handle? Does this individual have assistants? If so, what are the assistants authorized to handle?
- Can the vendor successfully accommodate multiple bill-to and ship-to addresses?
- Where will the sales representative assigned to work with the library be located? How quickly will this person respond to the library's questions and problems? How often will he or she visit the library?
- In the event the library transfers its account to the vendor, what services would be provided to facilitate the account transfer?
- In the event the library transfers its account to the vendor, what procedures would the vendor use to notify publishers of the change of vendors? [Note: this question applies to standing orders and serials.]
- In the event the library transfers its account away from the vendor, how would the vendor handle the cancellations of all titles for the library? [Note: this question applies to standing orders and serials.]

Management Reports Management reports are an important component of the vendor's overall service package. These reports provide information about the library's current expenditures with the vendor or its historical expenditures (e.g., for the last three years) and can be divided by elements such as country of origin or information contained in the library's original order (such as fund code). Reports can be arranged in alphabetical order, by ascending or descending price, or according to publisher. Other reports cover fulfillment rate, fulfillment time, or the number of titles supplied in a given subject.

Based on the library's preferred method of having management report information presented, it may decide to require certain management reports and specify their format. Both vendor and library system software is becoming increasingly flexible, making even highly customized reports easier to obtain and manipulate. To better understand standard reports offered by the vendor, the library may choose to ask for a description and sample of each report available. It should also verify whether a cost is associated with any of the reports and whether the vendor limits the number of different reports or the number of times that the library can receive a single report annually at no cost.

Computer-Based Services Computer-based services from vendors encompass a wider range of capability than ever before. For some time, libraries have required more from vendors than delivery of the right title, in the right format, at the right time, with excellent customer service at every step along the way. Libraries now require vendor systems interfaces and electronic services and capabilities. The required elements of the RFP in this area should be reasonable, cost effective, and appropriate to the library's needs today and to its anticipated needs during the contract period.

Computer-based services to consider may include ease of use and special features of the vendor's system, such as interfaces with the library's system, bibliographic utilities, or electronic products; inventory status; order, claim, cancellation, payment data, or status report transmissions; ability to provide bibliographic records in full MARC or processing level format; ability to provide name, subject, and series authority records; management reports; and a host of other options. Some of these services are suitable for a category of RFPs such as approval plans or serial subscriptions, while others apply to all categories. Some sample questions to consider follow (adapted from Wilkinson and Thorson 1998, 140–41):

- How many library clients does the vendor have that use [specify the integrated library system that the library uses]?
- Will the vendor assign a project manager to the library for testing of new interfaces and programs?
- Is the vendor's host system "view only" or can the library update and change its own records? If so, what kinds of records and updates are possible?
- What features does the vendor have under development for its host system? Describe.
- Does the vendor provide publisher dispatch data electronically?
- Does the vendor handle license agreements for libraries? For consortia?
- How does the vendor handle copyright regarding the electronic access environment?
- Describe the vendor's interest in partnering with the library on future computer or systems innovations.

Approval Plans, Firm Orders, and Standing Orders   Many libraries choose to combine their domestic approval plan, firm order books (ordered on a title-by-title basis), and standing order nonperiodical serials (such as yearbooks or series) with one vendor. Increasing the number of items the library orders from a single vendor can increase the library's discount amount. Placing its firm and standing orders with the approval plan vendor can reduce the chances of receiving duplicate material. Since the vendor will know what titles it has or will supply on standing order, and it knows what titles the library has placed a firm order for, it will not duplicate those titles on the approval plan.

Approval plan vendors work with the library to set up a profile of books to send to the library based on subjects, publishers, prices, geographic emphases, and intended audience levels (as discussed in chapter 5, "Acquiring Books and Media"). These books are of primary interest to the library. Books that are of secondary interest to the library are often made available for the library's consideration through a bibliographic form, also referred to as a bibliographic slip. Titles of secondary interest may include those over a specified dollar amount, reprints, translations, or in subject areas that are secondary to the library's collection emphasis. These notification slips contain all the bibliographic information the library needs to determine if it wishes to place an order for that title. The notifications may come in paper form, but increasingly, they are made available to libraries electronically.

In addition to domestic approval plans, the library may have any number of specialized approval plans for materials in area studies (e.g., Latin American, African, Asian, etc.), in the fine arts (e.g., art exhibition catalogs or music scores), in science and technology areas, or for media such as video tapes, DVDs, or music CDs. Such specialized approval plans can be broad based within the specialty, such as all of Latin America, for example, or narrowly defined, such as northern Brazil. Though many approval plan vendors carry some materials from foreign countries or in foreign languages, for full coverage of a special area the library should use a vendor that specializes in those materials.

Some sample questions relating to domestic approval plans, firm orders, and standing orders follow (adapted from Wilkinson and Thorson 1998, 143–45). Some of the questions in the serials section that follows are also applicable for standing orders, which are nonperiodical serials. The library will need to compose additional questions for specialty approval plans based on the characteristics of the type of material involved.

   ❖   What types of approval plans does the vendor offer (general, specialized, or both) and how many are operational at one time? [Ask the vendor to specify what percentage it runs for your library category: for example, academic libraries.]

- What is the basis for subject classification and profiling approval plans?

- Can specific publishers be limited by subject or nonsubject treatments via the vendor's profiling method? If so, how?

- How closely does the vendor monitor publisher credentials?

- What are the vendor's sources for title selection for approval plans?

- What sources are used for coding approval plan titles by subject? At what point are titles coded?

- How are coded approval plan titles matched to the library's profile?

- Describe the vendor's primary approval plan profiling tools or documents.

- What techniques are used to monitor the approval plan profile?

- When approval plan profile changes are required, how are they accomplished and how long does it take for shipments to reflect the adjustments?

- How are new subject terms added to the vendor's subject classification plan? How are libraries notified of the changes?

- Can specific imprints of one publisher be excluded from that approval plan?

- How does the vendor determine how many copies of a book to buy for its approval customers?

- What is the length of time from receipt of a book by the vendor until it is sent to the library for approval? For standing orders?

- What return rate is expected for approval plans? Is there a maximum acceptable percentage for new plans? For existing plans?

- How many titles did the vendor provide for approval plans last year?

- Does the vendor provide bibliographic forms to its approval customers? If so, please provide sample forms. Can it provide these forms electronically?

- How are bibliographic forms prepared? Book in hand? From CIP (cataloging in publication)? Other?

- What are the average and maximum turnaround times for the vendor to provide bibliographic form selection orders?

- How long does a title remain in the vendor's database?

- What is the time lag between date of publication and the library's receipt of a bibliographic form selection notification? For standing orders?

The RFP will include a section on pricing for the approval plan, firm orders, and standing orders. In this section of the RFP, the library asks vendors about discounts offered and other financial aspects. The library should indicate if it expects this pricing to be the vendor's best and final offer or if there will be any negotiation involved later in the process. Pricing is an area where the library needs to work very closely with the purchasing officer to ensure that all requirements and questions follow all appropriate policies of the institution and laws of the state. Some sample questions follow (adapted from Wilkinson and Thorson 1998, 142, 145).

+ What discount is offered for approval plans, bibliographic forms or slips, firm orders, and standing orders? Describe in detail.

+ Does the vendor provide escalating discounts for funds deposited on account against approval or standing order shipments?

+ Describe the vendor's invoicing practices in detail. Send a sample invoice. How are discounts shown on invoices?

+ Is a penalty imposed for late payment of an invoice? If so, indicate the time period and amount of the penalty.

+ Describe the vendor's practices for credits in detail. Send a sample credit.

+ Does the vendor ever add service charges to approval plan or firm or standing order invoices? If so, please explain under what circumstances this would occur.

+ Describe the vendor's return policy.

+ For returns, can titles be lined off an invoice, the total adjusted, and the adjusted total paid? Or does the vendor use some other procedure?

+ Enumerate and describe in detail the costs associated with value-added services that the vendor offers to approval plan customers (e.g., for providing full MARC records, partial records, cataloging, table of contents, shelf-ready materials, authority control, etc.)?

+ Is there a special handling charge for materials ordered on a "rush" basis (e.g., overnight, two-day, etc.)?

+ In the case of a foreign vendor, does the vendor charge a conversion fee for paying in U.S. dollars? How are changes in exchange rates handled?

Serials Subscription Services   Serials, unlike books, are intended to continue indefinitely; however, they change their titles, merge with other

titles, split into two or more titles, and either suspend publication temporarily or cease altogether with sufficient regularity to deter some people
from even considering becoming a serials librarian. They are available in
paper, microform, or electronically and include popular magazines, scholarly journals, newspapers, proceedings, annuals, and so on. Because they
are generally published more quickly than books, the articles that they
carry are often the latest information available on a given subject; thus,
they are in high demand. Selecting a vendor that will supply them on time
and with a minimum of problems is critical.

When writing the RFP for a serials vendor, be sure to consider all
aspects of the serials operation in a balanced manner. Give careful consideration when deciding what to require as opposed to what the library
desires from a serial vendor. Too often the library is tempted to write the
RFP from the perspective of its last bad experience. For example, does the
library really want to require the vendor to notify it each time the vendor
receives a new order, or is this a reaction to a previous vendor that either
did not always place orders in a timely fashion or perhaps lost an important order altogether?

Many of the time frames in the sample questions that follow can be
specified by the library in a "profile" that the vendor produces based on the
library's instructions after the library becomes a customer of the vendor.
This often applies to the "within how many days" questions. In addition,
much of this information is available on the vendor's system, so that the
library can access it at any time. For example, information on memberships and "titles in combination" are available this way, as is information
about the status of orders, claims, and payments. Still, some librarians
may prefer direct notification, either electronically or via a paper report at
some specified interval. A variety of sample questions regarding serials
orders, claims, cessations, and cancellations follow (adapted from Wilkinson and Thorson 1998, 149–50):

+ Will the vendor provide confirmation that a new serials order has
  been placed? If so, within how many days?

+ Will the vendor seek a common start date for all periodical titles
  (e.g., January) and a common expiration date (e.g., December)?

+ Will the vendor supply information about "comes with" titles and
  memberships, and will the vendor notify the library of options to
  buy titles in combinations, when available?

+ Within how many days does the vendor process new serials
  orders?

+ How many days should the library generally allow before expecting receipt of the first issue of a new serials order?

- Within how many days after the vendor's receipt of a serials order should the library expect an invoice?
- If the vendor is unable to supply a title, within how many days will the library be notified? Will the reason be included?
- Will the vendor accept expedited orders for serials? How does the vendor handle them differently from regular orders?
- How are claims for serials processed by the vendor?
- Within how many days of receipt are serials claims processed, and what is the average turnaround time for processing claims?
- Are serials claims ever held and batched by the vendor?
- How is the library notified as to the status of claims? Within how many days will the library be notified?
- Describe the features of the vendor's serials claim reports. Provide a sample.
- Can the vendor provide the library with statistics on its serials claims?
- For serials claims submitted to the vendor within the time period designated by the publisher, will the vendor agree to supply the missing issue or issues at no additional cost to the library, even if the publisher does not honor the claim?
- How will the vendor deal with a pattern of receipt of duplicate serials issues by the library?
- In the event of a title change, cessation, split, or merger, will the vendor notify the library exactly what the last piece to be received will be (e.g., volume, number, year, month)?
- When a title changes, will the library be given a choice of not subscribing to the new title, or will the vendor automatically enter a subscription for the new title for the library?
- When a title ceases, what effort will the vendor make to secure a refund for the library?
- Will the vendor notify the library of "suspended" publications? At what point are serials considered "dead" and procedures for a refund initiated?

Unlike pricing for the approval plan, firm orders, and standing orders that offer discounts (generally some percentage of what the publisher gives them), serials vendors impose service charges. This difference is because publishers do not offer discounts on most serials, and even where they do—mostly on science and technology titles—the discount is shrinking with each passing year. Serials vendors operate on a very small margin of profit and often have very little negotiating room with their service charge.

In this section of the RFP, the library asks vendors about the service charges imposed and other financial aspects. The library should indicate if it expects this pricing to be the vendor's best and final offer or if it expects to negotiate later in the process. In addition, the library should provide the vendor with a sample list of serials titles. This consists of a representative list of serials titles that the library wishes to purchase from the vendor to whom the contract is awarded. Generally, the sample list should include approximately 10 percent of the library's serials titles, accurately reflecting the library's mix of titles (not just its humanities titles or just its science and technology titles, unless the library collects in just one area, as may be the case in specialized libraries). The list will help the vendor make an informed response to the service charge portion of the RFP.

As with the approval plan, in serials pricing the library needs to work very closely with the purchasing officer to ensure that all requirements and questions follow all appropriate policies of the institution and laws of the state. Some sample questions follow (adapted from Wilkinson and Thorson 1998, 142, 145).

- What would the vendor's flat service charge be for the library's serials account? [To assist the vendor in determining the service charge, the library should state the approximate dollar value of its account and provide a sample list of titles (or the full list).]

- What other service charge options does the vendor offer besides a flat service charge for the library's serials account? Specify and explain how each service charge option would work.

- Does the vendor provide early-payment credits? Describe and enumerate any early-payment percentage schedules.

- Describe the vendor's invoicing practices in detail. Send a sample invoice. How are service charges shown on invoices?

- Will supplementary invoices state the reason for the additional charge?

- Is a penalty imposed for late payment of a serials invoice? If so, indicate the time period and amount of the penalty.

- Describe the vendor's practices for credits in detail. Send a sample credit.

- Enumerate and describe in detail the costs associated with value-added services that the vendor offers to serials customers (e.g., serials check-in, license agreement assistance, etc.)?

- In the case of a foreign vendor, does the vendor charge a conversion fee for paying in U.S. dollars? How are changes in exchange rates handled?

Evaluation Form   The RFP task force will develop an evaluation form, containing the various point-weighted criteria for each factor of the RFP. These factors vary by library and may have different headings or may be combined differently, but they generally include vendor management, customer service, management reports, computer-based services, pricing, and any other section included in the RFP.

Preliminary Review of the RFP

Once the RFP document has been written, the task force begins the final step in phase 1 of the planning process: review of the RFP by the library and the purchasing officer. First, the RFP task force conducts a review for completeness and accuracy of the document. Depending on the library's organizational culture, the task force may want to submit it to the library dean or director for reading, especially if that person or a designate does not serve on the task force. Then the RFP is sent to the purchasing officer for final review. That person will review it for completeness and adherence to all pertinent policies, regulations, and laws. If needed, he or she will return it to the task force for revision.

The purchasing officer will attach any needed documentation and stipulations such as due date, format for the vendor's proposal, number of copies required, and so on; assign a proposal number to the RFP; and mail it to vendors. The timeline should allow sufficient time for vendors to respond fully to the request. Vendors should be given a minimum of thirty days to respond, and, when possible, forty-five to sixty days is desirable.

Evaluating Vendor Proposals

Evaluation of vendor proposals begins as soon as the deadline for submission has passed and the purchasing officer releases them to the library. However, the planning for the evaluation process has been done as the RFP was written. The evaluation criteria have been clearly delineated in the RFP, reflecting the value the library places on each section of the request.

Many libraries give the most weight to customer service elements. Although price—either discount for approval plans and firm order books or service charge for serial subscriptions, payment terms, early payment credit, late payment fee, exchange rate, and charges for optional service— is important, most libraries do not weigh it as heavily as customer service. Most librarians agree that it is not wise to "evaluate mainly on the basis of speed, price, and accuracy" (Alessi 1992, 118).

The weight given to other factors, such as vendor management, management reports, computer-based services, and other elements, varies by library. The task force should keep the library's needs and priorities in mind at all times and not be swayed by features or services that it does not need or will not use.

After all the months of planning for and writing the RFP, once the proposals are in, the task force can finally evaluate the proposals and recommend a vendor or vendors to its administration and to the purchasing officer. If the RFP was well considered and the required and desired elements and questions were clear, the evaluation process should not be daunting.

Obviously, the first step is for each RFP task force member to read carefully each vendor's proposal, review any appendix materials, and scrutinize all samples included in the package. Adequate time needs to be set aside for this task so that it is not rushed, causing some important aspect to be overlooked.

The RFP task force will use a standardized form containing the various point-weighted criteria that it prepared when the RFP was written. Each member of the task force will use the form to evaluate each vendor proposal. Libraries may devise any weighting system they like. One simple system is to assign a percentage to each category (e.g., 40 percent to customer service or 10 percent to vendor management) with the total for all categories adding up to 100 percent. Asking evaluators to assign a percentage score to each category and then to explain what criteria they used to arrive at that score helps to keep everyone on track and objective.

Carefully checking all vendor references is an important step in the process. The task force should prepare a list of questions to ask each reference. The task of calling or emailing references can be divided among the members of the task force.

Once each evaluator has completed the evaluation form, taking into consideration the vendor proposals, its references, and the vendor's on-site visit, if there was one, the form goes to the RFP task force chair. All evaluators' forms are tallied, their scores are averaged, and the chair prepares a recommendation document. The chair provides this document to the appropriate person in the library (dean or director, management group, etc.) and then to the purchasing officer. The recommendation document should open with a statement listing all vendors submitting proposals and the criteria used for evaluating them. It should contain a clear, concise statement naming the vendors being recommended for the contract or contracts, the reasons for their recommendations, and the averaged evaluation score for each vendor along with the cost comparison. In addition, this document should discuss the considerations that led the task force members to their recommendations.

When the library is producing more than one RFP, it may be useful to devise a recommendation form. Used in addition to the evaluation form, it is a standardized form containing the types or categories of RFPs for which the library is soliciting vendor proposals—for example, domestic approval plan, art catalog approval plan, and so forth. The form provides space for the evaluator to recommend a vendor for each RFP category (e.g., vendor X for science and technology approval plans, and vendor Y for European serials). This one-page recommendation form clearly states to the person tabulating the results which vendor the evaluator is recommending for each type of RFP.

Awarding the Contract

Once the purchasing officer has read and agrees to the RFP task force's recommendation, the purchasing department or other group in the parent organization officially awards the contract. This is usually done by mail. All vendors submitting proposals will be notified of the award.

In most cases, the RFP specifications, the vendor's proposal, and any attachments will form the contract. Some states or institutions require a separate contract document. When required, preparation of this document is the responsibility of the purchasing department or legal counsel's office.

EVALUATING VENDOR PERFORMANCE

Libraries have been conducting evaluations of vendor performance for decades. A historical view of vendor evaluation methodologies and studies from 1955 to 1987 can be found in an annotated bibliography prepared by the Acquisitions Subcommittee of the Library Committee of the Association for Higher Education of North Texas (Vendor Study Group 1988, 17–28). More recent articles and books abound on approval plans, firm orders, serials subscriptions, and electronic data evaluation techniques. In 1994, *Library Acquisitions: Practice and Theory* devoted an entire issue (vol. 18, no. 1) to articles on the subject.

Why Libraries Evaluate Vendor Performance

The library is obligated to expend its materials budget wisely. One benefit of the lengthy, arduous RFP process is to obtain the best vendor services for the library at a fair price. "The library must ensure that the vendor meets all the mandatory conditions of the contract" (Hirshon and Winters 1996, 140). The library is in the best position to see that vendors live up to the spirit and detail of the contract. Acquisitions librarians are obliged to see that the vendor meets all contract conditions from the beginning, or the library may forfeit its right to enforce them later.

"Acquisitions librarians are required both legally and professionally to safeguard the budgets over which they have control and to assure themselves that dollars are being spent wisely and efficiently" (Cargille 1999, 94). Many benefits are associated with vendor performance evaluation. Good communication from the beginning sets the tone for the library's relationship with the vendor. Although formal vendor performance evaluation usually begins several months after the vendor receives the library's account so that there will be some data available to evaluate, early detection and resolution of minor problems prevents dissatisfaction later when the formal evaluation process begins. For example, approval plan profiles often need minor adjustments, or after serial titles are transferred to a new vendor some may not start with the issue expected, requiring the missed issues to be claimed quickly to avoid creating gaps in the collection.

Vendor Performance Evaluation

In the early stages of a new vendor contract it may be helpful for the acquisitions librarian to have a conversation with acquisitions staff about their impressions of the vendor's performance. This informal approach may uncover initial concerns before they escalate into problems. However, as soon as enough time has elapsed for sufficient data to be collected, a formal evaluation should be conducted. The formal vendor evaluation will either confirm or call into question the staff's perceptions. "It is reasonable to check one's intuitive judgments occasionally with fact" (Cargille 1999, 94).

The first decision the library must make when planning for a formal vendor performance evaluation is to determine who will perform the evaluation. Usually it will be the acquisitions librarian, but the serials librarian may perform the evaluation for serials vendors. In some cases the collection management librarian may serve as the evaluator or may team with the acquisitions librarian on the project. A staff member from one of those departments may also be chosen.

Before the library embarks on the vendor evaluation, it should consider which vendors it will survey (e.g., its approval plan vendor or its serials vendor) and what it hopes to learn as a result of the process. "Accountability and value for [the] dollar are two issues frequently discussed" in vendor performance evaluations (Black 1994, 58). For example, is the library trying to determine if the vendor is applying the correct discount on its approval plan, firm orders, or standing order, or on all of them, or the correct service charge on its serial subscriptions? Is it monitoring rejection rates on its approval plan or tracking timeliness of the receipt of its firm order books? Is it tracking customer service response time, or reviewing completeness and accuracy of the vendor's management reports? The library may want to survey its vendors in all these areas.

Next the evaluator will decide when the evaluation will begin, its duration, and what method of evaluation will be used. Numerous articles and books have been written on vendor evaluation methods. The most often cited and perhaps the definitive source to date is the American Library Association's *Guide to Performance Evaluation of Library Materials Vendors* (1988). Another useful source is the Vendor Study Group's annotated bibliography of vendor evaluation appearing in *Library Acquisitions: Practice and Theory* (1988).

There seem to be as many variations on the theme of vendor performance evaluation as there are libraries conducting evaluations. Evaluations range from simple one-factor studies to complex data analyses on multiple factors. Some of these factors include discount, service charge, average cost per volume, number of titles ordered, number of titles received, number of days between order placement and receipt, number of claims, number of cancellations, number of vendor problems, type of vendor problems, percentage of approval titles rejected, reason for rejection of approval titles, bibliographic accuracy on approval forms, and accuracy of management reports. This is only a partial list of factors; each library will add its own to produce an evaluation tailored to best fit its needs.

The library can use its integrated library system to provide statistics on myriad factors; however, some data will still need to be collected or confirmed manually. For example, the ILS can give the length of time it takes for materials ordered from bibliographic forms or firm orders to be supplied after they are ordered or the number of serials claims sent to the vendor in a given period of time. Before embarking on data collection using its system, the librarian performing the evaluation should review the system's capabilities. Remember, the data available from the integrated library system is constrained only by the system's limitations, and the evaluation factors and process are constrained only by the librarian's imagination.

CONCLUSION

Libraries use vendors to acquire books, serials, and media in all formats. Vendors function as an extension of the library's staff, saving time and money. Their relationship has evolved over the years, but libraries and vendors remain dependent on each other. Library vendors range from broad based to highly specialized; more than 260 library vendors are selling materials to the U.S. market.

Some libraries may be permitted to select vendors on an informal basis; however, increasingly, libraries are required to use a more formal competitive procurement process. The request for proposal process, though labor intensive and time consuming, is the most thorough, objective method available for libraries to use to select vendors.

Selecting the best vendor to handle the library's approval plan, firm and standing orders, serial subscriptions, and so on is only part of the responsibility of the library. Acquisitions librarians must ensure that the vendor is fulfilling its obligations to the library by conducting vendor performance evaluations and by working with the vendor to correct any deficiencies. "It is through the combined efforts of library and vendor staff together, each striving to produce the best possible service, that we ultimately progress toward our respective goals" (McLaren 1999, 86).

REFERENCES

Alessi, Dana. 1992. Vendor selection, vendor collection, or vendor defection. *Journal of Library Administration* 16: 117–30.

American Library Association. 1988. *Guide to performance evaluation of library materials vendors.* Chicago: American Library Association.

Black, Graham. 1994. Why do evaluation? *Library Acquisitions: Practice and Theory* 18: 57–60.

Cargille, Karen E. 1999. Vendor evaluation. In *Understanding the business of library acquisitions.* 2nd ed. Edited by Karen A. Schmidt. Chicago: American Library Association.

Dowd, Frank. 1991. Awarding acquisitions contracts by bid or the perils and rewards of shopping by mail. *Acquisitions Librarian* 5: 63–73.

Fisher, William. 1993. A brief history of library-vendor relations since 1950. *Library Acquisitions: Practice and Theory* 17: 61–69.

Guide to performance evaluation of library materials vendors. 1988. Chicago: American Library Association.

Hirshon, Arnold, and Barbara A. Winters. 1996. *Outsourcing library technical services: A how-to-do-it manual for librarians.* New York: Neal-Schuman.

McLaren, Mary K. 1999. Vendor selection: Service, cost, and more service! In *Understanding the business of library acquisitions.* 2nd ed. Edited by Karen A. Schmidt. Chicago: American Library Association.

Porter-Roth, Bud. 1991. How to write a request for proposal: A step-by-step outline for analyzing your needs and soliciting bids. *Inform* 5: 26–30.

Presley, Roger L. 1993. Firing an old friend, painful decisions: The ethics between librarians and vendors. *Library Acquisitions: Practice and Theory* 17: 53–59.

Schatz, Bob, and Diane J. Graves. 1996. Request for proposal or run for protection? Some thoughts on RFPs from a librarian and a bookseller. *Library Acquisitions: Practice and Theory* 20: 421–28.

Shirk, Gary M. 1993. Contract acquisitions: Change, technology, and the new library/vendor partnership. *Library Acquisitions: Practice and Theory* 17: 145–53.

Vendor Study Group. 1988. Vendor evaluation: A selected annotated bibliography, 1955–1987. *Library Acquisitions: Practice and Theory* 12: 17–28.

Wilkinson, Frances C., and Sever Bordeianu. 1997. In search of the perfect cover: Using the RFP process to select a commercial binder. *Serials Review* 23: 37–47.

Wilkinson, Frances C., and Connie Capers Thorson. 1998. *The RFP process: Effective management of the acquisition of library materials.* Englewood, CO: Libraries Unlimited.

Chapter 5

Acquiring Books and Media

Libraries purchase more than $4 billion of books each year (Schuman and Harmon 1999, 25). To acquire these materials for their users, libraries must establish clear procedures. "The book-ordering process is a complex one, but the steps involved are very simple and can be performed by clerical staff with a minimum of training if the operation is well thought out and each step planned, and if all steps in the various procedures are carefully monitored" (Eaglen 2000, 111). In this chapter, we discuss the methods of acquiring books and other monographs in printed or nonbook formats such as videotapes. The acquisitions of serials and electronic resources is discussed in subsequent chapters. Although the procedures of acquiring books and of acquiring media differ in some details, many of the basic procedures for both formats are similar; later sections in this chapter describe some of the processes that are unique to multimedia.

WHERE TO PURCHASE BOOKS AND MEDIA

Libraries purchase materials from three basic sources: publishers of the items, retail booksellers, and vendors or wholesalers. Each source has advantages and disadvantages; libraries will decide which sources they prefer after considering their needs and the type of materials being ordered. Regardless of the type of vendor libraries select, all vendors should supply the items correctly and rapidly, report delays or problems quickly, provide accurate invoices, and give libraries reasonable discounts.

Publishers

Some publishers, primarily those that publish reference sources, sell their materials directly to libraries; they do not sell materials through vendors. Most trade publishers sell their materials primarily to bookstores and wholesalers but will also sell directly to libraries. Libraries can establish accounts with these publishers or purchase materials using an institutional credit card. Publishers usually are the most likely source to have the books in stock or to be able to inform libraries when items are out of print or out of stock. Occasionally when a publisher states that an item is out of stock, a wholesaler may still have copies in its warehouse; a wise librarian will check more than one source for items reported out of print or out of stock. Publishers often give a small discount to libraries, sometimes between 10 and 20 percent; publishers frequently give booksellers and wholesalers discounts between 40 and 60 percent. Publishers also frequently add shipping and handling costs to the charges, resulting in higher costs than libraries would have paid to wholesalers. Libraries that place numerous orders with a large number of publishers may find that the shipping costs add up rapidly and that their staff spend a great deal of time setting up vendor records and processing individual invoices. If publishers are able to ship items on a rush basis, they can supply the materials quickly; however, Internet bookstores and some major wholesalers and vendors are now able to respond equally rapidly.

Bookstores

Libraries may be able to purchase materials directly from bookstores in their communities. The discounts will vary; some stores may give libraries large discounts while others will not give any discounts at all. These bookstores may be an excellent source for local and regional materials that are rarely handled by national and international vendors. Specialized stores that focus on specific subjects or genres are valuable resources for those types of materials. To deal with local stores, libraries may need to establish an account with them or have staff members purchase the materials and get reimbursed by the libraries. In most cases, staff must visit the stores and bring the materials back because delivery is rarely available.

Internet Bookstores

Some booksellers, such as Amazon.com (http://www.amazon.com, accessed June 1, 2003), exist only on the Internet. These sources may offer a variety of materials, including media as well as books. They offer very rapid delivery and will usually either set up accounts for libraries or accept institutional credit cards. The shipping and handling charges will vary, as will the discounts. If items are needed immediately, these booksellers are one of the faster ways for libraries to obtain the desired materials.

Booksellers that specialize in specific subject areas, such as Latin America or science fiction, often have Internet sites. Such booksellers can be invaluable resources when libraries are attempting to locate highly specialized materials. Specialized dealers may be located in such resources as *American Book Trade Directory, Literary Market Place,* or AcqWeb (http://acqweb.library.vanderbilt.edu, accessed June 1, 2003).

Vendors and Wholesalers

Vendors or book wholesalers purchase materials from publishers and sell them to libraries. They deal with most major publishers and many society and small presses as well. Some vendors handle books and media, while others specialize in specific formats such as videotapes. Vendors usually offer discounts to libraries that are higher than those available from most publishers and bookstores. The primary reason for libraries to use vendors is convenience. "Consolidation of orders for items from many publishers with one or several vendors saves the library time and money" (Miller 1992, 6). Vendors can consolidate orders, obtain materials from many publishers, and send the items to libraries in one shipment with one invoice. This consolidation saves money by reducing shipping costs and saves staff time by reducing the number of multiple shipments and invoices. Some publishers are unwilling or unable to sell materials directly to individuals or to libraries; vendors can frequently deal with those publishers to obtain the desired materials. Vendors that have warehouses stocked with materials may be able to supply needed materials very quickly and may have items that have been declared out of stock by their publishers.

Many vendors deal with a wide range of titles, subjects, publishers, and formats; others specialize in a format or a subject such as children's literature. Some vendors have extensive collections of materials in their warehouses, whereas others keep primarily currently published materials and best-sellers. When vendors do not have items ordered by libraries in their current stock, they order the materials from the publishers.

Most vendors have lists of the publishers with whom they will not do business. Some publishers refuse to work with vendors because the vendors require that the publishers give them discounts. Some vendors refuse to deal with specific publishers because the publishers do not give sufficient discounts in order for the vendor to make enough profit on the materials. Vendors should supply libraries with a list of publishers with whom they do not work.

When libraries deal with vendors regularly, they should establish a customer profile with each vendor. Libraries should give the vendors the addresses to which materials should be sent, the addresses to which the bills should be sent, and the names of library staff with whom they will be working. Most vendors will also ask libraries to establish some guidelines that define when libraries must be consulted about price changes or varying editions. Some libraries will tell vendors to ship materials that cost within $10 or 10 percent of the estimated price, while others have higher figures. When both paperback and hardback editions are available, some libraries specify which edition must be provided, while other libraries will accept whichever edition is available more rapidly. Libraries should tell their vendors that any orders that cannot be filled within a specific time should be canceled. Many libraries tell vendors to cancel orders for materials published in the United States if the orders have not been filled after ninety days. International orders take longer to fill; six months may be more appropriate for those materials. When setting up their profile, libraries should also tell the vendors how their invoices should appear and how many copies of the invoices they require.

Libraries should expect all vendors to fill orders promptly and correctly; to notify them when items cannot be supplied; to give them reasonable discounts; to ship materials carefully; to provide accurate, clear invoices; and to process any returns efficiently. Libraries should evaluate the performance of their vendors regularly, considering such factors as percentage of items delivered correctly, time between ordering and receipt, discounts, and customer service.

ECONOMICS

The economic issues involved in purchasing books and media are complex; the list price set by the publisher is only one factor. For more information about the economics of the publishing industry, please see chapter 3, "The Publishing Industry." Two factors that have the most direct impact upon acquisitions are price discounts and charges for shipping and handling.

Discounts

Most publishers give discounts to booksellers and libraries; these range from only a few percent to more than 50 percent, depending upon the publisher and the purchaser. Some publishers do not discount their materials to anyone. Publishers generally give libraries discounts of between 10 and 20 percent, while booksellers often receive discounts of around 50 percent. Most vendors give libraries discounts of between 10 and 20 percent. Vendors may offer flat discounts—negotiated percentages that apply to all materials they provide—or they may offer discounts that vary according to the discounts the vendors themselves receive on specific types of materials. Libraries attempting to determine which method is best need to analyze the types of materials being purchased, the percentage of each type of materials purchased, and the types of discounts given on each category of materials.

Library systems that order many copies of individual titles may receive a discount based on the quantity of the copies ordered. This discount may be valuable for large public library systems ordering large numbers of best-selling books.

Shipping and Handling Costs

Vendors and publishers usually charge shipping and handling costs to the libraries, and the amounts charged vary widely among companies. Some companies base their handling costs on a percentage of the cost of the materials; if an item is very expensive and very small, such as an expensive videotape, the shipping costs can be quite high. Libraries should determine whether the shipping and handling costs are charged for each item within a shipment or for the total shipment. Some vendors will pay for the shipping costs for regular shipments of approval plan books; when approval plan items are rejected and returned to the vendors, the libraries pay the shipping costs to return the materials.

STEPS IN THE ORDERING PROCESS

If the steps in the process of ordering materials are carefully structured, libraries can obtain and process the desired materials promptly. The orders must be received, the items must be clearly identified, the vendors must be selected, the orders must be sent to the vendors, and the funds must be encumbered.

Receiving Orders

In one-person libraries, the librarian may be responsible for identifying, ordering, and processing materials. In large research libraries, collection development personnel may identify the materials to be acquired and send the information to the acquisitions department. Information may be forwarded in almost any manner, from handwritten notes to electronic lists. Some libraries create special forms for selectors to fill out; others accept publishers' catalogs or advertisements annotated with information about the desired funds or locations. Each library must decide which methods are most efficient for its operations. Specially designed forms may encourage selectors to provide all the desired information, but they cost money to produce.

Acquisitions departments should keep track of the number of orders submitted so as to evaluate the workflow and the appropriate staffing level. Integrated library systems will track the number of orders actually placed, but since not all requests sent to acquisitions will actually become orders, the acquisitions staff must count the number of all items searched separately. Some libraries maintain statistics for specific types of orders including those not ordered because the libraries already owned the items or those ordered but later reported to be out of print.

Searching and Verifying Orders

Selectors or patrons who send requests for materials to acquisitions may include all the information needed to order the items or may provide partial or inaccurate information. Acquisitions personnel must first identify the items fully before placing the orders. In some libraries, selectors may do extensive searching before sending orders to acquisitions; in others, acquisitions personnel are responsible for all searching.

Orders accompanied by publishers' catalogs, advertisements, or printed records from vendors' databases generally contain accurate information about the items, author, and publisher. Acquisitions staff may need to verify whether the items are already published or are still in print, but the basic information about the author, title, publisher, and price is generally accurate. Some requests will not include all the information needed to create an order; others will have inaccurate information. In these cases, the acquisitions staff must verify the information before sending orders to vendors. Staff may use a variety of sources, such as *Books in Print*, vendors' online databases, publishers' print and online catalogs, Internet booksellers, or WorldCat, to find complete information about the requested items.

Verification may be extremely important for titles published in both the United States and the United Kingdom. Publishers often issue the same items in both countries but change the titles slightly. Acquisitions staff should identify such title variations in order to reduce unintentional duplicate orders. In most cases, ordering from U.S. publishers will be faster and possibly less expensive. If the U.S. version is out of print, acquisitions staff should check to see if the U.K. version is still available.

Before items are ordered, the acquisitions staff must check library records to determine whether the library already owns the requested items. In most cases, searching library catalogs under the author and title will be adequate. Conference proceedings and works authored by associations may require more extensive searching. For items that are part of a series, the staff should determine whether the library has a standing order for the specific series. Some libraries do extensive searching to identify all possible duplicate requests; others have discovered that the percentage of duplication is so low that extensive searching is unnecessary. No model fits all libraries; the amount of preorder searching required depends on the organization of each library and the amount of searching done before the orders reach acquisitions.

Libraries should establish general procedures for handing requests that might be identified as duplicates. For example, some libraries use processing forms that allow selectors to tell acquisitions staff to return any duplicate orders to the selector or to order the duplicates because added copies are needed. Selectors may also tell acquisitions personnel to order a title only if the library does not own a later edition.

If items are ordered for specific individuals, the acquisitions staff should have a procedure to allow that information to be maintained through the processing and cataloging workflow in order to notify the requestor when the item is ready to be circulated. Some integrated library systems allow such notes to be added to the records of items that are being ordered and processed.

Information Needed About Materials Being Ordered

Many books have similar or identical titles, just as many authors have similar names. To ensure that the library acquires the correct title, selectors need to provide sufficient information to identify the desired materials. The acquisitions staff must verify any incomplete information before sending the order to the vendor. The most useful information includes the author's name, the full title including any subtitles, and the International Standard Book Number (ISBN). The ISBN is a unique number supplied by the publisher that identifies the specific item. Each edition of a book will have a separate ISBN; the number for the paperback edition will be different from the number for the hardback edition.

When only selected volumes of a multivolume set are needed, the order must include the numbers or titles of the specific volumes, with the ISBN for the individual volumes if they were assigned in that manner. If the library already has some volumes of the set, including the call number for the set in the order record helps to avoid confusion when the volumes are received and processed.

Additional information should include the publisher's name and location. A shortened form of the name may be acceptable, but abbreviations can create difficulty in identifying the item. For example, using "M.L.A." as a publisher creates problems because at least three different societies use that abbreviation. If selectors are requesting materials from small publishers or associations, they should include the address if possible; if it is not included, acquisitions personnel should ask the selectors if they can provide the information since that will enable them to obtain the materials more quickly.

The selectors should specify which format or edition is preferred. Many titles are available in hardback and paperback editions; if the hardback edition is no longer available, the library may wish to accept the paperback edition. Movies are available in videotape and DVD formats. Many best-sellers are available in print and audio formats. Libraries may want a specific edition of a work or prefer the most recently published edition. Children's books are sometimes available in reinforced bindings designed for library use. If selectors do not specify which editions they desire, acquisitions staff should consult with them before placing the orders. If libraries do not specify which versions are preferred, the vendors may ask the libraries before filling the order, which will delay the arrival of the materials, or they may supply the items most easily available, possibly supplying the wrong format. If selectors request editions that are out of print, and acquisitions staff discover that reprinted editions exist, acquisitions staff should ask the selectors if the reprints are acceptable; reprints may be preferable because the paper and binding may be better than those of the original publications.

Orders should include the estimated price. Prices frequently change because of publishers' decisions or changes in the exchange rates for international materials. Vendors should be given a range that is acceptable to the libraries; many libraries will accept a price that varies $10 or 10 percent from their original estimate. If the price increases are more than the specified amount, the vendors should consult the libraries before shipping the items.

Libraries must tell the vendors how many copies of items are desired. Many libraries order only one copy of a title, while many large library systems order multiple copies.

Libraries must make any special instructions, such as requests to rush the items, clearly visible on orders.

Orders to vendors must include the address to which materials are to be shipped. Invoices for books and media are generally included in the boxes with the materials. If libraries need to have the bills sent to a separate address, that information must be clearly indicated.

When to Order Materials

The fiscal calendar and the financial policies of the institution determine the timing of the acquisitions cycle. If the fiscal year runs from July through June, most ordering will be done between August and April. Some institutions allow libraries to carry over funds that have not been spent by the end of one fiscal year, keeping the funds in the libraries' accounts for use in the next fiscal cycle; this allows libraries to purchase materials throughout the fiscal year. If institutions do not allow encumbered or unspent funds to be held over into the following fiscal year, orders need to be sent to vendors approximately three months before the end of the fiscal year to ensure that allocated budget is completely spent before the financial cycle ends. In such cases few orders will be sent to vendors during the last two months of the fiscal year because the materials probably would not be received before the financial accounts are closed for the year.

Because books go out of print rapidly, sometimes within a few months of publication, libraries should order most books at the time of publication. Sometimes libraries may decide to order materials before they are officially published in order to increase the libraries' chances of getting copies of items with small print runs. "Orders should be placed on a weekly basis, even daily if at all possible. A monthly order cycle is bad enough, but those institutions such as school, academic, and certain public libraries—which order books only once or twice a year—should be forewarned that fill rates for such orders will be unbelievably low—through no fault of the vendor, in most cases" (Eaglen 2000, 93).

Determining the actual time of publication can be challenging, however. Publishers' catalogs are frequently optimistic about the announced publication dates. Patrons may see titles listed as published and request that the library acquire materials that may not have actually been published at that time. Libraries can check WorldCat or vendors' databases to determine whether titles have really been published; these resources may also include the revised dates of expected publication. Libraries may order items that are expected to be published in the near future, adding notes in the order records to notify patrons when the items are received. If the publications have been delayed indefinitely, libraries may request that patrons check again in a few months.

Vendor Selection

Vendors of library materials are listed in such directories as *Literary Market Place* and *AV Market Place* and on AcqWeb (http://acqweb.library. vanderbilt.edu, accessed June 1, 2003). The Acquisitions Section of the Association for Library Collections and Technical Services is revising directories of vendors in Asia and the Pacific, Africa and the Middle East, and Eastern Europe. Some vendors specialize in specific subjects, languages, or formats, while others handle materials in all areas. Libraries may decide to deal with several vendors or may concentrate their orders with only a few companies. Some states have lists of approved vendors; libraries using vendors participating in such systems may receive higher discounts or other additional services. In some states, libraries intending to spend more than a prescribed amount, such as $10,000, with one vendor may be required to put in a formal request for proposal or bid. For more information about vendor selection, see chapter 4, "Domestic and Foreign Vendor Selection and Evaluation."

Sending Orders to Vendors

Orders may be printed and mailed to vendors, sent by email or fax, ordered online at Internet bookstores, or transmitted electronically from libraries' integrated library systems to vendors' databases. The printed purchase order or emailed message should include the complete bibliographic information about the desired items, the libraries' purchase order number for the items, any specific instructions, the shipping address, and the billing address.

Vendors may acknowledge receipt of orders that are sent electronically with email messages or with messages from their systems. Libraries should specify in their profile what kind of acknowledgment they require. A few publishers may require that libraries pay for the materials in advance; they refuse to ship materials until they have received payment. While most such publishers do indeed supply the materials, some never do. Libraries must be cautious when prepaying; if the materials are never delivered, the money is lost. Some publishers requiring prepayment will accept payments on institutional credit cards; this practice provides some assurance that the materials will be sent.

Creating Records of Ordered Materials

Libraries keeping a manual system or an internal system that uses a personal computer need to keep a record of all the information about materials on order in local files. Libraries with integrated library systems may have acquisitions modules that create records in the system. Whether the system is manual or part of an integrated library system, the information should include the bibliographic record that includes the author, title, publisher, and date; the vendor; the estimated cost; and the date of order. Other information may include the funds used to pay for the items, the locations where the items will be housed, and any relevant notes such as the name of the selector.

Encumbering Funds

Encumbering funds means setting aside the money that will be required to pay for the materials when they arrive. Integrated library systems can encumber funds when orders are placed. Libraries using a manual system must create procedures that track the amount of money committed and the amount remaining. Libraries should be able to adapt any basic accounting software program for personal computers to create a program that can track their encumbrances and expenditures. Systems can be as simple or as complex as the organization requires. Libraries may divide their money into separate funds for various formats or subjects. Some libraries have several funds; others have only a few.

Libraries should encumber items at the publishers' list prices. The actual prices that libraries pay will be different from the list prices most of the time; the costs for shipping and handling and the discounts given by vendors will result in prices that are somewhat unpredictable. List prices are estimates, but they are generally close enough to final prices for initial budget analyses.

Sorting Mail

In addition to receiving the books, media, and serials that have been ordered, acquisitions units receive advertisements, catalogs, gifts, fliers, and bills. Personnel must sort the mail carefully to separate materials into the proper categories. In larger libraries, advertisements generally are sent to the selectors in the collection management department. Sometimes mail arrives that looks exactly like an invoice, having a very small note stating it is a notification, not an invoice; acquisitions personnel must watch carefully for these misleading advertisements.

Unscrupulous Publishers

Some unscrupulous publishers send libraries materials they have not ordered. They may include invoices and may say that the items are being sent on approval or for review. They may state that the materials should be returned within a few days if the libraries decide they do not wish to pay for the materials. Such unsolicited and unordered materials should be treated as donations. According to the U.S. Postal Office, such materials may be kept as gifts, without payment by the libraries. For more information, see http://www.usps.gov/websites/depart/inspect/merch.htm (accessed June 1, 2003).

Other publishers may call or email libraries and ask that personnel verify information describing the libraries in order to include the libraries in forthcoming business directories. Frequently the publishers then send the directories stating that the phone calls or emails were orders for them. Acquisitions staff should inform such companies that their libraries will refuse to pay for such items and that they will report the fraudulent practices to the U.S. Postal Office or other appropriate authorities. In addition, libraries should alert their colleagues about potential abuses by posting information on such electronic discussion lists as ACQNET-L and COLLDV-L; librarians can and should monitor these lists for information about new or repeating problems.

Delivery Times

Libraries can expect to receive nearly all of the materials they order within one to three months. "When dealing with a reputable wholesaler who maintains an adequate inventory, librarians can expect receipt of an initial shipment of 75 to 80 percent of the materials within two weeks" (Eaglen 2000, 80). The time will vary with the type of materials, the information libraries provide, and the service of the vendors. Many vendors working with academic libraries usually deliver materials within six to eight weeks. Books that were published recently by major publishers generally will be delivered more rapidly than older materials from small publishers since some vendors may have the newer materials in their warehouses. "For most books, a period of ninety days from purchase order date should be the maximum allowed" (Eaglen 2000, 95). International materials will take considerably longer because the shipping methods usually require more time than most domestic shipments. Some vendors automatically cancel orders that are unfilled after six months, while others keep trying to fill orders indefinitely; libraries must inform the vendors what action they want from them.

Vendor Reports

If delays occur in supplying items to libraries, the vendors should notify the libraries about the problems. The acquisitions personnel should enter this information in the record, indicating what the problems are and when the vendor anticipates delivering the items.

Vendors may report that items are out of stock or out of print. While these reports are frequently accurate, sometimes they are wrong. Another vendor may still have the last remaining available copies. Vendors sometimes do make mistakes, cannot locate items, or receive inaccurate information from publishers. Libraries can sometimes verify whether items are unavailable by checking with the publisher or with the information about warehouse supplies of some vendors provided in *Books in Print Plus*. If libraries find that some vendors are consistently inaccurate when reporting that items are out of print, the libraries should switch to more efficient vendors.

Claiming

Claiming is the process of asking vendors about the status of an order. Integrated library systems can generate lists of items that were ordered before a specified date and have not yet been received. Using these lists, acquisitions personnel can ask the vendors for reports on the status of these orders. Occasionally orders do get lost in the mail, either electronic or physical, and the claims may be the first notice the vendor receives.

Some vendors can respond to claims sent to them electronically; sending claims by email can be a rapid means of communication. Vendors should respond in a timely manner, even if their initial answer is simply to say that they received the message and will investigate. In many cases, the vendors will need to communicate with their suppliers, which requires additional time. The vendors should tell the libraries the results of their investigations.

STEPS IN THE RECEIVING AND PAYMENT PROCESS

After items have been identified and ordered, they will arrive at the libraries. The materials must be unpacked, identified, and received. Acquisitions personnel must verify that the invoices are correct and approve them for payment. Finally the materials will be physically processed.

Receiving Materials

When a package arrives from a vendor, it must be opened promptly. Most vendors put the invoice in the box; the first step is to find the invoice and match the items in the box to the invoice. Sometimes items may be listed on the invoice but not included in the shipment, or vice versa. When the invoice and the shipped items do not match, the errors must be investigated and corrected before the invoice can be paid.

After the invoice has been matched against the items in the shipment and any errors corrected, the next step is to find the original records of the orders for each item. The acquisitions staff must match the order records to the received items to make certain that the correct items were received and that the prices are within the guidelines established by the library.

Even the most careful vendors and libraries make mistakes occasionally. Sometimes entire shipments will be sent to the wrong library or the wrong branch in a library system. When that happens, libraries should verify the shipping address with the vendor.

Most problems involve incorrect titles being shipped or exceptional increases in the costs of items. One common cause of receiving an incorrect item is an error in the ISBN. Many vendors use the ISBN to identify titles; if a number is incorrect the library will not receive the item it ordered. Different editions of books, such as the hardback and paperback editions, have different ISBNs; acquisitions personnel must be careful when entering the data to ensure that they use the correct number for the desired edition.

Prices differ from the estimated prices when the publishers change prices or when the currency exchange rates change. Mistakes also occur when the data are entered into the systems. Libraries should tell their vendors that they will accept price increases within a specified range; the vendors should notify the libraries when prices increase beyond the agreed-upon amounts.

Acquisitions staff should check items to see that they are in perfect condition. Items with major flaws such as blank pages and missing sections should be rejected, and the vendor should be asked to replace them. Items with minor damage, such as a slightly bent corner, may be kept. If the damage does not affect the content, many libraries will not spend the staff time to return items that have only minor damage.

Acquisitions personnel must be careful not to damage materials being received. They should not use temporary sticky notes on materials being added to the collection; such notes leave residue on paper and remove ink from newsprint. Staff should also avoid using rubber bands on items; the rubber bands may cut into the edges of the materials and damage the paper.

Acquisitions personnel may be responsible for marking the materials with their library's ownership label and for inserting security devices. Materials are frequently marked with the library's name at this time to reduce the possibility of theft of items waiting to be cataloged. Materials should not be marked with the library's ownership label until the acquisitions personnel verify that the items are indeed what the library ordered. Books that have been marked cannot be returned to vendors.

Invoices

Invoices are bills from vendors for materials that have been sent to libraries. They should include all information necessary to identify the materials, including authors, titles, and purchase order numbers. Invoices should arrive in the shipments and be easy for staff to find. Libraries should work with vendors to ensure that the invoices have the appropriate information in a clear and legible document. Vendors may provide multiple copies of invoices; libraries must decide how many copies they actually require. Each added copy of an invoice will cost the vendor money and will require library staff time to handle; libraries should request the minimum number of copies that they actually need. When acquisitions personnel have verified that the invoices are correct, they approve them for payment. In some libraries, invoices will be sent to the fiscal services section of the institution for payment; in other libraries, the libraries may issue the checks.

Clearing Order Records

The acquisitions personnel must annotate the records in integrated library systems to show that the invoice has been approved and is to be paid. The system will then remove the encumbrance for the items, deduct the amount paid from the specified fund, and indicate that the items have been paid. In manual systems or those managed on personal computers, acquisitions personnel must subtract the encumbrance and show the payment. In integrated library systems, order records for books are usually kept in the system at least until the items have been cataloged. Some institutions require that order records be kept for at least one full fiscal year. Acquisitions personnel must learn the regulations of their institution and the capabilities of their integrated library system.

Returning Items

Libraries may return items that are damaged, were sent by mistake, exceed the established guidelines concerning price increases, or are items rejected from approval plans. In nearly all cases, libraries pay the shipping costs to return items. Libraries must pack materials carefully to ensure that items are not damaged in shipping; if vendors receive damaged shipments, they will not give libraries credit for the materials. Returned items should include specific information describing why they are being returned, copies of the invoices, and statements telling the vendors whether replacements or credit memos are desired.

Each library will establish guidelines concerning when items should be returned. Some libraries return very few items; they have found it more efficient to order replacement copies and discard the rejected items rather than to ship the rejected items back to the vendors. Others return items frequently. Each library must determine the balance between the cost of paying for rejected items and the staff time required for returning items.

Shipping materials to international vendors is expensive; libraries may save money by keeping the items and informing the vendors that similar items should not be supplied. The postal regulations concerning international shipments are very detailed; libraries must learn those regulations before sending materials abroad.

If clear patterns develop, such as materials from one vendor frequently being shipped in poor boxes resulting in damaged shipments, the library should notify the vendor. If the vendor does not correct the problem, the library should consider changing vendors.

Some vendors will allow libraries to alter invoices by lining off amounts for the defective items; libraries can then pay the revised amount. Other vendors may insist on having defective items returned before they issue new invoices. The first option is quicker and easier for libraries, and they should request that service from their vendors.

Credit Cards

Some organizations authorize libraries to use institutional credit cards to purchase materials. Credit cards are extremely useful when the libraries purchase materials from used book dealers or bookstores. They may also be useful for international orders; however, libraries must be aware that exchange rates vary, which means that prices may vary from the original estimated prices.

Institutions generally limit the number of individuals authorized to use the cards and require detailed documentation of the purchases made on the cards. Most organizations set limits on the amount of money that may be charged for individual items and for the total monthly use of the card. Some organizations require that libraries create separate records for each credit card, listing all purchases along with the title, amount, date of the order, date of the payment, and name of the vendor. Others require libraries to provide their fiscal services departments with the original receipts from the dealers; these receipts must list the title, author, and price for each of the individual items ordered. Libraries must work with their fiscal services units to ensure that all necessary records are provided.

Payment

Fiscal services units of the libraries may be responsible for issuing the checks to pay vendors; in other institutions, payment may be done by fiscal units that are not part of the library. The invoices should be handled swiftly so that the vendors may be paid promptly. Acquisitions personnel must learn the practices of their institutions, and learn how long it takes for checks to be sent to the vendors. Some vendors give discounts to institutions that pay their bills within thirty days or other negotiated time periods; acquisitions personnel must know how swiftly their institutions process checks before promising that they can meet such time lines. If libraries fail to pay the bills promptly, many vendors may charge interest on the unpaid amounts, charge higher prices in the future, require that the library pay in advance for materials, or even refuse to deal with the library.

Most vendors, especially smaller independent dealers, operate on a very small profit margin. When libraries are slow in paying invoices, the companies may be harmed financially. Libraries and institutions that are consistently late in paying their vendors are engaging in poor financial management. Libraries that deliberately delay paying their bills because of internal library mistakes such as overspending are behaving unethically. If libraries frequently delay payments because of mistakes by a vendor, they should evaluate that vendor's performance and consider switching to another company.

VENDOR EVALUATION

Acquisitions personnel should evaluate their vendors' performance to determine whether the libraries are receiving the desired quality of service for a reasonable cost. Among the factors that personnel should evaluate are the average time in which items are delivered, the percentage of orders filled, the costs of the materials, the percentage of errors, and the quality of the customer service. "Any vendor whose fulfillment error rate exceeds 1 or 2 percent should not be in business; any library book purchaser who accepts such shoddy performance should be doing something else" (Eaglen 2000, 20). For more information about vendor evaluation, please see chapter 4, "Domestic and Foreign Vendor Selection and Evaluation."

ADDITIONAL SERVICES OFFERED BY VENDORS

Some vendors provide additional services such as searching for out-of-print titles, physical processing, and electronic resources. When items are declared out of print, some vendors can automatically transfer libraries' orders to dealers that specialize in searching for out-of-print materials. Some larger vendors will handle the physical processing of books, stamping them with the libraries' ownership marks, inserting security devices, and labeling them. Others will catalog materials and notify online bibliographic utilities such as OCLC (the Online Computer Library Center, Inc.)

to add the libraries' ownership symbols to the appropriate records. A few vendors offer approval plans, providing libraries with materials in specific areas shortly after publication; some will deliver these materials cataloged and ready to be shelved. Many larger vendors have electronic databases that allow libraries to verify bibliographic records, order materials online, and check the status of their orders. Vendors usually charge additional fees for these services; libraries must compare the costs paid to the vendor with the costs of doing the work themselves.

USES OF THE INTERNET IN ACQUIRING BOOKS

The Internet has transformed many parts of the acquisitions and publishing process. Publishers post their catalogs on their webpages rather than printing and mailing many copies to libraries. Rather than mailing fliers with announcements of new books, companies send email notices to subject selectors. Vendors have created databases that enable libraries to order materials online and to check on the status of orders. Acquisitions personnel use electronic discussion lists to seek information about publishers or systems. Internet bookstores enable libraries to verify bibliographic information about books, compare prices of books, receive email notices about new books in specific subject areas, order materials online, and locate out-of-print books.

AUTOMATIC PURCHASE PLANS

Libraries may establish agreements with vendors in which the vendors supply materials automatically without having the libraries issue individual orders for all the items. Such plans may include materials published by specific companies or materials in specific subjects or formats. The major types of these automatic purchase plans are standing orders, blanket orders, and approval plans.

Standing order plans are generally established between publishers and libraries. Publishers send the libraries all their new publications or the publications in specific areas. The library will keep all the materials; only defective items may be returned. Libraries can also purchase standing orders through approval plan vendors to receive a larger discount and to reduce possible duplication with titles provided on approval plans.

Blanket order plans are usually established between vendors and libraries. Vendors send newly published titles to libraries; the materials may be about a specific subject or may be published in a designated country or region. The libraries will return defective items but usually will keep all the materials.

Vendors establish approval plans to allow libraries to review materials before deciding which items to purchase. Libraries and vendors create profiles that define what subjects, publishers, and formats should be provided to the libraries. The vendors may send the books, or they may send bibliographic notification forms for materials that are not supplied as books. Libraries review the materials and return items they do not wish to purchase.

Libraries may hire approval vendors to supply them with materials that are physically processed and cataloged. They use the same method of profiling materials that is used in approval plans; however, the items that are received are automatically purchased, and items cannot be returned.

APPROVAL PLANS

For many years booksellers have supplied books to libraries for review and possible purchase, but approval plans, which are a more systematic method of this service, are a relatively recent development. These plans are contractual agreements between libraries and vendors in which the vendors agree to supply current materials or bibliographic notification forms to the libraries. Organized approval plans began in the 1960s when the Richard Able Company began providing books to a large number of libraries. Libraries' budgets were experiencing rapid growth, and approval plans allowed libraries to spend those funds and keep up with the increase in the number of materials being published. Libraries worked with Richard Able to define what the libraries wanted to purchase by creating detailed profiles that described the subjects, publishers, and formats the libraries desired.

Approval plans vary widely in size and scope. They may be limited to narrow areas, such as those covering the literature of an individual country, music scores, or art exhibition catalogs. Such plans are most useful to special libraries or research libraries that collect extensively in those areas. Another type of approval plan provides extensive coverage of most U.S. and U.K. trade publishers, handling materials in all subject areas and in many formats. Large academic and research libraries are the most frequent users of these general plans.

Approval plans require that libraries work with vendors to define what types of materials are desired. Libraries and vendors create profiles that describe the types of materials the libraries want to purchase. Profiles may be based on subject categories or on specific publishers. Most plans combine several factors, including subjects, publishers, prices, physical formats, languages, geographic emphases, and intended audience levels. Careful profiling is required to ensure the success of approval plans. "A close working relationship between vendor and librarian is required for the plan to be effective" (Flood 1998, 3).

Libraries decide which types of items should be supplied as books; they may also receive bibliographic notification forms describing materials of secondary interest. Notification forms may be appropriate for items such as those costing more than a specified price, reprints, or translations. The notifications may be printed or electronic bibliographic forms; some libraries may compile lists of such titles by searching the vendors' online databases. The libraries may order these items from the approval vendor; however, using one vendor's forms to place orders with another vendor is unethical.

Approval plan vendors profile items based on information received from publishers, estimate how many copies will be needed depending on the profiles created by their customers, and order the books. When the items are received, they are processed and sent to the approval plan customers. Libraries review the materials, decide which items will be purchased, and return those items that are rejected. Most approval vendors ask that the rejection rates be under 10 percent. If the rejection rates are higher than that, the libraries should work with their vendors to refine the profiles. Libraries should return rejected items as soon as possible, preferably within a month; this allows the vendor to supply the items to other libraries or return them to the publishers.

Some approval vendors have online databases that allow libraries to order materials online, verify the status of orders, and determine whether items are already published—or already out of print. Most have the ability to transmit electronic files containing bibliographic records for the items being supplied on approval. Many vendors can transmit invoices electronically. Some vendors will catalog and physically process materials; these items cannot be returned to the vendor. Approval plan vendors provide statistical reports describing the libraries' purchases and the materials handled by the vendors. They can also project how much money libraries might spend by creating cost estimates for hypothetical profiles. Some vendors' databases show why items were not supplied to their customers. Many databases are now interactive; librarians may request and view reports online.

Approval plans allow libraries to review the actual materials, rather than relying on reviews. These plans also provide materials shortly after they have been published, reducing delays in obtaining materials and ensuring that the materials will be acquired before they go out of print. Because vendors handle huge numbers of items, they discover materials that might be missed by selectors. Selectors do not have to spend as much time reviewing catalogs of publishers that are covered by the approval plans; they can concentrate on publishers and areas not included in the plans. Materials are supplied at a discount negotiated with the libraries; these discounts vary with the amount of money projected to be spent by the libraries and the types of materials expected to be supplied. Approval plan vendors can help libraries build strong basic collections easily. General approval plans are most useful for large libraries that are collecting materials in a wide range of subject areas.

On the negative side, libraries may find themselves purchasing materials that they might not have ordered because selectors sometimes find it harder to reject a book than to discard an advertisement. The libraries do pay the cost of returning materials, both in shipping costs and in staff time to handle the returned items. Approval plans do delegate some of the responsibility for selection to companies outside the library. Approval plan vendors do not provide all types of materials; they cannot be the only source of materials for the libraries. Some publishers will not agree to give discounts to approval vendors; therefore, the vendors may not supply items from those publishers. Consequently libraries must monitor the publication lists of such companies in order to acquire their publications separately from the approval plans.

Libraries must monitor the plans to ensure they are performing correctly. Approval plans that are created accurately and are functioning properly will supply libraries with materials they need, promptly after the publication of the items, and at a reasonable discount. If approval plan profiles are incorrectly structured or if selectors do not identify materials that are not supplied on approval, important materials will be missed, inappropriate materials will be supplied, and the libraries will waste money.

PRESERVATION

"The main role of the acquisitions librarian in preservation is to help acquire materials in usable condition, and to refer newly received materials in poor condition for review or treatment before they are added to the collection" (Hamilton 1993, 6). Acquisitions personnel should watch for materials that have been damaged in shipping and notify vendors if a pattern of ongoing damage emerges. When receiving materials, acquisitions personnel should watch for damage that may include loose pages, loose sections of pages, bindings that are separating from the text or are upside down, or sections that are blank or incorrectly printed. Most libraries do not have enough time to check all items extensively, but taking a short time to detect obvious defects will avoid the cost of purchasing replacement copies later when patrons discover that the items are damaged or defective.

Acquisitions personnel should follow basic preservation techniques. They should not use rubber bands, paper clips, or sticky temporary notes on materials that will be added to the library's collection. They should handle materials carefully and shelve them properly, seeing that books are supported on the book trucks and shelves and that large books are shelved flat or on their spines.

Some materials are very fragile and therefore require special handling. They may need to have protective covers or boxes made before the materials are processed. Acquisitions personnel must be able to identify such materials and know what steps to take to protect them.

ACQUIRING MEDIA

Libraries acquire media materials such as videotapes, audiotapes, software, DVDs, or electronic books using the same methods by which they acquire books; however, some additional issues are involved. Some vendors handle print books and many types of media, while others specialize in specific formats such as music. *AV Market Place* lists many of the media vendors. Electronic discussion lists provide information about the selection, processing, and use of media. For information about VIDEOLIB and VIDEONEWS, see http://library.berkeley.edu/MRC/vrtlists.html (accessed June 1, 2003).

Format

When ordering media, libraries must be very careful to specify the format that is needed, for example, indicating whether software must be compatible with IBM clone or Apple computers. Movies may be available as DVDs or videotapes. Videotapes produced in the United States, Canada, and Mexico are recorded in the NTSC standard, while those produced in other countries use either the PALS or SEACAM standards. If vendors cannot supply the desired format, libraries may need to request permission from the copyright holder to transfer the item into the needed format and then arrange to have the transfer done.

Physical Processing of Media

Media such as videotapes that may be damaged by magnetic devices should not be exposed to security systems. Libraries may decide to label these materials with a warning note that alerts people to this danger.

Videotapes and other media may arrive in thin cardboard or paper cases. Libraries should replace these temporary cases with plastic ones or other cases that will better protect the materials.

Legal Issues: Licensing and Registration

Some books now include access to Internet sites that provide updated information. The password information or registration numbers are included in the books. Libraries should ask the publishers whether the access is restricted to one user. If more than one person may use the same password, the information could be included in the book or the record. If access is restricted to one user, librarians may try to create a generic registration that any patron may use, or they may decide to remove the access information before the item circulates.

Some software companies may require libraries to sign licensing agreements; other software may include notices that opening the packages or using the material implies that the libraries accept the licensing agreements. Libraries must learn the procedures and policies of their institutions in dealing with contracts and licensing agreements.

Other software requires that owners register their ownership with the publisher. Libraries must investigate such products carefully. Some companies state that their items are to be used only by the individual who purchases the software; they do not allow the items to be resold or loaned to other individuals. Libraries may be able to purchase versions that allow the libraries to make the items available to many patrons by creating an institutional registration.

Some videotapes or DVDs may include a label stating that the items are licensed for noncommercial or private home use only, and that any public performance or copying is prohibited. The "fair use" exemption of the U.S. copyright law allows some use of copyrighted materials by libraries without explicit permission. This exemption allows some videotapes that are labeled for home use to be used in classrooms or in instructional sessions. It does not allow libraries to use videotapes designated for home use in public programs (Scholtz 1995, 104–8). If libraries are purchasing items that will be used for public performances, they should ask the publisher whether such rights are granted. If the items were ordered for the purpose of showing them in public programs, and the copyright holder refuses to grant permission, the libraries may not use the items in that manner. This information should be noted in the record or in a file in acquisitions. Some publishers charge higher prices for media sold for public performances.

Libraries may not make multiple copies of media and circulate them instead of purchasing additional copies. They may make a backup copy of most media in order to keep a copy in reserve in case the first copy is damaged. They may not add to their permanent collections any unauthorized copies of programs recorded from television or radio broadcasts, just as they cannot add a photocopy of a copyrighted book without permission.

See chapter 7, "Acquiring Electronic Resources," for further information about licensing issues.

GOVERNMENT PUBLICATIONS

"A large percentage of the materials published throughout the world emanates from local, state or provincial, national, and international agencies and governments. Their publications vanish, or reappear with new titles and frequencies, making acquisitions as much a matter of luck as the application of specialized training, experience, and diligence" (Magrill and Corbin 1989, 51). Government publications include materials such as statistical reports, investigative reports, archaeological surveys, consumer advisory reports, and music recordings. Many large research and academic libraries have departments that handle the acquisition of government publications. In some libraries such a department may deal with state and federal documents, but the acquisitions department may acquire documents from all other governments. Many government publications are printed and distributed through depository programs; the documents are rarely available for sale. Most vendors handle only a few major government publications; they rarely deal with local or international government publications.

The major electronic discussion list for U.S. government documents is GOVDOC-L (listserv@lists.psu.edu). Documents Data Miner (http://govdoc.wichita.edu/ddm, accessed June 1, 2003) is an Internet site listing collection management resources for federal document collections. The Government Documents Round Table (GODORT) is a section of the American Library Association that promotes the use and discussion of government publications. Some useful guides to U.S. government publications include *Introduction to United States Government Information Sources* by Joe Morehead (Greenwood Publishing Group, 1999) and *Using Government Information Sources: Electronic and Print* by Jean L. Sears and Marilyn Moody (Greenwood Publishing Group, 2001).

Publications issued by the United Kingdom and the United Nations may be purchased directly from the respective publication office. For the United Kingdom, see http://www.tso.co.uk/ (accessed June 1, 2003). For the United Nations, see http://www.un.org/Pubs/sales.htm (accessed June 1, 2003). The publications office for Canadian government information is the Canadian Government Publishing Office; see http://publications.gc.ca/pubindex-e.html (accessed June 1, 2003).

CONCLUSION

Acquiring books and media is a complex process composed of numerous individual procedures; the individual steps are usually not complex. Acquisitions personnel must create the individual steps that make up the total process. They must establish procedures that allow materials to be acquired swiftly and yet provide all the information needed by other departments that will process the materials and the financial transactions. Acquisitions personnel must evaluate the procedures continually to ensure that they remain efficient and current. In order to establish efficient procedures to acquire materials, acquisitions personnel must know their institution's financial practices and policies concerning contracts, and they must be able to analyze workflow and organize activities into logical sequences.

REFERENCES

Eaglen, Audrey. 2000. *Buying books: A how-to-do-it manual for librarians.* 2nd ed. New York: Neal-Schuman.

Flood, Susan, ed. 1998. *Guide to managing approval plans.* Chicago: American Library Association.

Hamilton, Marsha J. 1993. *Guide to preservation in acquisitions processing.* Chicago: American Library Association.

Magrill, Rose Mary, and John Corbin. 1989. *Acquisitions management and collection development in libraries.* 2nd ed. Chicago: American Library Association.

Miller, Heather S. 1992. *Managing acquisitions and vendor relations: A how-to-do-it manual.* New York: Neal-Schuman.

Scholtz, James C. 1995. *Video acquisitions and cataloging: A handbook.* Westport, CT: Greenwood Press.

Schuman, Patricia Glass, and Charles Harmon. 1999. The business of book publishing. In *Understanding the business of library acquisitions.* 2nd ed. Edited by Karen A. Schmidt. Chicago: American Library Association.

Chapter 6

Acquiring Serials

A serial is "a publication in any medium issued in successive parts bearing numerical or chronological designations and intended to continue indefinitely. Serials include periodicals, newspapers, annuals (reports, yearbooks, etc.); the journals, memoirs, proceedings, transactions, etc., of societies; and numbered monographic series" (Gorman and Winkler 1988, 622). Serials may appear daily, such as newspapers, or at irregular and unpredictable intervals, such as collected works of writers. "Serials are remarkably like people in that they are born, change names, marry, divorce, have offspring, and finally die. Serials also have been known to come back from the dead and resume living, often in a different format or with a different focus" (Puccio 1989, 4). These characteristics of serials are true regardless of whether the format is print (paper), electronic, or microform. This chapter primarily discusses print serials, while chapter 7, "Acquiring Electronic Resources," addresses electronic serials and books.

The exact number of serials being published is constantly changing. *Ulrich's Periodicals Directory* online lists approximately two hundred fifty thousand serials currently published worldwide (http://www.ulrichsweb. com/ulrichsweb/, accessed June 1, 2003). In 1999–2000, U.S. libraries spent almost $800 million on serials (R. R. Bowker 2001, 397–405). Members of the Association of Research Libraries spent more than $500 million for serials in 2000 (Association of Research Libraries 2001). Academic libraries generally spend well over half their acquisitions budgets on serials. Serials are everywhere; they are in the very pores of the library.

Serials may be acquired in the acquisitions department, in a separate serials department, or in a department that combines ordering and cataloging operations. Please see chapter 1, "Organization of Acquisitions Departments," for information about the structure of acquisitions and serials units. Regardless of where the serials operation is located, serials acquisitions includes identifying and verifying the existence of the item, ordering it, receiving it, checking it in, paying for it, and renewing it, claiming it, or canceling it as needed. In some libraries, serials cataloging may be included within the acquisitions department. "A serials acquisitions operation that uses sound methods is the basis for effective serials collection development and user services" (Chiou-sen 1995, 65).

The process of acquiring serials is a continuing one. Books are identified, ordered, received, paid for, cataloged, and shelved. Unless problems are discovered, technical services departments do not deal with books after they are cataloged until the items are withdrawn. Serials are identified, ordered, received, paid for, cataloged, renewed, claimed, recataloged after the titles change, and renewed again until they cease or are canceled. Technical services deal with serials constantly; the process never ends. This chapter describes the procedures involved in obtaining serials.

WHERE TO PURCHASE SERIALS

Libraries purchase serials either directly from the publisher, from subscription services, or from consortium arrangements. Most serials purchased through consortial arrangements are electronic journals and are discussed in Chapter 7, "Acquiring Electronic Resources." In addition to purchasing serials, libraries acquire serials as gifts, from exchange agreements, and from depository agreements. Each source has advantages and disadvantages; libraries will decide which sources are preferable after considering their own needs. Regardless of whether a serial is purchased or received through an agreement, it should be shipped in a timely fashion, subscriptions should be started with the issue requested, delays or problems should be reported quickly, invoices should be clear and accurate, and returns or credits should be easily processed.

Publishers

Publishers will sell their serials directly to libraries, and most also sell their serials to subscription services, who then sell them to libraries. Why do libraries purchase serials directly from publishers? Some publishers, such as local newspapers and some small societies, especially regional ones, will not do business with subscription services. Some subscription services will not do business with some publishers. Sometimes publishers offer packages of their publications to libraries at a reduced rate that may not be available through subscription services. Organizations may offer their publications through institutional memberships, providing publications that are either not available except through membership or are more expensive to nonmembers.

Libraries that order serials directly from the publisher must carefully monitor their mail and the information provided inside the serials received to ensure that they locate renewal notices and invoices. Not all communications from the publisher are easily found or identified. For example, some newspapers simply insert a card with pricing information inside the paper with no indication that the card was meant to serve as an invoice; some magazines insert an invoice inside the issue, where it may not be easily found.

A few very small libraries may not use subscription services in order to save the service charge imposed by the service. This practice is not a cost-effective option for larger libraries.

Subscription Services

A subscription service, sometimes called a subscription agency, subscription agent, or a serials vendor, is a commercial business that processes serials orders for all types of libraries. Subscription agents have a long history; W. H. Everett and Son Ltd. began business in the late eighteenth century; Dawsons and Faxon began in the nineteenth century. Subscription services provide a variety of services for librarians including placing orders with publishers, processing renewals, consolidating many publisher invoices into one or several vendor-generated invoices, processing claims, and providing a variety of specialized customer and computer-based services such as online interactive databases. Subscription services maintain detailed records and provide management reports for titles that the library has on order with them.

The advantage of subscription services is the savings they provide to the library in reducing workloads, reducing the number of staff, saving space, and saving equipment. Once the library places an order with the subscription service, the service performs the clerical procedures associated with dealing with many different publishers for orders, claims, and problems. Subscription services can ensure that the library's subscriptions are automatically renewed, avoiding gaps in issues. They can invoice the library at the times that are most appropriate for its budget cycle. "Agents are frequently in direct contact with publishers and, as a result, amass a great deal of knowledge about publisher whims and procedures. Agents learn quickly which publishers demand prepayment and which have specific ordering requirements; they know when subscription periods can and cannot start; and they usually maintain up-to-date files of publishers' addresses or details of distribution centers, where relevant. Agents can offer expertise in a wide variety of languages, especially if the company is based in the appropriate country, e.g. Japan or Poland, and can communicate with publishers in their respective languages. Detailed knowledge of national or local publishing practices can also prove a valuable asset" (Pilling 1988, 129–30). In addition, subscription services can pay foreign publishers in their local currencies.

Subscription services, libraries, and publishers are all negotiating their roles in the rapidly changing serials industry. Some publishers are exploring new business models by creating packages of their print and electronic journals; these publishers sell their packages directly to libraries and library consortia rather than going through subscription services. Publishers may offer lower prices to libraries than the subscription services may be able to offer, but libraries that deal directly with such publishers must process invoices from those companies separately. The invoices from publishers are usually single-line invoices for the complete packages of journals; the individual titles are not listed in an electronic format that can be loaded into the libraries' systems. Libraries that need to document the prices and subscription status of specific titles must enter the information into their system manually. The collection management reports created by subscription services become less useful when libraries subscribe to many titles directly from the publishers. Libraries may save some money with the lower prices, but they may see an increase in the staff time required to process and monitor the invoices. Removing large numbers of titles from the lists handled by the libraries' subscription services may also lead to increased service charges from those agents if the size and nature of the accounts change. Subscription services are expanding their automated systems and their efforts to assist libraries in handling electronic journals. The role of subscription services in dealing with consortial purchasing of electronic resources is in flux. Libraries, publishers, and subscription services are all attempting to find their way as virtual collections develop rapidly.

Subscription services may specialize in a specific subject area, such as medicine; in a specific geographic area, such as Eastern Europe; or in a specific format, such as microforms, or they may handle all formats, subjects, and geographic areas. Subscription services do not handle all types of materials; for example, most services will not supply regional publications such as newspapers from small towns.

Subscription services provide publishers with benefits similar to those received by libraries: efficient consolidation of orders and renewals, handling of international currencies, assistance with claims, knowledge of the library market, and distribution of information.

Libraries may decide to consolidate all their serials titles with one subscription service, or they may divide their titles among multiple services.

Some libraries divide their accounts by geographic regions; titles published in Latin America are ordered from subscription services in those regions, while titles published in Europe are ordered from services in that area.

Serials include titles that are published annually or irregularly, as well as periodicals that are published on regular schedules. Both serials subscription services and book vendors can supply most annual or irregular materials; libraries may use either type of company to handle these serials. Libraries that have separate units responsible for acquiring books and acquiring serials must decide which unit will handle these materials. Whatever policy is established, the units must maintain continual communication in order to minimize confusion. Deciding whether items are or are not serials is sometimes a matter of interpretation; personnel in separate units must work closely when processing such materials.

Librarians can find lists of serials vendors at Internet sites including AcqWeb (http://acqweb.library.vanderbilt.edu), ulrichsweb.com (http://www.ulrichsweb.com/ulrichsweb/), and the Association of Subscription Agents (http://www.subscription-agents.org) (all accessed June 1, 2003).

Gifts, Exchanges, and Depository Agreements

Libraries may acquire serials in ways other than purchasing, primarily through gifts and exchange programs. In larger libraries, gifts and exchange programs are frequently located in acquisitions departments. For more information on the structure and operations of these programs, please see chapter 9, "Gifts and Exchange Programs." Depository programs are arrangements in which organizations or governments send copies of their publications to libraries. Some depository agreements require the libraries to retain all the publications; other arrangements allow some materials to be discarded. Gifts, exchanges, and depository programs do allow libraries to obtain materials without paying money for their direct purchase; however, the programs do require staff time to acquire, preserve, and process the materials.

Gifts

Gifts of serials may include scattered issues of titles, complete back files of titles, or donated subscriptions. Donors may be individuals, organizations, or the publishers of the titles. Libraries must evaluate gifts carefully, remembering the costs of processing, preserving, and storing the materials. Libraries should have policies describing the types of materials that will or will not be accepted as gifts; all donations should meet the criteria established in the collection development policies of the libraries.

Many libraries will not add scattered issues of titles to their permanent collections unless the items are in areas in which the libraries collect comprehensively. If the libraries receive donations of the complete collections of titles that are not already owned, libraries frequently decide to add those materials.

Individuals or publishers may offer to donate subscriptions to periodicals. Librarians must evaluate the potential title to determine whether it meets the collection policies of the library. Some libraries may wish to add the publications of religious denominations or associations advocating specific social issues, whereas others do not acquire materials in such areas. Each library will have different policies that should be documented and shared with potential donors.

Donors may offer to provide subscriptions for a year, anticipating that the libraries will purchase subscriptions to the donated titles after that time. Libraries should inform the donors about their policies and their abilities to purchase the desired titles. Libraries should encourage donors to provide the titles for more than one year; some libraries refuse donated subscriptions unless the donor will agree to purchase the titles for at least three years. Donors may give the libraries money to purchase the titles through the libraries' regular subscription services, or the donors may purchase the titles themselves and have them sent to the libraries. Either method can work, depending upon the institutional policies and fiscal services practices.

Libraries should create order records for the donated titles that include the names of the donors and the length of the subscriptions. Gift serials should be checked in like other serials. If the gift is a new title, a check-in record will need to be created. Donated subscriptions may require more staff time to claim since the records of the payments will be under the names of the donors; libraries may need to include the specific information from the mailing labels when inquiring about problems. Donated subscriptions may stop unexpectedly if the donors decide they will no longer purchase the titles. Subscription renewal notices are generally sent to the purchasers; the libraries may be unaware that the subscriptions have expired until the issues stop arriving.

Gifts of serials can save money since the libraries do not purchase the subscriptions, but they do require staff time to evaluate, process, preserve, and monitor. Libraries must balance the savings in money against the cost in time required to handle the materials.

Exchange Programs

Exchange programs usually involve trading the publications of an institution for those of another organization; some exchange programs may also exchange duplicate or unwanted materials. Libraries must identify exchange partners, agree with the potential partners about what titles will be exchanged, and monitor the materials to ensure that the program is relatively balanced. If libraries establish exchange programs with international organizations, the acquisitions staff may need foreign language skills to handle some correspondence.

Libraries should create order and check-in records in their integrated library systems for titles received on exchange. The records should include the names of the exchange partners and notes on whether missing issues should be claimed. Some organizations can supply missing issues; others do not attempt to replace issues.

Depository Programs

Depository programs are arrangements in which institutions or governments provide their publications to libraries. Most of the publications received on depository programs are serials, and like other serials they will require that order and check-in records be created in the library's integrated library system for them. Libraries may decide to receive all the publications issued by the institution or to receive only selected materials. Libraries may receive the materials at no purchase cost, or they may pay an annual fee. Libraries establish depository programs in order to acquire materials that cannot be purchased through other methods and to acquire all materials issued by an institution.

Depository agreements may require that the library sign a contract. In such cases, the library must review the terms of the agreement carefully and must follow institutional policies governing the legal requirements for signing contracts.

Governments may require that libraries promise to keep the depository materials permanently and make them available to all interested researchers. Libraries must review depository agreements carefully; those libraries with limited space may not be able to retain all materials indefinitely, and libraries not usually open to the public may not be able to allow unaffiliated users access to the materials.

ECONOMICS

The serials industry is a multibillion-dollar international industry that runs to a huge extent upon trust. Libraries trust that subscription services will pay the publishers for the materials and that the publishers will provide the materials to the libraries; subscription services trust that the libraries will pay their invoices promptly and that the publishers will deliver the materials to the libraries; and publishers trust that the subscription agents and libraries will subscribe to their materials. Because most serials publishers do not give discounts, subscription agents charge fees for their services in order to make a profit. The profit margin for sub-scription services is very small. Prepayments and deposit accounts are the norm, unlike in the books industry, where payments are made when the materials are received. Publishers may establish different levels of prices based on the type of library or individual subscribing to their titles. Inter-national publishers may charge libraries in the currency of the publisher or of the library.

For more information about the economics of the publishing industry, please see chapter 3, "The Publishing Industry."

Service Charges

In the book publishing industry, publishers give large discounts to ven-dors and bookstores. In the serials publishing industry, few publishers give any discounts to vendors, and those discounts are quite small. The absence of discounts means that subscription services must charge fees to provide services and make profits. "An efficient, well-managed agency can return a pre-tax profit of from half of one percent to five percent of annual sales" (Basch and McQueen 1990, 53).

The most common type of service charge is a fee that is determined by cal-culating a percentage of the total dollar amount of the titles handled by the subscription agent. The percentage may be charged on each title, so that the invoice will have the service charge included in the price of all the individual titles, or it may be a separate figure added at the end of each invoice. The size of the percentage may vary somewhat, depending upon the size and nature of the account. If a large number of standing orders are included in the account, the service charges might be slightly lower because the sub-scription services may get large discounts on those materials from their publishers. An account that includes a high percentage of scientific, techni-cal, or medical serials may have a lower service charge than an account that consists primarily of humanities titles. Humanities titles cost far less than the scientific titles; the profit margin for the subscription services is some-what higher when they handle more expensive titles.

Because the profit margin for subscription services is quite small, the range of the service charges offered by the major companies is very small. When libraries negotiate with companies, they should remember that the prices charged by competing companies vary only slightly.

Prepayments and Deposit Accounts

The cycle of payments for serials varies somewhat with the size of libraries and the practices of the subscription services, but nearly all periodicals and most other serials require that libraries pay for the subscriptions in advance.

Prepayments

Most large libraries and library systems use subscription services to handle their subscriptions; these services maintain extensive databases containing information about serials titles and pricing. The subscription services work closely with publishers to obtain information about serials price increases in the summer and early fall. Because some publishers do not set their subscription prices until late in the calendar year, subscription services may not have some current prices until late fall. When publishers set their prices late in the year, subscription services must enter the information into their databases at their busiest season and libraries have inadequate information and insufficient time to decide about renewals. The Association of Subscription Agents continues to urge all publishers to establish prices by early summer to prevent such problems. Subscription services pay the publishers in the fall, which means that libraries must pay the subscription services before late fall. Many subscription services offer libraries incentives to pay their renewals in the summer or early fall; these incentives may be a decrease in the percentage of the service charge or a discount on the total cost of the renewal invoice.

Libraries that prepay early must remember that the prices for some serials have not been set and that the amount of the renewal invoice is an estimate. Most subscription services take the amount spent by the library in the previous fiscal year, subtract major cancellations, and add a percentage factor for the estimated inflation for the coming year. This figure is generally a close approximation, but it may be somewhat inaccurate. If an estimate is too low, the library may have to send the subscription service additional money later in the year; if an estimate is too high, the subscription service may have money remaining in the library's account at the end of the fiscal year. If the library did not prepay enough money, the subscription service will issue a supplemental invoice; this may arrive late in the fiscal year, making accounting and budgeting difficult for the library. If money does remain unspent, a library may request that the subscription service send the money to it, or it may request that the money be applied to its account for the coming year. Libraries should compare their records with those of the subscription services each year to verify that the numbers agree; any discrepancies must be reconciled.

Some subscription services offer libraries the option of a guaranteed price. The subscription services estimate the prices and invoice libraries for that estimate and will not send any supplemental invoices. Because the subscription services wish to continue in business, they will estimate prices that will cover unanticipated increases, so the total costs may be slightly higher than the amount that would have been paid if the libraries had paid individual invoices throughout the year. The subscription services and libraries work together to balance the accounts each year. The major advantages for libraries are the elimination of multiple invoices and the ability to allocate funds evenly throughout the year.

Deposit Accounts

Some businesses, associations, and government offices will establish deposit accounts for libraries. The libraries send money to these organizations, and the organizations supply the libraries with materials that are charged against the deposited money. Many such organizations will give libraries some discount on the price of the materials. Libraries must be able to track the materials received on such deposit accounts, record the costs of the materials, and subtract the amounts from the deposit accounts. When the deposit accounts begin to be depleted, libraries must send additional funds; some organizations will ignore orders that they receive when the deposit accounts are exhausted, while some will notify the libraries that the deposit accounts must be replenished before the orders will be processed. The discounts can be helpful, but the record keeping can be complicated; libraries must evaluate whether the cost savings on the materials are balanced by the time required to maintain the deposit accounts.

Dual Pricing

Some publishers list multiple prices for their journals. The individual subscriber pays the lowest price; corporations, institutions, and libraries pay much higher prices. The publishers state that the price differentiation is justified because the copies sent to libraries and institutions will be read by a large number of people. Libraries object that they are subsidizing the costs of those copies sent to the individual subscribers. Libraries must be aware of the differences in costs and verify the correct rates when ordering titles.

Shipping and Handling Costs

Serials publishers usually include all shipping and handling costs in the annual subscription costs, unlike book publishers, which add such charges for each title to the invoice. Shipping and handling charges are frequently added to invoices for annual publications and other materials received on standing order, as well as for purchases of back issues of periodicals.

STEPS IN THE ORDERING PROCESS

The process of ordering serials is composed of several steps, including verifying the existence, price, and publisher of a title; deciding when and from whom to order the serial; and creating records of the order. When libraries clearly identify the activities required to process orders, materials can be ordered and received more rapidly.

Preorder Preparation

Before ordering serials, acquisitions personnel must check library records to determine whether the library already owns the requested titles. In most cases, searching periodical titles is relatively straightforward; however, conference proceedings and publications of associations may require careful searching to be certain that libraries are not receiving the items already.

When acquisitions personnel receive a request to order a serial, they must verify the title, the publisher, and the price of the serial. Many serials have similar or identical names and change publishers frequently. Serials change titles frequently. Many scholarly serials move among academic institutions. The corporate mergers and company purchases in the serials industry in the last two decades have resulted in many serials being purchased by a few large corporations. Serials prices change frequently, and some increases may be very large; librarians must establish the current prices before ordering titles. In order to verify the bibliographic and pricing information, librarians can consult sources such as publishers' Internet pages and catalogs, *Ulrich's Periodicals Directory,* the *Serials Directory,* or the online databases of serials subscription services used by their libraries. These sources will also provide the ISSN (International Standard Serial Number), a unique number identifying each serials title; librarians should provide this number to subscription services when ordering serials to minimize any confusion over which serial is being ordered. Some subscription services have online databases that include control numbers they have assigned to each title; when libraries include those numbers in their orders, the titles can be supplied more rapidly.

Librarians should tell the publisher or subscription service when they want the subscription to begin. Some publishers will begin sending issues as soon as they receive an order; others will wait until they receive payment; and still others will wait until the beginning of the next volume or year. Some publishers may honor requests to begin with a specific issue, but other publishers may not. If a publisher does not begin the subscription with the desired issue, the library may need to send a separate order to the publisher or to a dealer in back issues of serials in order to acquire the desired issue.

When libraries order a specific edition of a serial, such as only the newest edition, and do not desire to continue to receive subsequent editions, they must specify on the order that only the latest edition is being ordered. If libraries do not state that they wish to purchase only that individual volume, the publisher may continue to send future editions. To avoid misunderstandings and to ensure that the correct issues are received, libraries must express their wishes clearly. Some publishers will assume that an order for the "latest edition" means the last edition that was published, while others will assume that libraries are ordering the edition that will be published in several months. Libraries should include explanatory messages with their orders when such confusion is possible.

When to Order Materials

Although serials may be ordered at any time, some libraries place new subscriptions in the fall in order to start receiving issues at the beginning of a calendar year. Some subscription services and publishers allow libraries to purchase subscriptions for multiple years. This process frequently lowers the annual subscription costs. Before arranging multiyear subscriptions, librarians must check with the fiscal services units of their institutions; some organizations cannot commit funds for more than one year unless the agreement has specific clauses allowing the arrangement to be terminated if financially necessary. While the annual subscription costs for multiyear subscriptions are usually lower, they can create problems for libraries that face unexpected serials cancellation projects. If libraries need to cancel subscriptions, obtaining refunds for portions of multiyear subscriptions can be very difficult.

Subscription Services Selection

Subscription services vary in size and scope; some handle serials of all types, while others specialize in a geographic region such as Latin America, a subject such as medicine, or a format such as microforms. Librarians may be able to select a serials subscription service or may find that a company already has been selected by their institution. Some states have contracts that require public and state-supported libraries to place all subscriptions with companies that are identified as state-approved services. Some large institutions may require that all their branches use one subscription agent. Some states require official requests for proposals or bids when libraries intend to spend more than a prescribed amount, such as $10,000, with one vendor. Please see chapter 4, "Domestic and Foreign Vendor Selection and Evaluation," for more information about the bidding process.

Creating Records of Ordered Materials

Libraries with integrated library systems may have acquisitions modules that create records of all orders placed. Libraries that have manual systems or have created an internal system operating on a personal computer must record all information about serials that have been ordered. Whether the system is part of an integrated library system, a manual system, or an in-house computer system, the information about orders should include the bibliographic record with the title and the publisher, the vendor, the estimated cost, and the date of order. The record should show whether the order is for an ongoing subscription or for individual issues of a serial. The funds used to pay for the items, the locations where the items will be housed, and any relevant notes, such as the name of the person requesting the serial, may also be included. Orders for replacement or additional issues of titles owned by libraries should include the call numbers and the record order numbers from the integrated library system.

Libraries sometimes become institutional members of organizations in order to acquire the publications of the organizations. Staff should create multiple records for such memberships; one record is needed for the membership payment and additional records are needed for the individual titles received. The membership record should list the titles received; the records for the individual titles should state that the titles are received as part of a membership and that the payment must be made to that membership order record.

Sending an Order

Libraries may print and mail orders, fax them, or place them online through the vendor's database. Many large subscription services have online databases; libraries may search titles, identify those that are to be ordered, and instruct the subscription services to place the orders. Libraries rarely order serials by telephone; using services' databases or email is usually more effective for ordering titles that are needed immediately. Printed orders and email messages must include the complete bibliographic information about the desired items, the libraries' purchase order number, any special instructions, and the libraries' shipping and billing addresses. The shipping address is the place to which the actual issues must be sent; the billing address is the place to which the invoice must be sent.

Invoices for serials are usually not included in the shipment with the issues of serials, unlike the process for books and media, where invoices are packed with the items. While the shipping and billing addresses may be the same for smaller libraries, they are frequently different for larger orga-nizations. Many libraries, especially large systems with multiple branches, have serials issues sent to individual locations and have the invoices sent to a different address. Libraries must make certain that the subscription agents have the correct information.

Subscription services may acknowledge the receipt of orders by email, by messages on their online systems, or by print mail. Libraries should inform their agents what types of acknowledgments are preferred.

Encumbering Funds

Encumbering funds means setting aside the money that will be required to pay for the materials when they are billed. Integrated library systems can encumber funds when orders are placed. Libraries using a manual system must create a procedure that tracks the amount of money com-mitted and the amount that remains. Smaller libraries should be able to adapt any basic accounting software program for personal computers to create a program that can track their encumbrances and expenditures.

The encumbrances for serials titles are generally an estimate of the cost. Most libraries encumber funds when beginning new subscriptions for seri-als or for orders of back issues. Libraries usually do not encumber funds in their systems for renewals.

Encumbrances are usually based on the publishers' list prices; the esti-mates rarely include the service charges added by subscription services. When the invoice is received, acquisitions personnel authorize payment, the encumbrance is removed, and the payment is entered into the system.

Credit Cards

Some libraries have institutional credit cards that they can use to make purchases. Such cards are used most frequently for books and media but occasionally may be used for serials as well. Some publishers will accept credit cards when libraries wish to purchase individual issues of a serial. Some publishers of general magazines also accept credit card payments for subscriptions; this may be useful when libraries need a new subscrip-tion started immediately.

Ordering Back Issues

Libraries may need to obtain replacements for missing issues or to acquire older issues of a serial to supplement a new subscription. Many publishers can sell copies of recent issues to libraries, but few have extensive files of their older issues. Larger serials subscription services have small collections of back issues of some titles that are available to their customers. Some serials are available in microform, enabling libraries to acquire the complete files of a title at a relatively reasonable price. Some companies specialize in selling older issues of serials to libraries. Lists may be found at the Back Issues and Exchange Services Internet site (http://www.uvm.edu/~bmaclenn/backexch.html) or AcqWeb (http://acqweb.library.vanderbilt.edu) (both accessed June 1, 2003).

Obtaining Irregular and "Pseudoserials"

While most periodicals are published at regular intervals, other serials may have an unpredictable schedule. Publishers may issue books that have a related theme in a numbered series; other serials publishers produce issues when they acquire enough material or enough money to create new issues. These "pseudoserials" have some, but not all, of the characteristics of serials. Many libraries treat such materials as serials in order to track the receipt of the issues. Both subscription services and book vendors can supply most of these materials; libraries must decide which method is more convenient for the libraries.

Some publishers, especially small regional associations, may not accept standing orders for irregular serials. Libraries attempting to order pseudoserials may decide to create a method of tracking these titles so that they may order the issues at the appropriate time. Such records may be simple card files or notes created in the order records in integrated library systems (Carter, Stephenson, and Wilkinson 1996, 13).

STEPS IN THE RECEIVING AND PAYMENT PROCESS

After items have been identified and ordered, the issues will begin arriving at the libraries. The serials must be opened, identified, received, and checked in; the invoices must be verified and paid; and the issues must be physically processed.

Receiving Serials

Serials arrive with address labels on the issues or on the mailing envelopes. Serials personnel should open the mail, separating the advertisements and catalogs from the serials issues. The mailing labels should remain with the serials until the issues are checked in; if any problems with the issues show up in the process, the subscription services or publishers will need the information included on the mailing labels to resolve them. Sometimes issues are sent to the wrong branch of a library system, and sometimes libraries receive duplicate issues. The numbers on the mailing labels can help identify the exact records, enabling the subscription services or publishers to find and correct the necessary information more easily.

Nearly all libraries use serials check-in systems—whether manual methods, systems using personal computers, or integrated library systems—to record what serials issues are received. The data generally include the volume, issue number, issue date, and date of receipt.

When checking in the first issue of a new subscription, staff should find the order record for the title and verify that the issue is actually the title that was ordered and that the subscription begins with the issue number and date requested by the library. If the library requested that a new subscription begin with issue number one of a volume, and the first issue that arrives is number six, the library will need to order or claim the other issues separately.

When checking in issues of an existing subscription, staff should review the records to verify that the previous issues have been received. If issues are missing, staff may need to claim those issues.

Libraries mark serials in a number of different ways. Some integrated library systems generate labels that include the title, call number, location, date of receipt, or name of the library. Annual volumes may receive permanent iron-on labels, while periodicals may receive pressure-sensitive labels. Some libraries insert security devices in individual periodical issues; others have security devices inserted by the companies when the journals are bound.

Approving Serials Invoices for Payment

Invoices, the bills from subscription services or publishers for the serials, are generally reviewed by acquisitions personnel, approved for payment, and forwarded to the fiscal services unit of the institution. Librarians must learn the policies and practices of their institution in order to know what information the fiscal services unit requires.

Unlike the book publishing industry, in which invoices are usually included with the books, invoices for serials arrive separately from the issues. When libraries order new subscriptions, the invoices frequently arrive before the first issues of the serials are received. Prepayment is common in the serials publishing industry; some publishers will not begin sending issues until they receive payment. Acquisitions personnel must verify that the invoices are indeed for subscriptions that were ordered by the library, that the invoices are from the sources from which the library ordered the materials, and that the prices are what were expected. Some advertisements resemble invoices, and some unethical publishers send invoices for materials that were never ordered by the library. Acquisitions personnel must watch for these traps. Some serials increase rapidly in price; if the price is dramatically different from the estimated price, acquisitions personnel should consult the selector before authorizing the invoice for payment.

Some large subscription services provide electronic invoices that can be loaded into integrated library systems. Librarians must work with their agents and their technology departments to ensure that the systems are compatible so that these invoices can be processed efficiently.

Publishers may send multiple renewal notices and invoices. Acquisitions personnel should verify that the invoices have not been paid before approving payment. Acquisitions personnel must be careful in approving payments to avoid paying for a title more than once.

Librarians should tell their subscription services how many copies of invoices to send and what information to include. Most libraries require that invoices include the service's name, address, and Federal Identification Number; the library's ship-to and bill-to addresses; the service's account number; the library's purchase order number; the serial's title, ISSN, and volumes or dates ordered; and the costs and service charges. Some libraries require that the library's fund information be included. Libraries can specify the size of the invoices, limiting either the number of items or the total dollar amount contained on one invoice.

Most subscription services can invoice libraries in the currency of their choice. Most U.S. libraries prefer to be billed in U.S. currency, expecting that the subscription services will deal with the currency conversion mechanics.

Timing of Invoices and Supplemental Invoices

Many libraries operate on fiscal years that begin in July and end in June; the fiscal cycle of most U.S. government libraries begins in October and ends in September. Most publishers operate on a calendar year, beginning new volumes in January. Most subscription services pay the publishers in late fall; the subscription services expect libraries to pay the major invoices in the summer or early fall. Libraries that are canceling serials need to notify their subscription services about their plans, including the approximate dollar totals, by late spring and then provide the lists of titles being canceled by early fall. Some libraries renew their subscriptions in early summer because subscription services offer discounts for early prepayments. Libraries may receive supplemental invoices later in the year if their prepayments were not sufficient to cover the price increases.

Publishers may increase the size of journals by adding pages to issues or publishing more issues in a volume during the middle of the subscription year. Such increases frequently result in price increases appearing on supplemental invoices. Acquisitions personnel should inform the selectors of such price changes. Most libraries will pay the increases that come during the year and review the titles for possible cancellations for the next subscription year. Some libraries refuse to accept supplemental volumes and return them to the publishers, refusing to pay for unauthorized materials.

Standing orders for annual publications and monographic series are frequently not included in prepayments for subscriptions. These materials are processed as books, with the invoices supplied when the items are sent to the libraries. These materials arrive throughout the year, and the invoices must be paid when the items are received.

Claiming Serials

When libraries do not receive issues of serials, they claim them, generating reports that are sent to the subscription services handling the titles, or to the publishers of those titles ordered directly from their publishers, asking that the issues be supplied.

Libraries discover that issues of serials have not been received in a variety of ways. Some integrated library systems will generate claim notices automatically if the libraries have entered the expected publication frequency for the serials into the system. Staff checking in issues may notice that the issues prior to those being processed were never received. Patrons may ask librarians why the latest issues of their favorite titles have not arrived.

Some serials stop coming completely; others will skip a few issues and then resume arriving at the libraries. While some publishers notify libraries if issues will be delayed, many more do not volunteer that information until they receive questions from libraries or subscription services.

Librarians using subscription services can check the online databases created by the subscription services, online catalogs of other libraries, or the publishers' Internet sites for information about any delays in publication or for the date the issues were published. Librarians can use this information to determine whether claims need to be created.

Integrated library systems with serials check-in functions allow librarians to enter information about the publication frequency of titles into the system. One common guideline is to expect an issue when more than half of the publication interval has passed. For example, a monthly issue is late if it has not arrived two weeks after it was expected. When titles are not received at the expected time, the systems can generate claims. When serials change frequency, such as changing from quarterly to monthly, the pattern in the integrated library system must be updated.

Libraries will claim most missing issues in order to acquire complete files of the titles. In some cases, such as newspapers and ephemeral materials, libraries may not ask for replacement issues; instead, the libraries may request that their subscriptions be extended to compensate for the missing issues.

Publishers set time limits during which they will honor claims for missing issues; after the time limits have passed, the publishers may replace missing issues for a fee. The time limits vary depending on the frequency of the titles; many daily titles must be claimed within a couple of weeks, and monthly magazines must be claimed within three months. Claiming must be done promptly in order to replace materials before the publishers' deadlines have passed. This process is difficult because of the tendency of some publishers to ignore the first claims for issues. Many publishers have discovered that some libraries claim titles based only on the information generated from integrated library systems; many times the issues are being shipped just as the libraries are claiming the issues. Libraries, publishers, and subscription services are working to resolve this imbalance, but at this point, the situation remains difficult. As more publishers provide subscription services with publication status reports, libraries will be able to identify which issues need to be claimed immediately.

Libraries may claim issues from their subscription services by using the services' online databases, by email, or by regular print mail. Most publishers can be contacted by email or by print mail. Subscription services should keep librarians informed about the status of claims. Some services acknowledge claims by email or by messages on their online databases; libraries should tell their services what method of acknowledgment the libraries prefer. Subscription services should notify libraries promptly when issues are no longer available from the publishers.

Librarians should evaluate their claims in an effort to identify any patterns. If specific titles are frequent problems, resulting in a number of claims, are they all issued by the same publisher or handled by the same subscription agent? Missing issues and claims are an inevitable part of serials, but clear patterns may indicate that librarians should work with publishers or subscription services to resolve the issues.

Some publishers, especially those that publish general magazines with extremely high circulation such as *Time,* hire companies to distribute the magazines. These companies, called fulfillment houses, receive the issues, produce the mailing labels, and mail the issues. The publishers have no direct control over the process. Some fulfillment houses require that the mailing addresses meet very specific criteria; some demand that the addresses contain only three or four lines and that each line consists of no more than twenty or thirty characters. If an address exceeds those requirements, the fulfillment houses arbitrarily shorten it to fit their requirements. This treatment can result in periodicals intended for specific departments within specific libraries being sent to a general university address. The service declines, and the claims increase. Libraries that suspect that missing issues might result from the actions of fulfillment houses should check with their subscription services or the publishers. As a last resort, libraries have canceled titles and placed new subscriptions after creating a new form of their address that meets the restrictions of the fulfillment houses.

Renewing Serials

Libraries that purchase the majority of their serials from subscription services rely upon the services to renew the serials each year. Some libraries instruct services to renew all titles each year unless the libraries notify them of specific titles to be canceled. Other libraries instruct services to send the libraries lists of all their serials titles; the libraries review the lists annually and inform the services which titles are to be renewed. Either method works, depending on the libraries' structure and staffing; libraries must make certain that the services understand which method is needed.

Libraries receive many renewal notices from publishers, even for titles handled by subscription services. Acquisitions staff can check such notices to verify that the subscription service will renew the title; however, most of them can be ignored. If the renewal notices continue after the beginning of the calendar year, or if a notice states that it is a final notice, acquisitions personnel should ask the subscription service to verify that the subscription has indeed been paid. Usually the payment and the notices have passed in the mail, but occasionally the subscription service or the publisher has made a mistake. The sooner problems are detected and investigated, the better the chances are for a full run of the periodical.

Acquisitions personnel must watch for renewal notices from some publishers. Local and regional newspapers may include invoices inside the newspapers; some send postcards with their subscription costs, assuming that libraries will recognize the postcards as invoices. Some small magazines may include notes in the issues stating that these are the last issues of a subscription. Some libraries create lists of these titles, maintaining reminder files that can be checked each month to identify titles that need to be renewed.

The cycle of prepayments requires that most serials be renewed by late fall. If libraries or subscription services renew titles late in the year, publishers may not receive the payments before the first issues of the new year are published. If the publishers do not receive their payments on time, the libraries may miss issues. If the delays are a result of library or institutional problems, librarians must explain the results of the delays to their organization and find ways to correct the problem. If delays are a result of poor performance by subscription services, libraries should discuss the problem with the companies and, if necessary, consider switching to other services.

Sorting Mail

In addition to all the materials that libraries do order, acquisitions units receive advertisements, catalogs, gifts, fliers, and bills. Libraries receive huge amounts of mail; the process of sorting the materials properly can be difficult. Acquisitions personnel must sort the mail carefully in order to separate materials into proper categories.

Sometimes materials arrive that appear to be invoices but are not. The items may have a very small note stating that they are notifications, not invoices; acquisitions personnel must watch carefully for such misleading advertisements.

Acquisitions personnel in large systems with multiple libraries should watch the mail for issues that belong to other libraries. Libraries should copy the mailing labels, report the problem to the subscription service or publisher, and forward the issues to the correct libraries.

Many publishers now offer electronic versions of their serials. Acquisitions personnel should watch for notices about these products and send this information to the appropriate selector.

Staff sorting mail must be able to identify actual invoices, advertisements, and information about changes in publications. Much mail truly is junk; the remaining materials are vitally important and must be handled correctly.

Monitoring

Serials change over time. Titles merge or split. Publishers issue supplements and indexes. The volume and issue numbering becomes unpredictable, skipping or combining numbers. Titles move from one publisher to another. Publishers change addresses. Titles suspend publication, resume publishing, and cease. Prices change dramatically. Publishers add electronic access. Serials subscription services try very hard to track all the changes and keep their clients informed, but some changes slip past the services as well. Serials personnel must be alert to changes as they check in the issues. Some changes, such as mergers and cessations, will require changes in the bibliographic records. Large price changes and the addition of electronic access may require that serials personnel consult with the selectors to decide what actions the library will take.

Returning Serials

Libraries rarely return serials, even when they receive duplicate or defective issues. Duplicate issues usually result from errors made by publishers or fulfillment houses. When a system has several libraries, or when libraries have similar addresses, the addresses can get confused, resulting in issues going to the incorrect libraries. Most subscription services request that libraries send them copies of the mailing labels or the subscription numbers from the labels rather than returning the issues. This information helps the agents determine the cause of the problem. Sometimes defective copies of periodicals are replaced at no cost by the publishers or the subscription services. When the defective items are expensive annual titles or monographic series, the publishers may ask libraries to return the items. Libraries should ask their agents for permission before returning any issues. When issues are returned, the subscription services may issue the libraries credit for future purchases or may allow them to adjust the invoices.

Canceling Serials

Many academic and research libraries have been unable to continue purchasing the same number of serials that they once did due to the increases in journal pricing. Please see chapter 3, "The Publishing Industry," for information about the serials pricing crisis. Libraries have been canceling serials since the late twentieth century and continue to do so. Libraries must work closely with their patrons and with their serials subscription services when planning serials cancellation projects.

Service charges frequently depend upon the size and nature of the account; large cancellation projects may affect the size of the service charges paid by libraries. Many publishers refuse to refund payments; therefore, if the services have already paid the publishers, libraries cannot receive any refunds for titles they cancel late in the fiscal cycle.

Academic libraries should prepare their cancellation lists before the spring semester ends. Library liaisons can consult with the faculty during the year and provide acquisitions personnel with a list of titles that are to be canceled in late spring. Acquisitions staff will be able to process the cancellations, update all records, and inform the vendors of the necessary cancellations before the prepayments are due and long before the subscription services pay the publishers.

Clearing Order Records

Most libraries are required by their institutions to keep financial records for a specified number of years; maintaining the order records in integrated library systems can meet this requirement. For serials subscriptions, order records are always kept until the titles cease or are canceled. When a serials subscription is no longer active, some libraries remove the order record from the system. Deleting these records saves space in the databases and saves money by allowing the records to reused. On the other hand, many libraries find it useful to keep the order records for ceased and canceled titles. The records can show the price history for titles and can include notes explaining when and why titles were canceled. Irregularly published serials may issue volumes several years apart; if the order records are not retained, libraries may not realize they have standing orders for the titles. If libraries have enough available order records to maintain order records for ceased, suspended, and canceled titles, they should keep that information.

PAY-PER-VIEW ARTICLES

As serials subscription prices increased dramatically in the late twentieth century, research libraries began frequent serials cancellation projects. Libraries improved their interlibrary loan operations in order to provide users with the information they wanted.

New technologies, such as improved fax and delivery operations, reduced the time required to provide serials articles and to locate books. Some libraries required their users to pay all charges for interlibrary loan; other libraries paid all fees from their budgets.

Databases of electronic resources developed rapidly. Companies that originally produced indexes and abstracts of periodical articles began adding the full-text articles to their databases. Publishers began producing electronic databases of their serials and books. Some publishers allowed libraries to purchase access to the indexing and abstracting portions of the databases without also acquiring access to the complete full-text resources. When libraries do not subscribe to the full-text files, they can purchase individual articles as their patrons request them. As with interlibrary loan, some libraries paid to purchase the articles for their patrons; others required their users to purchase the materials.

Some libraries have found that charging all interlibrary loan, document delivery, or pay-per-view costs to the collections budget is less expensive than paying for the subscription costs for all the titles requested. Although the materials are not added to the libraries' permanent collections, the items are provided to the libraries' users. Some libraries have canceled expensive serials and used the money from those cancellations to pay for interlibrary loan and document delivery services.

Budgeting for such projects can be difficult in the beginning because estimating the use and the costs calls for careful planning and some educated guesses. Once the projects have been established, the ongoing budgeting is less challenging.

Costs for pay per view and for copyright fees are rising, although not yet as rapidly as those for serials subscriptions have. Most interlibrary loan and document delivery systems can create lists of what serials titles are requested. Libraries can review those lists and identify which titles are requested repeatedly. The libraries can then obtain the subscription costs for those titles and decide whether subscriptions would be more cost effective.

PRESERVATION

The personnel who receive materials are the first ones responsible for ensuring that library collections are properly handled and preserved. Receiving staff should watch for materials that are damaged in shipping and notify the subscription services or publishers if a pattern of ongoing damage emerges. When materials arrive, acquisitions personnel should watch for damage such as pages that are loose, bindings that are separating from the text, or pages that are incorrectly printed. Although most libraries do not have enough time to check all items completely, taking a short time to detect obvious problems will avoid the cost of purchasing replacement copies later after patrons discover the defective issues. If the damage is relatively minor, libraries may decide to repair the item rather than attempt to acquire a replacement copy. If print periodicals are damaged, libraries may decide not to replace them if the contents are also available in electronic format or will be available in microform within a short time.

Acquisitions personnel should follow basic preservation guidelines. They should not use rubber bands, paper clips, or temporary sticky notes on materials that will be added to their library's collection. The sticky notes leave a residue on glossy paper and remove the print from newspaper pages.

Some materials are very fragile and require special handling. Acquisitions personnel may need to have protective covers or boxes made for some fragile materials before the items can be processed. Acquisitions personnel must watch for those materials and learn what steps to take to preserve the materials.

Serials may include computer disks, cassettes, or CD-ROMs. Acquisitions personnel may need to put such materials into cases that are preservationally appropriate before sending the materials to cataloging.

UNSCRUPULOUS PUBLISHERS

While most publishers are ethical and reliable, some unscrupulous individuals or companies try to take advantage of libraries. Some individuals or companies send libraries materials that the libraries never ordered. The packages may include invoices, or they may say that the items are being sent for review. The information may state that the materials should be returned within a few days if the libraries decide that they will not purchase the items; the deadlines for returning the materials are frequently impossibly short. By law, such unsolicited and unordered materials may be treated as donations. According to the U.S. Postal Service, such materials may be kept as gifts, without payment; for more information, see http://www.usps.gov/websites/depart/inspect/merch.htm (accessed June 1, 2003).

Other publishers may call, email, or send faxes to libraries, asking that library personnel verify information describing the libraries so that the information can be included in forthcoming business directories. These companies then send the directories to the libraries with invoices stating that the phone calls, emails, or faxes were actually orders. Some companies may even record the portion of the conversations in which the staff members agree that the materials may be sent to the library. Even though the staff members never intentionally agreed that the libraries would purchase the materials, some institutions will view such conversations as legal agreements to purchase the materials. Acquisitions staff should inform such companies that their libraries will report these practices to the U.S. Postal Service or other appropriate authorities. In addition, libraries should alert their colleagues about potential abuses by posting information on such electronic discussion lists as ACQNET-L and COLLDV-L; librarians should monitor these lists for information about new or continuing abuses.

Some publishers announce new serials and then publish only a few issues, if any. Most of these are simple cases of business failures, but some announcements are part of large organized fraudulent actions. Libraries should investigate new companies that ask for large sums of money as prepayment for serials that have not yet been published.

MANAGEMENT REPORTS

Subscription services can provide a variety of management reports that help libraries analyze their collections and expenditures. Some services have online databases that libraries can use to obtain some data and to produce reports tailored to their needs; other reports must be produced by the subscription services. Subscription services may be able to provide reports that show changes in the price of serials over several years; the reports may be arranged by title, by publisher, by country, or by subject. Other reports may show the titles received in selected languages, from specific countries, or in electronic format. Subscription services may also be able to provide lists of title changes or of new titles. Some services can provide libraries with information about the dates when issues were published. Libraries should ask their subscription services what reports are available and whether reports are free.

Integrated library systems can also produce management reports. Each system varies somewhat, but many systems can provide lists of titles received for a designated location, in a designated format, or that are charged to specific funds.

Electronic databases can produce usage statistics that show libraries which databases or specific serials titles were used by the libraries' patrons in a given time period. Some usage statistics are available online; others are provided in print by the database producer.

RFPS AND BIDS

Institutions may require libraries that spend more than some specified dollar amount with one vendor to use a formal process to select that vendor. When a formal process is required, generally the request for proposal (RFP) process is used. A task force, composed primarily of representatives from the acquisitions, serials, and systems departments, works with the institution's purchasing office to produce the RFP. The library decides what required and desired elements will be included in the request. Questions frequently include requests for the history and financial condition of the company; the number and backgrounds of the people who will be working with the library; the types of documentation and training that can be provided; the costs of all services; the ways in which the company will communicate with the library; the nature of the automated databases; and the types of materials that can be supplied by the agent. The committee must establish criteria, evaluate all responses fairly, and document the reasons for selecting the successful agent. See chapter 4, "Domestic and Foreign Vendor Selection and Evaluation," for more information on the RFP process.

SUBSCRIPTION SERVICES EVALUATION

Acquisitions personnel should evaluate the performance of their serials subscription services to determine whether the libraries are receiving the desired quality of services for a reasonable cost. Among the factors that personnel should evaluate are the average time in which orders are filled and in which claims are resolved, the service charges of the agents, the percentage of errors, the quality of customer service, the costs for access to online databases and special services, the quality and content of the agents' databases, and the ability of the agents to provide materials from a wide range of publishers.

Evaluations should be a regular part of library operations. Libraries must work closely with their subscription services and communicate any problems immediately. Assuming that the services can sense when the libraries are upset is an unreasonable expectation. For more information about evaluating subscription services, please see chapter 4, "Domestic and Foreign Vendor Selection and Evaluation."

CHANGING SUBSCRIPTION SERVICES

Libraries change subscription services in order to obtain better services or lower costs or because their institution awards the contract to a new company. Libraries must plan such a transition very carefully. The library and the subscription services must identify all titles being transferred. The former subscription service must cancel all the subscriptions, and the new agent must initiate the subscriptions with all the publishers. The process involves the library, both subscription services, and all the publishers, creating opportunities for mistakes and confusion even when everyone works extremely carefully to make the process successful. Everyone must change their records at the correct time to prevent libraries from receiving duplicate issues or missing issues entirely.

The former subscription service should provide the library with a list of all the titles handled by the service; the list is given to the new service, which will notify the publishers about the changes and ensure that the subscriptions will continue. The library may wish to compile its own list of titles to compare with the list from the subscription service in order to verify that all titles are included. The new subscription service is responsible for resolving problems during the transition, and it will work closely with the library. Some subscription services can provide considerable assistance to libraries during service changes.

Switching subscription services is always challenging for everyone concerned; however, careful planning can ease a difficult process.

ADDITIONAL SERVICES FROM SUBSCRIPTION SERVICES

Some subscription services offer "consolidation services," which means the subscription service subscribes to serials, has the issues mailed to the service, uses libraries' online systems to check the issues in, claims any missing issues, marks and labels issues according to the libraries' instructions, and sends the issues to the libraries in a completely marked, ready-to-shelve condition. This service can be very expensive, but it is a useful option for libraries that do not have sufficient staff to maintain a serials operation.

Large subscription services, especially those that do offer consolidation services, maintain a supply of issues of selected serials. Customers of these subscription services may be able to obtain replacement issues from those collections. The subscription services usually charge a nominal fee for the issues. The collections are comparatively small, but they may contain issues libraries need.

Large subscription services have online databases that can provide valuable information to their customers. Most of the databases are available free to the customer. Libraries can generate many reports from the online databases; a few reports must be created by the subscription services.

Subscription services may provide sample issues of serials. Libraries can review these issues to decide whether they wish to subscribe.

Larger subscription services may help libraries arrange access to electronic resources. The services can check the libraries' subscriptions and determine what journals are available in electronic formats and what access would cost. Some services will handle preliminary negotiations for the licensing agreements, informing publishers what clauses are likely to create problems. If libraries are able to give the subscription services the authority to sign contracts on their behalf, the services may negotiate the contracts and set up access for the libraries. Many purchasing offices are hesitant to delegate signing authority; librarians must work closely with their institutional purchasing and legal offices when considering this option.

Libraries should ask their subscription services about special services that may be available to them. Advances in technology are expanding the scope of services rapidly, and new services are being developed continually.

CONCLUSION

Serials publishing and serials librarianship are undergoing rapid changes. Publishers are adding electronic resources to their print materials; libraries are joining consortia to purchase access to databases; and libraries are purchasing individual articles instead of subscribing to printed journals. Several sources can help librarians learn about these rapid developments. The major periodicals related to serials acquisitions are *Serials Librarian, Serials Review, Library Resources and Technical Services,* and *Against the Grain.* In addition to the meetings of the librarian associations, two major conferences deal with issues related to serials acquisitions: the Charleston Conference (http://www.cofc.edu/cdconference) and the North American Serials Interest Group (NASIG) Conference (http://www.nasig.org) (both accessed June 1, 2003). Electronic discussion lists can provide invaluable information; the major electronic discussion lists for serials acquisitions are ACQNET-L (http://acqweb.library.vanderbilt.edu/acqweb/acqnet.html); SERIALST (http://www.uvm.edu/~bmaclenn/serialst.html) (both accessed June 1, 2003); and COLLDV-L (Listproc@usc.edu).

Communication is a crucial component in the successful acquisition of serials. Serials personnel must work closely with the systems, cataloging, collection management, public services, and fiscal services units. Personnel must also work closely with publishers and subscription services. When the units work together and communicate well, the processing of materials will proceed more smoothly.

Acquiring serials is a perpetual process. "Serials acquisitions is a complex and challenging responsibility. The work increases and never appears to diminish; patrons abandon the library seasonally, budgets are cut, staff members resign, but still the serials come into the department for processing" (Tuttle 1996, 149). Staff must follow procedures accurately and recognize problems as they appear. To resolve problems, the staff must be diplomatic, patient, and tenacious. Libraries must provide continual training to ensure that acquisitions personnel learn to deal with new resources and formats. Serials are a major source of current information, especially in scientific and technological areas; serials also consume a major portion of research libraries' funds. Serials and acquisitions personnel must deal with the challenging complexities of the materials in order to make the resources available to the libraries' users.

REFERENCES

Association of Research Libraries. 2001. ARL statistics. <http://fisher.lib.virginia.edu/arl/> (accessed September 1, 2002).

Basch, N. Bernard, and Judy McQueen. 1990. *Buying serials: A how-to-do-it manual for librarians.* New York: Neal-Schuman.

Carter, Christina E., Nina K. Stephenson, and Frances C. Wilkinson. 1996. Putting the house in order: Using INNOPAC to manage problematic reference serials and pseudoserials. *Reference Services Review* 24 (1): 13–20, 72.

Chiou-sen, Dora Chen. 1995. *Serials management: A practical guide.* Chicago: American Library Association.

Gorman, Michael, and Paul W. Winkler. 1988. *Anglo-American cataloging rules.* 2nd ed. Chicago: American Library Association.

Pilling, Stella. 1988. The use of serial subscription agents by the British Library Documents Supply Centre. *Serials Librarian* 14 (3/4): 127–31.

Puccio, Joseph A. 1989. *Serials reference work.* Englewood, CO: Libraries Unlimited.

R. R. Bowker. 2001. Library acquisitions expenditures, 1999–2000: U.S. public, academic, special, and government libraries. In *The Bowker annual: Library and book trade almanac, 2001.* 46th ed. 397–405. New Providence, NJ: R. R. Bowker.

Tuttle, Marcia. 1996. *Managing serials.* Greenwich, CT: JAI Press.

Chapter 7

Acquiring Electronic Resources

In the mid-twentieth century, researchers and computer scientists began to use computer technology to organize and retrieve information. Batches of punched cards were used to search databases of citations and abstracts such as ERIC in order to retrieve references on specific topics. Since the full documents were not available in an electronic format, researchers would take the list of citations to their libraries to find the complete sources. Electronic journals began to appear as text messages sent by email to distribution lists in the late twentieth century. The early version of the Internet was developed as a research and military tool; commercial use was initially prohibited. While some librarians were interested in the possibilities of these new developments of email and online access, few people predicted that these electronic resources would transform libraries and publishing. The changes have been revolutionary; today, libraries without electronic resources are practically unimaginable.

Libraries that formerly only purchased and received physical items now pay to view some materials that exist only as distant computer files. In many cases, libraries lease access to the materials, paying for the ability to use the materials only for the duration of the payments and losing access to all those materials when the libraries cease to subscribe. Libraries are learning new methods of dealing with these new materials, creating new techniques and new jobs to handle the electronic resources. "Undoubtedly, libraries today expend the greatest proportion of their management efforts and resources in providing access to the new electronic forms of information resources, and particularly networked electronic information" (Gregory 2000, 47).

Electronic resources may be in the form of journals, books, databases, or indexing and abstracting tools. Most electronic resources acquired by libraries are available over the Internet, although some resources are still published on CD-ROM. A few resources are free; however, most scholarly electronic resources are expensive. The resources may be leased, requiring annual subscription payments, or may be purchased outright. Electronic journals may be the exact counterparts of print journals, containing all materials included in their print versions. Other electronic journals have less materials than their print versions, while still others include additional materials not available in the print editions. Some electronic books may include supplemental materials, such as video clips of plays included in a book about the history of drama. Other electronic books omit illustrations or graphs that were in the printed books. All purchase decisions require research and evaluation.

To acquire electronic resources, acquisitions personnel must identify, order, receive, and pay for the materials, just as they do for books, serials, and media. Because the process of acquiring the electronic materials frequently involves verification of IP (Internet protocol) addresses, variable pricing ranges, and licensing agreements, the acquisition of electronic resources is more complex and time consuming than the process of acquiring other library resources. "The process of selecting and acquiring electronic journals requires more time, more staff, and a higher level of staff than when dealing with print journals....There is more decision making at every step, with the result that ordering electronic journals is far from routine" (Curtis, Scheschy, and Tarango 2000, 117).

This chapter examines the major steps in acquiring electronic resources, including the economics of the industry; relationships among libraries, publishers, and vendors; ordering, receiving, and paying for materials; and handling licensing agreements.

WHERE TO PURCHASE ELECTRONIC RESOURCES

Libraries can purchase or lease electronic resources from publishers, vendors, or consortia. Most of the larger subscription services and some of the larger book vendors can supply electronic serials and books just as they supply print materials to libraries. Some large approval vendors include electronic books in their approval programs, profiling the books in their databases and providing access to the items to their customers. In addition to the publishers and vendors that have supplied materials to libraries for many years, groups of affiliated libraries, known as consortia, now play a major role in the acquisition of large and expensive electronic resources. Consortia allow libraries to purchase access to electronic resources for all members of the group, which makes it possible for libraries to acquire resources they could not afford separately. Each method of purchasing electronic materials has advantages and disadvantages. For example, consortial purchasing can often allow libraries to acquire more resources at a lower price than an individual library could obtain, but it can reduce the library's control over the nature of the content and materials added to the collection when consortia purchase large collections of material.

Some publishers of electronic journals and databases are reluctant to work with subscription services, preferring to deal directly with libraries. Libraries that purchase electronic journals directly from these publishers may pay a slightly lower price than those libraries that use subscription services to acquire the same materials. The cost savings on these subscriptions may be counterbalanced by an increased workload required within the libraries. The library staff will have to process all orders, renewals, and cancellations for these titles individually because the titles are not available on electronic invoices similar to those provided by the subscription services. Most publishers cannot provide the types of collection management statistics that subscription services offer, forcing libraries to compile the data internally. Libraries must deal with any problems concerning payments or lack of service rather than have their subscription services work with the publishers on their behalf.

Subscription services have been deeply concerned about the trend of publishers dealing directly with libraries and have begun developing new services for both libraries and publishers in order to maintain their existence in the information industry. Some of these new services include advice to publishers about licensing contracts and assistance to libraries in negotiating these contracts. Other subscription services function as aggregators, creating programs that allow libraries to consolidate all their subscriptions to electronic journals using a standard gateway created by the subscription service. These gateway services verify the electronic addresses of journals continually, provide stable URLs for the libraries, and validate users who are authorized to have access to the materials. Most subscription services can provide lists showing which serials are available in electronic formats and notify libraries when new electronic versions of titles are available. Most librarians hope that subscription services continue to play a major role in the acquisition of electronic journals because acquiring electronic resources requires considerable amounts of staff time. "The most valuable service agencies can deliver is related to acquisitions rather than to direct delivery to the users. After so many years of a fairly simple and widely accepted business model for journal delivery, e-journals have caused acquisitions to become more difficult again, opening up a wide field for agency activities" (Weigel 2001, 51).

ECONOMICS

As the Internet began to grow rapidly, some people assumed that everything would soon be available there and that it would all be free. Both assumptions are wrong. Even as more and more information becomes available on the Internet, printed materials continue to be published, and most historical information has not yet been digitized. Most electronic resources cost as much as their paper versions, and many electronic databases are far more expensive than the paper versions ever were. Electronic resources rarely have predictable prices; the costs vary in accordance with a wide range of factors.

Pricing Models

Electronic resources may be sold, giving libraries perpetual access to the files, or leased, giving libraries access as long as they pay the annual subscription fee. Some prices are negotiable; libraries should ask publishers if the prices are firm. Prices may be based on the size of the library, the number of people who may use the resources, or the nature of the database.

When prices are based on library size, publishers may establish higher prices for universities granting doctoral degrees and lower prices for small community colleges. Prices may be based upon the size of libraries' budgets, either on the serials or book budgets or on the total amount of the budget.

Publishers that offer pricing ranges based on the enrollment of colleges and universities may use the actual number of students enrolled or they may use the number for the full-time equivalent enrollment. Some publishers will include staff and faculty in the total number of potential users, whereas others include only students.

Libraries may purchase limited subscriptions that allow a set number of users to access the resource at any one time. The number of these simultaneous users may be as low as one, or it may be much higher. The cost for unlimited simultaneous users is generally much higher than the cost for a limited number of users.

Publishers may set one price for access to their resources for large libraries with multiple branches, while setting a far lower price for access that is restricted to one machine or one building. Universities that have branch campuses must review the licensing agreements carefully to determine whether access may be extended to the branches without additional fees and negotiations.

Some large databases, such as JSTOR, require that libraries pay a large initial fee and much smaller annual fees. Some publishers charge one fee for access to current information and a different fee for older data.

Pricing can depend upon the level of the content. Databases that include full-text articles may have different prices for viewing a citation of an article than for viewing the full content of the article. Some libraries purchase unrestricted access to the citation and abstracting portions of such databases, but not the full-text portion; the users must pay to view the full content of the articles they wish to see or request the articles through interlibrary loan.

Some electronic resources exist only as electronic publications, but others have print versions. When both electronic and print versions exist, publishers have created several pricing models. Some publishers provide the electronic versions of journals at no cost or at an increase of perhaps 10 percent when the libraries subscribe to the print versions. If libraries subscribe to the electronic version without receiving the print version, some publishers charge less than they had previously charged for the print edition.

Library consortia frequently negotiate favorable prices for electronic resources. Publishers work with consortia because the consortia provide publishers with many users and relatively consistent income. Many libraries belong to more than one consortium, allowing them to compare prices in order to find the best combination of costs and resources.

Pricing of electronic resources is complicated; the pricing models vary widely and consistent standards do not exist. Libraries must decide what level of access they need for each resource and then discuss their options with the publishers.

Publishers' Costs

Publishers must spend money to build the infrastructure required to create and distribute electronic resources. Most publishers are still producing print versions of their journals while adding electronic versions. The process of digitizing materials is costly, especially when large files of retrospective publications need to be created. Publishers must still continue to acquire, edit, and organize materials; print the issues; and distribute the copies printed on paper. Simultaneously the publishers must create and distribute the electronic versions. They must deal with the creation and revision of licensing agreements, which requires additional staff costs. Publishers that issue their materials only in electronic format have fewer financial demands on their companies than do the companies publishing in both print and electronic formats. The publishing industry is in a major state of transition, with an unclear future.

Libraries' Costs

Most libraries maintain many journals in both print and electronic formats; few have stopped receiving large numbers of journals in print. Most libraries are paying for both print and electronic versions from budgets that are inadequate to supply either version at the level desired by library users. Some libraries have received additional funding for technology, whether through increased budgets from their institutions or from one-time funds, but many others have not benefited from such increases. Many libraries have shifted funds from their book or print serials budgets to purchase electronic resources.

In addition to the costs of purchasing electronic resources, libraries also have faced increasing costs to improve their electronic infrastructure and to purchase the additional computers needed to provide access to the electronic resources. The process of acquiring new electronic resources and making them available to users also requires that staff learn new skills. If new positions are created or changed to a higher grade level, libraries must pay increased salaries. Maintaining both print and electronic collections, improving the electronic infrastructure, and adding new electronic resources all combine to stretch many budgets to the breaking point.

LICENSING AGREEMENTS

When publishers began creating electronic products, they also began creating licensing agreements for the new products. Such agreements described the products, the parties to the agreement, the people authorized to use the products, the ways in which the products could be used, and the rights of all parties. Librarians learned that such agreements were contracts that were legally binding on their organizations and began working with their institutions to discover how to deal with these documents responsibly. "License agreements have become a fact of life in the electronic publishing world. Yet nothing about them is standard or predictable" (Davis 1999, 364).

"Licensing has become a part of life and day-to-day duties for librarians. The knowledge and skills of librarians in this area are growing rapidly. Knowing your library's goals, understanding clauses that appear in licenses and entering into the negotiation process with a flexible view and authority from your library will result in licenses that meet your needs" (Harris 2002, 115). Librarians dealing with licensing agreements must learn the policies of their institutions. Some organizations require their institutional lawyers to sign all contracts, while other organizations allow librarians to negotiate and sign the agreements. Librarians must work with their institutions to identify what clauses should be included in all agreements and what clauses are unacceptable.

Most publishers developed their own individual contracts, forcing all libraries to review and negotiate each contract separately. As the contracts increased in complexity and in numbers, librarians, publishers, and vendors began working together to create model contracts in an effort to reach consensus on basic issues of concern. For examples of these model contracts, please see http://www.library.yale.edu/~llicense/modlicintro.html or http://www.licensingmodels.com (both accessed June 1, 2003). These contracts are ideal models; publishers or libraries rarely use them without considerable modification. These models have improved communications and do help librarians and publishers understand some of the problems involved in licensing agreements.

Large subscription services are developing new roles for themselves in interpreting the terms of licensing agreements between libraries and publishers. Some services can perform part of the preliminary contract negotiations on behalf of libraries; the companies can explain to all parties which terms can be negotiated and which cannot. Some subscription services can negotiate and sign basic contracts on behalf of libraries if the libraries or their parent institutions are able to give the services the necessary legal authorization.

Obtaining Licensing Agreements

When acquisitions personnel receive requests to acquire electronic products, they must determine whether licensing agreements are required. Many publishers put their licensing agreements and terms of use on their webpages. If the contracts are not available on publishers' websites, acquisitions staff must request the agreements from the publishers before ordering the resources. The contracts must be received and reviewed before the invoices for the products can be paid.

Shrink-Wrap and Click-On Licenses

Manufacturers of computer software often use "shrink-wrap" licenses. The license agreements are printed on the package and may not be visible until after the package is opened. Some of these licenses state that the contract is accepted when the user opens the package; others may allow the user to load the program before the contract becomes binding. Some users have sued because they could not review or negotiate the contracts before purchasing the materials; so far, court opinions are divided about the legality of such licenses.

"Click-on" or "click-through" licenses are Internet contracts in which users must click on a box that states the users agree to the terms and conditions governing the resource in order to use the materials. Many users will simply agree, without ever reading the terms. Librarians must review the agreements to determine whether the libraries can accept the terms. Many publishers are willing to negotiate these agreements and provide libraries with revised contracts that must be kept in the libraries' files.

The Uniform Computer Information Transaction Act (UCITA) is a model of a law being proposed in many states. This law makes shrink-wrap and click-through licenses legally binding even if libraries and purchasers have not reviewed or negotiated the terms of the contracts, although state consumer laws may override UCITA. Only two states had adopted UCITA by 2002, but it continues to be proposed in many other states. Librarians and many other groups oppose UCITA in its present form (Neal 2000, 36–38). UCITA was revised in 2002; while some of the more restrictive clauses were removed, the proposed law still remains complex and controversial (Thirty-eight amendments 2002, 4). For current information, librarians should consult Internet sites such as the Association of Research Libraries (http://www.arl.org, accessed June 1, 2003).

Signature Authority

Librarians must learn who is authorized to sign contracts in their institutions. Some organizations allow library directors or department heads to sign licensing agreements; others require that all contracts must be signed by the institutional lawyers or purchasing officers. Agreements must be signed by the authorized individuals to be legally binding on all parties to the contracts.

Reviewing Licensing Agreements

Nearly all licensing agreements can be modified. Librarians must work with publishers to create contracts that meet the needs of both library and publisher in order to provide users with the information they need. Successful negotiations can take considerable time and may involve several exchanges of questions and responses. Librarians must be patient and persistent. Occasionally, although rarely, negotiations will fail because a proposed clause is unacceptable to one party; librarians must be prepared to end the negotiations if the licensing agreement is not acceptable, explaining exactly why they will not sign the contract. "Do not be afraid to walk away from the negotiations if they are going nowhere. Your ultimate goal is to obtain access to specific content, access targeted to your particular patrons. If you've determined that the final license agreement will not provide you and your patrons with the appropriate access, then perhaps you need to look for a different publisher. If you are not reaching your goals, then further negotiations are a waste of your time as well as theirs" (Harris 2000, 14).

Institutional practices on handling contract negotiations vary. Many organizations encourage librarians to review the contracts and inform the authorized signers of any concerns. Lawyers or purchasing officers may not be aware that libraries need contract clauses that address such issues as interlibrary loan or "walk-in" users who are not affiliated with the library. Other organizations allow librarians to do some preliminary negotiations and contract revisions with publishers before sending all the information to the individuals who handle the final review and signing.

The American Library Association, the Association of Research Libraries, and other library associations have created guidelines for handling licensing agreements. These principles address issues concerning the rights of users, libraries, and publishers. Please see http://arl.cni.org/scomm/licensing/principles.html (accessed June 1, 2003) for further information about these principles.

CLAUSES IN LICENSING AGREEMENTS

The clauses in licensing agreements define the rights of users, libraries, and publishers. The specific language varies from contract to contract, as will the length and complexity. Most clauses are relatively uncontroversial, but some clauses are unacceptable to many libraries. Librarians must read such clauses carefully to determine what must be negotiated. "Technical issues are easy to solve. We will really use the new media to their best extent only if we come to grips with the legal and business issues" (Weigel 2001, 59).

Definitions

Most contracts begin with clauses that describe the products being acquired, the parties in the agreement, and the people who are authorized to use the products. Some publishers may restrict the use of their products to students, staff, and faculty of academic institutions. Many libraries dealing with such restrictive clauses ask that publishers also allow access for walk-in users, allowing occasional use by visitors who are not affiliated with the institutions.

Confidentiality

Some contracts require that the cost of the resource be confidential. Institutions whose budgets are public information may not be allowed to accept such clauses.

Libraries must protect the confidentiality of their users. Publishers should be able to compile usage statistics, but they should not gather information that identifies individual patrons. Some publishers ask that users create individual accounts even for resources acquired by the institution; librarians should review such practices carefully to determine whether the requirements are necessary.

Governing Law

Many contracts include clauses that say the agreement will be governed by the laws of the state or country where the publisher is located. Most public institutions are legally forbidden to agree to be governed by the laws of any state or country other than the one in which they are located. Librarians must learn the policies of their institution and request that such clauses be deleted or changed as necessary. Nearly all publishers are aware that such clauses may be problems and are willing to make the needed changes.

Perpetual Access

Perpetual access clauses ensure that libraries will continue to have access to the materials that they paid for during their subscriptions even if the library cancels the subscription. Some publishers do provide such perpetual access; libraries should request this archival access during contract negotiations.

Obligations of Libraries

Licensing agreements may require that libraries inform all users about the terms or the agreements, monitor the use of the resources, or ensure that patrons may not use the resources for any commercial purposes. Librarians must review these clauses carefully to determine whether the conditions can be met. Many publishers will add clauses that state that libraries will make reasonable efforts to comply with the agreements. While some libraries find terms such as "reasonable" or "best efforts" too vague, others find them acceptable modifications to these statements of obligations; librarians should ask their institutional lawyers or purchasing officers if such terms are acceptable.

A few publishers ask that librarians be responsible for any use that any patron may make of the material or prohibit any commercial use of the information. Since librarians have no ability to determine what all their users may do, librarians should not accept such clauses.

Most publishers include clauses that state that libraries will cooperate with the publisher to resolve problems if any abuse, such as use by unauthorized patrons or excessive downloading of entire journal issues, is discovered. Most libraries accept these clauses.

Terms of Payment and Termination

Librarians must know how much time their institution needs to pay invoices or respond to renewal requests. Licensing agreements frequently state that invoices must be paid within a specified number of days; if librarians know that their institution requires a longer period, then the time period must be negotiated.

Some agreements remain in effect until libraries notify the publishers to cancel the contracts; other publishers require that libraries confirm their renewals each year. Libraries must determine which method is included in the contract and request any changes that are required.

Termination clauses define how and when contracts can be ended. Publishers should state what grounds would lead to termination, how they would notify the libraries that an agreement would cease, and when such notice would be given to the libraries. Libraries should request that termination notices be provided in writing and include a reasonable time for the libraries to respond.

Some publishers state that financial penalties will be applied if a library cancels a contract before the scheduled end of the agreement. Some institutions will not accept such clauses; librarians must consult their institutional purchasing officers or lawyers.

Acceptable and Prohibited Uses

Most contracts allow users to view, download, or print a copy of materials for personal or educational use. Some publishers allow materials to be included in electronic reserve services or provided on interlibrary loan, while others prohibit such uses completely. Some publishers will allow materials to be used in distance education if the libraries control access by using passwords. Librarians must identify their needs and discuss their options with the publishers.

Copyright and Fair Use Issues

The copyright laws of the United States allow libraries to make copies of portions of some materials and to send copies of some materials to other libraries. "Fair use" allows excerpts that are not substantial portions of copyrighted materials to be used for nonprofit educational purposes as long as the use does not damage the sales of the work (Davis 2001, 90–91).

Libraries may make copies of articles or portions of materials that are sent to other libraries for their users' educational purposes through interlibrary loan. Some publishers of electronic resources state that all interlibrary loan use of their materials is prohibited. Others allow libraries to print individual copies that may be used for interlibrary loan but prohibit any electronic version from being sent to another institution. Libraries must review contracts carefully to determine what is being stated, and they should ask that publishers recognize the rights to fair use and interlibrary loan. Some libraries request that all contracts include a clause that states that nothing in the contracts shall restrict the fair use rights of users (Soete 1999, 32).

The Digital Millennium Copyright Act (DMCA) is still being analyzed; lawsuits have already been filed challenging several portions of the law. The DMCA includes sections that prohibit the distribution of information about methods of circumventing encryption technology, such as programs designed to prevent the copying of DVDs. "The TPM [technological protective measures] and anti-circumvention provisions of the DMCA will most likely ensure that more works come with licenses and with an obligation to pay for each use or access. This change could hit libraries particularly hard because it challenges the way in which libraries function as archives of our published history. Libraries must be prepared to review contracts for the acquisitions of digital works more closely than ever before and bargain for full access rights" (Lutzker 1999, 2).

Copyright law is a complex and rapidly changing area; librarians should consult with their institutional experts and professional colleagues about new developments.

Liability and Indemnification

Liability clauses sometimes state that libraries are liable for any unauthorized use of the resource by patrons of the libraries. Because libraries cannot be responsible for the actions of third parties, most libraries refuse to sign such statements. Most public institutions are legally prohibited from agreeing to accept general liability clauses.

Indemnification clauses frequently state that libraries will pay the publishers for any monetary damages resulting from the improper use of their resources by the libraries' patrons. Again, most public institutions are legally prohibited from signing such indemnification clauses; all libraries should consult with their institutional lawyers before signing contracts that include such clauses.

Sources of Information

Licensing agreements are legal documents, and many librarians are not familiar with the technical language used in such agreements. Several sources of help are available for librarians dealing with these agreements. Among the most useful Internet sites are LIBLICENSE: Licensing Digital Information: A Resource for Librarians (http://www.library.yale.edu/~llicense) and Licensing Issues (http://www.arl.org/scomm/licensing/) (both accessed June 1, 2003).

ORDERING ELECTRONIC RESOURCES

Searching and Ordering

The ordering process for electronic resources begins with identifying the title that is to be acquired, just as the process for ordering books and serials does; however, the process for acquiring electronic resources is more complex. "The acquisitions process for any e-journal is long, expensive, and overly complex. The cost comparison between ordering a print journal and subscribing to an e-journal is a factor of ten to one if not fifty to one" (Tonkery 2001, 90). Acquisitions personnel must work closely with selectors, systems personnel, publishers, and vendors when ordering electronic resources.

For all types of electronic resources, acquisitions personnel must identify the costs, the desired level of access, and the technical support required to support the resource. Acquisitions personnel may also be responsible for obtaining and reviewing licensing agreements and contracts; these documents must be reviewed and approved before acquisitions approves the invoices for payment. "Librarians will also need to maintain a high degree of flexibility in this era of electronic resources. Old assumptions are constantly being challenged, and new ways of doing business are constantly being developed. As with early automation in the cataloging arena, organizational structures and reporting lines will need to change to accommodate team participation in the selection of electronic resources. Librarians may additionally find that their libraries are now members of multiple, and possibly overlapping and/or competing, consortia set up to purchase needed or desired electronic resources at the lowest possible cost" (Gregory 2000, 92).

Identifying Costs

Some electronic resources are purchased while others require annual subscriptions. Still others combine the purchase and subscription models by requiring a large initial purchase fee and smaller annual maintenance fees. In addition to verifying the initial or annual costs, acquisitions personnel must learn whether the library is acquiring permanent access to the resources. In some cases, access to the information ceases when the library stops subscribing, while other publishers provide perpetual access to the information that was available while the library was subscribing to the resources.

Levels of Access

Only the students and employees of the institution purchasing the resources may use some Internet resources; other resources may be available to anyone using the libraries. A few electronic resources are available only on one computer; many other resources are available to all authorized users from any computer. Libraries may purchase unlimited access to resources or may purchase a specified number of simultaneous users, with the price varying according to the number of users. While wider access is sometimes more expensive, most libraries feel that limiting an electronic resource to one machine is not practical. Acquisitions personnel must determine the costs for the different levels of access and consult with the appropriate selectors when questions arise. Once the level of access has been decided, acquisitions personnel should annotate the order records and any local tracking databases with the information describing the access that has been purchased.

Technical Support

Acquisitions must work closely with the systems department in order to determine whether new electronic resources can be supported by their institution. Some resources that are in non-Roman alphabets require special software to display the materials accurately. Some databases consisting of full-text books require special software to view and print the materials. When databases require passwords to access them, systems departments may be able to create programs that make it simpler for the users by including the passwords in the log-in programs. Acquisitions personnel must communicate with systems personnel when new resources are being considered to ensure that the resources can be readily used by patrons.

Most publishers of resources available on the Internet provide access that is based on the identification of libraries' IP addresses; acquisitions personnel must supply the publishers with the current numbers. When the IP address of a library changes, acquisitions must send the new number to all the publishers. When the IP number of a publisher changes, acquisitions must inform the appropriate systems, cataloging, and public services departments of the changes.

Licensing Agreements

In some libraries, acquisitions personnel are responsible for obtaining and reviewing licensing agreements; in other institutions, their lawyers sign all such agreements. These contracts were discussed in a previous section of this chapter; please see that information for details about handling these legal documents.

Librarians need to keep copies of all licensing agreements after they have been signed. Libraries or institutions sign the agreements and return them to the publishers. Publishers sign the documents and send copies to the department that signed the agreement for the institution. If the agreements are sent to the institutional lawyers or purchasing officers, acquisitions personnel may need to ask those departments for a copy of the agreement for the library's files. Libraries that maintain local tracking databases may be able to scan contracts and link them to the records in their databases.

Types of Electronic Resources

Electronic resources include books, journals, databases, and publishers' packages. Each type of resource may present different challenges to acquisitions personnel.

Electronic Books

Many academic libraries acquire electronic books from companies that digitize books issued by many different publishers. In addition, libraries purchase electronic books from large book vendors or through consortial programs. Acquisitions personnel may create order records for these books when the items are acquired individually. When libraries purchase large numbers of titles in a group, they frequently purchase catalog records that can be loaded directly into their online catalog. In such cases, the only order record is for the purchase of the entire package. Some libraries do not add records for their electronic books to their catalog at all, relying on links to the website of the distributor for access to the materials.

Some libraries purchase and circulate electronic books with the specialized handheld devices that are required to read such books. These readers are currently available in competing, incompatible formats that are still somewhat expensive. Many libraries are waiting for the technology to stabilize and for a dominant format to become evident before they invest much time or money in the devices.

Some electronic books can be read on PDAs (personal digital assistants). Because the viewing area on those devices is small, many readers do not find this technology comfortable for reading long passages of text. This technology may be more useful for reference tools or periodical articles than for books.

Electronic Journals

Electronic journals may be provided with subscriptions to print journals or may exist only as electronic titles without any print counterparts. These journals may be available individually or may be included in large collections created by publishers or aggregators. When electronic journals are available individually, acquisitions personnel may place subscriptions directly with the publisher or from a subscription service and create order records for the individual titles. Many libraries do not create order records for the individual titles included in the large packages compiled by aggregators. Some aggregators frequently add and remove titles from their packages, often with minimal notice. Libraries that need to track the individual titles in these packages are exploring commercial products to monitor such changes and to create lists of all the titles in the packages, allowing libraries to load the information into their online catalogs or databases at regular intervals. Some aggregators sell catalog records of all the titles included in their packages; libraries can add these records to their catalogs.

Some electronic journals are not identical to their print counterparts. Some publishers do not include the letters or announcements that appear in the print versions, while other publishers include additional materials that are available only in the electronic versions. When publishers provide information about the differences in formats, acquisitions personnel should annotate the order records or the local tracking databases with that information.

Electronic Databases

Electronic indexing and abstracting databases frequently include some full-text content. Patrons may look for information about a topic, get several citations, and view the complete article or book online. Some publishers have different prices for access to the citations and for access to the full-text content; acquisitions personnel must verify the prices for the appropriate levels, consulting with selectors to determine which version of the resource is desired.

Some electronic databases are available only from the publishers; others are available from several vendors. Because the structure and the searching techniques of the databases may vary among vendors, acquisitions personnel must work with selectors to identify the correct vendor.

Electronic Packages

Some societies and publishers offer packages that include most or all of their publications. In some cases, associations offer several different packages with content that varies based upon subject or upon the cost of the packages. Acquisitions personnel must determine what materials are included in the desired packages. If the packages include journal titles, the libraries may need to cancel any existing subscriptions for those journals. Some libraries create order records for each title included in each package. Creating these records is time consuming but enables libraries to know exactly which titles they are receiving from which source.

When to Order

Librarians must learn the fiscal schedule and financial policies of their institution. Some institutions allow libraries to carry over funds that have not been spent by the end of one fiscal year, keeping the funds in the libraries' accounts for use in the next fiscal cycle. These libraries can combine funds from two budget cycles in order to purchase extensive resources. Some publishers will allow libraries to divide payments for very expensive databases among multiple years. Librarians must verify that their fiscal service departments allow such multiyear commitments; many institutions will require statements that the payments for the subsequent years will be made only if funds are available. Such statements are not intended to allow libraries to cancel the contracts unless they are faced with major budget reductions or bankruptcy; libraries must reassure publishers that these clauses are legal requirements and that the libraries do not intend to cancel the agreements arbitrarily.

Vendor Selection

Fewer vendors provide electronic resources than provide print books and serials. Most electronic journals are available directly from their publishers or from any of the major subscription services. Electronic books may be purchased from the larger book and approval vendors or from their publishers. Many large electronic databases and resources are available from their publishers, from a few vendors, or through consortia. Libraries may join consortia, such as SOLINET or the Greater Western Library Alliance, and purchase large electronic packages, such as all the electronic journals of a specific publisher or a collection of thousands of electronic books. In some states, libraries intending to spend more than a prescribed amount, such as $10,000, with one vendor may be required to write a formal request for proposal or bid request. When libraries are purchasing resources from the publishers or copyright holders, they may be able to describe the process as a "sole source" purchase by documenting that the resource is available only from the one source; this eliminates the requirement of submitting a bid. For more information about vendor selection, please see chapter 4, "Domestic and Foreign Vendor Selection and Evaluation."

Order Records

Order records should include the title, publisher, estimated cost, vendor, and fund information. Most integrated library systems have fields for notes in the order records; such a note may include the name of the person negotiating the contract for the publisher, the number of authorized simultaneous users being purchased, or the IP ranges provided to the publisher. Acquisitions personnel need to update order records to include the current vendor and contact information.

Local Tracking Databases

The processing of electronic resources involves selectors, acquisitions, cataloging, systems, and public services. Because of the number of people participating in the process, some libraries that acquire many electronic resources create internal files to track them. While integrated library systems may include a great deal of information about electronic resources, they usually cannot include all the information related to the negotiations for each of the resources in a manner that can be searched easily. Tracking databases based on software such as Microsoft Access allow several fields to be sorted and matched. The files may include not only the authors, titles, publishers, and universal resource locators (URLs), but also the history and status of the negotiations for the licensing contracts, contact information, passwords, authorized user definitions, and contractual restrictions on interlibrary loan. Some databases include scanned versions of the complete contracts and any email communications about the resources. These databases should be accessible to all personnel who process electronic resources, as well as those staff such as interlibrary loan personnel who may need to verify contractual issues about the resources. Creating and maintaining such files does take time; having all the information in an easily accessible form can save a great deal of frustration and time when problems appear.

Encumbering Funds

Integrated library systems encumber funds when orders are placed. By the time the funds are encumbered, the libraries usually know what the final price of an electronic resource will be; variations in price that result from service charges for serials and discounts for books are generally not a factor in the pricing of electronic resources. The major exception involves consortial purchase of large databases. In cases where the final price of a database is determined by the final number of participants, the numbers of libraries or users may change during negotiations, causing the price to change as well. In these cases, the estimated price and the final price will vary; changes should be noted in the order record.

RECEIVING, BEGINNING ACCESS, AND PAYING

Printed materials rarely accompany Internet resources; frequently the only physical item received is an invoice. CD-ROMs and disks are received by acquisitions just as any print materials are; the item is received, matched to the order record, and sent to cataloging.

Initiating Access

Some publishers will send the libraries email notices to announce when access to the resources is available. Other publishers apparently assume that libraries check the resources regularly to discover when their access begins. Libraries should request to be notified when access does actually begin and should also check the resources frequently.

When acquisitions personnel determine that access has indeed begun, they must notify other departments. Each library must establish procedures for processing electronic resources. Acquisitions usually needs to inform the systems department that maintains the technical access and the cataloging department that maintains the online catalog. Acquisitions may also need to notify the personnel who maintain the local tracking database, the selectors who requested the product, and the personnel who will publicize the new resources.

Invoices

Acquisitions personnel must review invoices, approve them for payment, and forward them to the fiscal services department of the institution. Staff must verify that invoices are for the correct items; some publishers offer several packages distinguished by letters or codes that are easily confused. Acquisitions personnel must also determine whether the library is being invoiced for the level of access that was requested; costs frequently increase dramatically for additional simultaneous users or extended networks. Acquisitions personnel must verify that invoices are from the correct vendors; libraries subscribing to a package through a consortium may occasionally receive invoices from both the publisher and the consortium. When this accident occurs, acquisitions personnel must resolve the duplicate billing quickly.

Acquisitions personnel must update the order records to show the actual payments and the dates on which the invoices were approved for payment. Order records for electronic resources that will have annual payments should be kept in the integrated library systems. Order records for electronic resources that are one-time purchases may be purged according to the requirements stated by the fiscal services department.

Credit Cards

Acquisitions personnel may find using institutional credit cards useful when they order less expensive items, especially those issued by smaller publishers. Most electronic databases and packages are quite expensive and exceed the limits placed on most institutional credit cards.

MAINTAINING ACCESS

Just as print serials occasionally stop arriving and must be claimed, access to electronic resources sometimes stops without notice. In some cases, the publisher or vendor fails to receive its payment, and acquisitions personnel must check the records to determine whether the invoice was processed and when payment should have arrived. If the service interruption is not due to problems with payment, the library's acquisitions or systems personnel may need to contact the publisher or vendor to begin the process of identifying and resolving the problem.

URLs of electronic resources can change unexpectedly, requiring systems personnel to update the information. Some libraries use software programs that check all URLs at regular intervals to identify problems. Other libraries rely on publishers' notices or information from patrons to discover such changes.

When libraries change their IP ranges, all vendors and publishers must be notified; this process is frequently handled by the acquisitions and systems departments. Some subscription services handle the maintenance of URLs and IP addresses for libraries using the gateway services created by the companies.

VENDOR EVALUATION

Acquisitions personnel must work with collection management, public services, and systems departments to evaluate the vendors providing electronic resources. Acquisitions staff can provide information about customer service, technical support, and changes in pricing. Depending upon the structure of the library, acquisitions personnel may also contribute information about changes in the content of the resources and the percentage of time the resources were unavailable.

ROLE OF CONSORTIA

Library consortia have existed for many years, providing expedited interlibrary loan for members and doing limited cooperative collection development. As electronic resources developed, libraries discovered that sharing electronic resources was far simpler than sharing print resources had been. Many large electronic resources that are prohibitively expensive for individual libraries become affordable when several libraries work together and share the costs.

Some states have consortia that negotiate for products on behalf of all the academic libraries, for example, or on behalf of all libraries that are open to the public. These consortia have successfully acquired extensive electronic collections that provide their members with greatly expanded resources; among the more notable is OhioLink (http://www.ohiolink.edu, accessed June 1, 2003).

Some consortia are funded by special state allocations; many are funded by membership contributions from the individual libraries. The consortia negotiate with publishers on behalf of their members, offering an expanded number of customers and a stable level of funding to the publishers in exchange for increased access to electronic resources or for lower prices.

Consortia may have a formal governing board that coordinates all purchases, paying the publishers and billing its members. Other consortia negotiate the price and arrange for publishers to bill the members directly. Most consortia have legal documents describing their structure and the obligations of members; librarians must learn who has the authority to sign such documents for their institutions. Some consortia have full-time staff members who handle all negotiations; others depend on staff from the consortia members to do all the work of the group.

Consortia with strong organizational structures can compile information about what licensing agreement terms are unacceptable to each of their members and negotiate acceptable contracts with publishers and vendors. If this coordination does not exist, each member must review the contract and make necessary changes, which must then be reviewed by all other members of the consortia. This process of creating, reviewing, and revising contracts can take months.

Consortia frequently allow libraries to acquire extensive resources at reduced prices. The process of agreeing on which products should be acquired and of negotiating contracts can take considerable time, but the benefits can be substantial.

PRESERVING AND ARCHIVING ISSUES

Books printed on paper hundreds of years ago can still be used by patrons. Materials created on magnetic tapes and disks a few decades ago are useless without the appropriate equipment and software; some information has vanished because the technology no longer exists to read the information. The life span of technical formats is very short: Beta videotapes and 5 1/4–inch computer disks have already disappeared, and VHS videotapes are endangered by DVDs. "Preservation concerns regarding electronic resources are far from being adequately resolved. For the foreseeable future, concerns are very real regarding continued hardware and software availability for reading the present generation of electronic materials. Access to licensed material involves both these issues and the legal right of future access to material that was previously licensed" (Gregory 2000, 92). Libraries, publishers, and vendors are discussing issues of preservation and archiving of electronic resources, but the concerns have not yet been resolved.

Licensing agreements should include clauses that describe what procedures exist to archive the materials and to provide libraries with access to the content if the publisher goes out of business or if the journals are sold to different publishers. Some publishers promise to archive their materials themselves to preserve the content indefinitely; others contract with consortia such as OCLC (Online Computer Library Center, Inc.) to archive their publications. Other publishers promise to provide archival copies of their materials in formats such as CD-ROM; libraries must decide which formats are acceptable.

Preservation of physical media, such as disks, tapes, and CD-ROMs, begins with acquisitions personnel. Staff must handle such materials carefully, putting them in appropriate envelopes or boxes, and protecting the materials from magnetic security devices that can damage tapes and disks.

COMMUNICATION

The work that acquisitions does with all materials affects many other areas of the library system, and the work involving electronic resources affects almost all areas. This impact makes extensive communication essential. Acquisitions librarians must work with systems, collection management, and public services to ensure that all records and information about electronic resources are accurate and understandable. Acquisitions personnel must communicate with publishers and vendors about the resources being requested, the costs, the number of users, the technical requirements, and the licensing agreements. Acquisitions must inform systems departments of the technical requirements needed to support the resources. The institutional legal and purchasing departments may be involved in the negotiation of contracts and licensing agreements. Public services and library patrons must be informed about access to new resources and about any restrictions on the use of the resources. Acquisitions must provide public services with the information about copyright and use restrictions that must be shared with patrons. Consortial members must know what resources are being considered. Communication is vital in acquiring electronic resources and making them available to the users of libraries.

MANAGEMENT REPORTS

Most publishers and vendors supply statistics that show how frequently patrons use the databases. Such resources are frequently available online, accessible to authorized personnel. The data may show the use of individual titles within a package, how long patrons were using a database, or when patrons were denied access because the library reached the number of authorized simultaneous users. Acquisitions personnel should include the information describing access to such statistics in the order records or in the local tracking database.

EDUCATION AND TRAINING

Acquisitions staff gather considerable information about electronic resources during the ordering process and must share that information with staff who maintain the resources and those who teach the library's patrons how to use the resources effectively. Acquisitions personnel should help inform library staff in other areas about the electronic resources being added and about the contractual and legal issues related to the use of these resources. "Librarians will need to call upon all their technical, service, professional, and human resource skills if they are to thrive in this new and rapidly changing environment" (Gregory 2000, 97).

Acquisitions personnel must be trained in how to acquire electronic resources. Librarians can attend workshops about negotiating licensing agreements and then train their colleagues. Electronic resources and tools change rapidly; training must be a regular component of the jobs of all acquisitions personnel.

DOCUMENT DELIVERY AND PURCHASING ARTICLES

Some databases that include citations and abstracts may also include the full text of articles. Libraries may subscribe to the complete resources including the full-text content or only to the citations and abstracts. Libraries that subscribe only to the citation portions may require that patrons who want the full-text articles either use interlibrary loan or purchase the articles themselves from the database creators. Some libraries establish deposit accounts with the database creators in order to allow patrons to purchase the individual articles. Many libraries that have created such deposit accounts fund them with money they saved from serials cancellation projects. Libraries must evaluate the costs of such services, comparing the costs of acquiring the individual articles with the costs of subscribing to the journals.

CONCLUSION

Printed books and serials have existed for centuries, changing very little in their basic formats. Electronic resources appeared a few decades ago and have already gone through several changes in format. Publishers now ask whether they should continue to issue print versions of encyclopedias, indexes, or scientific journals. Acquisitions librarians must deal with IP addresses, passwords, and licensing agreements.

The continual changes in electronic resources lead to ongoing changes in libraries. The transformation of acquisitions work means that personnel must be able to deal with new technology, analyze contracts, and work with publishers. Libraries may need to create new positions and train staff for higher levels of responsibility in order to handle these new tasks.

Librarians can learn of current developments in the areas of electronic resources, licensing, and copyright by monitoring library science journals, attending conferences, and consulting Internet resources such as those of the American Library Association (http://www.ala.org), the Association of Research Libraries (http://www.arl.org), or LIBLICENSE (http://www.library.yale.edu/~llicense) (all accessed June 1, 2003).

Electronic resources are an integral part of libraries, and librarians must deal with the complex issues related to such resources in order to provide materials to their users. "Like the mythological shape-shifters, electronic serials will continue to evolve, changing their characteristics to best meet the needs of librarians, publishers, and the community of readers" (Bluh 2001, xii).

REFERENCES

Bluh, Pamela M., ed. 2001. *Managing electronic serials: Essays based on the ALCTS Electronic Serials Institutes, 1997–1999*. Chicago: American Library Association.

Curtis, Donnelyn, Virginia M. Scheschy, and Adolfo R. Tarango. 2000. *Developing and managing electronic journal collections: A how-to-do-it manual for librarians*. New York: Neal-Schuman.

Davis, Trisha L. 1999. Licensing in lieu of acquiring. In *Understanding the business of library acquisitions*. 2nd ed. Edited by Karen A. Schmidt. Chicago: American Library Association.

———. 2001. The Digital Millennium Copyright Act: Key issues for serialists. *Serials Librarian* 40 (1/2): 85–103.

Gregory, Vicki L. 2000. *Selecting and managing electronic resources: A how-to-do-it manual for librarians*. New York: Neal-Schuman.

Harris, Lesley Ellen. 2000. Deal-maker, deal-breaker: When to walk away. *Library Journal Supplement: Net Connect* 125 (January): 12–14.

———. 2002. *Licensing digital content: A practical guide for librarians*. Chicago: American Library Association.

Lutzker, Arnold P. 1999. In the curl of the wave: What the Digital Millennium Copyright Act and Term Extension Act mean for the library and education community. *ARL: A Bimonthly Report* 203: 1–5.

Neal, James G. 2000. The fight against UCITA. *Library Journal* 125 (15): 36–38.

Soete, George J. 1999. *Managing the licensing of electronic products*. ARL SPEC kit no. 248. Washington, DC: Association of Research Libraries.

Thirty-eight amendments to UCITA pass, petition for downgrade shelved. 2002. *Library Hotline* 31 (33): 4, 6.

Tonkery, Dan. 2001. Seven common myths about acquiring and accessing e-journals. In *Managing electronic serials: Essays based on the ALCTS Electronic Serials Institutes, 1997–1999*, edited by Pamela Bluh. Chicago: American Library Association.

Weigel, Friedemann A. 2001. Electronic serials into the millennium. In *Managing electronic serials: Essays based on the ALCTS Electronic Serials Institutes, 1997–1999*, edited by Pamela Bluh. Chicago: American Library Association.

Chapter 8

Acquiring Out-of-Print and Antiquarian Materials

WHAT DOES "OUT OF PRINT" MEAN?

When an item is out of print, it is no longer available from a library's usual vendors or from the publisher. The phrase may also mean that the publisher has decided not to issue any more copies or that the publishing rights have reverted to the author. Frequently, librarians will learn items are out of print when vendors report that they cannot supply them. Sometimes an item that is reported out of print or out of stock with one vendor may be acquired from another vendor or from the publisher, who may have some of the last copies still available. Depending on the nature of the item and local circumstances, area bookstores might also have copies available. If no copies remain available, the library must decide whether to attempt to obtain the item from the out-of-print market.

WHY DO BOOKS GO OUT OF PRINT?

While some items stay available for many years, others go out of print very quickly. Best-sellers sometimes do sell millions of copies and stay in print for years, but few books are expected to be best-sellers, and even fewer actually fulfill that hope. The average number of copies printed of most books is usually rather small. The number of copies printed of each title varies widely depending on the type of book and publisher. In 1992, the average print run for nonfiction books was between 1,000 and 1,500 copies, and between 2,000 and 6,000 copies for most fiction books (Brunet and Shiflett 1992). In the late 1990s, university presses often printed between 1,000 and 2,500 copies (Greco 1997, 207). That number appears to continue to decline in the twenty-first century. Smaller independent publishers sometimes print more copies, often doing print runs that range from 2,000 to 5,000 copies (Book Industry Study Group 1999, 22). If the average trade book sells around 5,000 copies, it is a moderate success, and those selling more than 7,500 copies are exceptional (Greco 1997, 202). A book that is expected to be a best-seller will have a much larger first printing, sometimes of several thousand copies and occasionally even a million copies, and books that sell exceptionally well will be reprinted. Most items, however, will have smaller print runs, and consequently go out of print quickly. About 90,000 titles go out of print every year (Hilts 1999, 46). Among the many reasons for this are taxes that must be paid on inventory in the United States, the size of print runs, and the demand for the individual titles. Large publishers that require that each title make a profit may declare a title out of print when its sales drop below 2,000 copies per year (Schiffrin 2000, 118). The reasons items are out of print are seldom relevant when librarians attempt to acquire the materials in order to replace missing items, acquire added copies of heavily used materials, or support new areas of interest.

OBTAINING OUT-OF-PRINT MATERIALS

When an item has been identified as out of print, the librarian must decide whether to continue trying to obtain it. The next steps depend on the nature of the item and the desires of the individual who requested that the item be purchased.

When publishers decide to declare a title out of print, they dispose of their remaining copies, which are called remainders. They may have the copies pulped and the paper recycled, sell the copies to dealers who specialize in selling the last copies of items, or sell them to the author. Dealers in remainders often sell items at greatly reduced prices. Because they have limited quantities of most books, the titles may be sold quickly. Authors who purchased their books from the publishers before the books were sold to dealers or destroyed may sell copies directly to libraries.

Librarians might request an out-of-print item on interlibrary loan, photocopy it, bind it, and add it to the collection; however, this requires permission from the copyright holder if the item is still under copyright. This process requires time to identify the copyright holder, who is frequently the publisher, and to correspond with the copyright owner. If the original publisher has been purchased in one of the numerous corporate mergers, additional time and effort will be needed to verify the current owner of the copyright. If the copyright holder is the author, the library must attempt to locate him or her.

Libraries may be able to obtain a copy of an item that is out of print from a company that prints copies of books on demand; however, most such companies do not have a large number of titles. The print-on-demand industry is still small; comparatively few titles are available so far.

All of these methods require time, and some may be costly. The out-of-print market may be the least expensive and quickest method of obtaining such items.

TYPES OF OUT-OF-PRINT DEALERS

Dealers in out-of-print and used materials acquire books from publishers, individuals, authors, and other dealers. These dealers may be able to supply libraries with books that are unavailable from publishers or vendors. The thousands of dealers of used, out-of-print, and rare books vary as much as libraries do. They range from neighborhood bookstores to international dealers who specialize in a subject or format. Landesman (1999, 181–84) identifies types of dealers, including book scouts who search for items to sell to dealers; general and specialized dealers; and bookstores and dealers who sell their books on the Internet. Some dealers issue catalogs in print or on the Internet, while others do not. Some dealers may have bookstores, while others operate only by mail from an office in a dealer's home. Some will search a library's "want list" for years; others will not handle such lists at all. Dealers sometimes specialize in specific types of materials such as maps or back issues of serials, while others handle a wide range of subjects.

DEALING WITH THE OUT-OF-PRINT BUSINESS

Librarians searching for out-of-print items will frequently find that several different dealers offer the items at a very wide range of prices. Since many dealers put their catalogs on their Internet sites, librarians can compare costs easily. The dealers use a number of criteria to set their prices. The two main factors are the condition and the identity of the item. Items that are unmarked and undamaged will be more expensive than those with torn dust jackets or signatures of the owners. An item without a dust jacket will be cheaper than the same item with the jacket. The more damage to an item, the cheaper the price will be. The first printing of the first edition of an item will generally be more valuable than a later printing. Acquisitions personnel must know whether the library needs a copy for the general circulating collection or for a special collection of rare books before purchasing the item.

Libraries may find items of interest in dealers' catalogs received in the mail or posted on the Internet, or they may receive a message that a title of possible interest is available. Selectors or acquisitions staff should first search their library's catalog to determine whether an item is already owned before ordering it. Librarians should always call or email the dealer to verify that the item is still available before sending payment; it is always possible that the desired item may have been sold before the library's request is received. Some libraries put records of an order in their system before they verify whether the item can be acquired; others wait until they have confirmation from the dealer.

Most dealers will reserve materials when they receive a telephone or email request; they usually hold the material for a few weeks until they receive the purchase order from the library. They then ship the material to the library and include the invoice in the package. Some dealers require prepayment; librarians must know their institution's regulations governing prepayments. Some dealers will accept payment by credit card; these dealers usually ship items immediately.

When an item is received, acquisitions staff should check it carefully to determine whether it matches the description. Used items may be worn, but any major damage should have been included in the dealer's description. Acquisitions should return any items that were not described correctly by the dealers.

Many out-of-print dealers are small operations dependent upon prompt payments to survive. While all invoices should always be handled as rapidly as possible, swift processing of those invoices from small companies is especially important. Acquisitions staff should tell dealers how long the institution usually takes to issue payments; this will reassure the dealers and reduce anxious inquiries to the library from the dealers.

ADDITIONAL SERVICES OF OUT-OF-PRINT DEALERS

In addition to selling materials and searching for desired items, some dealers appraise materials for tax purposes. Library users frequently ask librarians to appraise materials or to provide referrals to appraisers; librarians will want to know which dealers may be available to do this. Librarians may find appraisers listed in local telephone directories, by consulting local used book stores, or by consulting resources such as the *American Book Trade Directory.*

Some dealers will take unwanted materials from libraries and sell them, dividing the profit with the libraries. Dealers may also offer libraries credit for such materials; the credits may then be applied to future purchases from those dealers. Since institutional guidelines vary on these types of transactions, librarians must determine their institutional regulations before discussing the possibilities of selling materials with the vendor. Some institutions prohibit libraries from selling materials removed from their collections unless the materials are reviewed by the governing institution, which may give permission to dispose of them. These policies may, or may not, also apply to materials given to libraries that have not been added to the processed collections. When dealers purchase materials from libraries, they often pay approximately one-third of the price that the dealers might later charge for the materials. Dealers may not wish to purchase materials with library markings, labels, or stamps; if they do, they will usually pay much less than they would for unmarked materials.

LOCATING OUT-OF-PRINT DEALERS

When libraries decide to attempt to acquire out-of-print materials, they can look for listings of dealers in reference sources, either printed or Internet; consult the professional associations; or search Internet sites that list the stock of many dealers. Here are some of the major print directories that list out-of-print dealers:

+ *American Book Trade Directory*, published by R. R. Bowker (New Providence, New Jersey).

+ *Sheppard's* book directories, published by Richard Joseph Publishers (Franham, Surrey, England); editions cover North America, the British Isles, Europe, Australia and New Zealand, Japan, India, and the Orient.

+ *Antiquarian, Specialty, and Used Book Sellers*, edited by James M. Ethridge and Karen Ethridge, published by Omnigraphics (Detroit, Michigan).

The following are major online sources listing dealers:

+ AcqWeb, <http://acqweb.library.vanderbilt.edu> (accessed June 1, 2003).

+ Abebooks, <http://www.abebooks.com> (accessed June 1, 2003).

+ BookFinder.com, <http://www.bookfinder.com> (accessed June 1, 2003).

+ WorldBookDealers, <http://www.worldbookdealers.com> (accessed June 1, 2003).

The major organizations of rare and out-of-print dealers have Internet sites that list their members:

+ Antiquarian Booksellers' Association of America (ABAA), <http://abaa.org> (accessed June 1, 2003).

- International League of Antiquarian Booksellers (ILAB), <http://www.ilab-lila.com> (accessed June 1, 2003).
- Antiquarian Booksellers' Association (ABA), <http://www.aba.org.uk> (accessed June 1, 2003).

OUT-OF-PRINT DEALERS ON THE INTERNET

Like most of the information industry, the out-of-print market has been changed dramatically by the Internet. Only a few years ago, librarians searching for out-of-print titles had very few alternatives. They could watch for the desired items in dealers' catalogs, put lists of the titles they wanted in *A. B. Bookman's Weekly*, or arrange for dealers to search for the items. In all cases, success was generally low, the process frequently took a long time, prices were often high, and determining the fairness of a quoted price was extremely difficult. The Internet has changed this process greatly. Libraries that formerly found out-of-print searching too expensive and time consuming are now able to locate many materials rapidly through Internet resources.

Some dealers who formerly issued print catalogs of selections from their stock now have more extensive listings on their own websites. Other dealers who never issued catalogs now post portions of their holdings on the Internet. These websites include small dealers with specialized collections as well as huge stores with materials in a wide range of subjects such as Powell's Books (http://www.powells.com, accessed June 1, 2003).

Given the number of dealers now online, checking each site could take a great deal of staff time. Rather than searching each dealer's individual listing, librarians can begin a search by going to some of the sites that search a large number of dealers' listings. Among these sites (all accessed June 1, 2003) are BookAvenue (http://www.bookavenue.com), Book-Finder (http://www.bookfinder.com), Abebooks (http://www.abebooks.com), and WorldBookDealers (http://www.worldbookdealers.com). Another source is Amazon.com (http://www.amazon.com), which began business by selling new books over the Internet. In 2000, it added the option of buying used books on its website; the sellers include both individuals and dealers.

Searching Web Dealers' Sites

Most dealers' sites can be searched by author, title, or subject, or a combination thereof. Some sites allow advanced searches that add type of edition or price range to the search parameters. Before searching for titles on websites, librarians must determine whether they need a specific edition.

Many items are issued in the United Kingdom and in North America under slightly different titles; if the library will accept either edition, the chances for locating a copy are increased. Many items are printed in both cloth and paper editions; librarians must decide which version is acceptable.

Some sites search a number of dealers' listings and then present a list of all items that meet the search criteria. The librarian can check for the specific edition, the price range, and the physical condition in order to choose the items that meet the criteria and then contact the individual dealer directly. Examples of these sites are Abebooks (http://www.abebooks.com) and BookFinder (http://www.bookfinder.com) (both accessed June 1, 2003).

Other sites allow libraries to purchase from a range of individual dealers through the central site. Again, librarians enter their desired criteria, and the system searches a number of catalogs and presents a list of results. Librarians select the desired items and place an order with the central site. This site then handles the ordering and the billing from the individual dealers for the library. The individual dealers mail the items to the library, and then the central site bills the library on one invoice. This arrangement simplifies the paperwork for both sides, providing only one vendor account and one bill for the library. Examples of such sites include Alibris (http://www.alibris.com) and BookAvenue (http://www.bookavenue.com) (both accessed June 1, 2003).

Some dealers have the ability to take orders on their website through a secure server that allows credit cards to be used safely. Others do not have that capability and prefer that libraries pay by check or credit card after the availability of the items has been confirmed.

Web Advantages and Cautions

The Internet allows out-of-print dealers to reach many more libraries and collectors than was previously possible. Dealers no longer have to compile, publish, and mail catalogs, hoping to reach the right audience. The Web allows librarians to find items previously unobtainable—they no longer have to review numerous catalogs searching for an elusive title; nor do they need to prepare and present a want list to several dealers. Searching for out-of-print items is easier and faster than before the presence of dealers' catalogs on the Web. The Web also allows both dealers and librarians to compare prices for items, something rarely possible before the Internet.

The listings on the Internet are extensive, but few dealers are able to list their entire stock. Many dealers find that listing everything requires more time than they have available. Because the listings are not comprehensive, libraries searching for specific titles that are very difficult to find may still find it necessary to work directly with a dealer who specializes in the desired subject area.

The Internet does not provide solutions to all problems, and it has created some new concerns as well. Anyone can claim to be a dealer and post a list of titles with inadequate or inaccurate descriptions. Sellers may range from well-established dealers with extensive collections to people with no knowledge of books beyond their hope to dispose of an inherited collection for a substantial amount. Librarians should always check the received items carefully to see that the dealer filled the order correctly. The bibliographic information should match the edition that was ordered, and the physical condition should be acceptable. In some cases a copy formerly owned by a library, referred to as an "ex-library" copy, may be acceptable in spite of the markings and labels, as long as the description of the item indicated the condition. If the description was inaccurate, and the item is unacceptable, the library should return the item to the dealer.

The reputation of the dealer is a crucial factor, especially when ordering expensive items. The Antiquarian Booksellers' Association of America was founded in 1949 to promote ethical standards in the antiquarian book trade in America; it has a code of ethics for its members on its website (http://abaa.org, accessed June 1, 2003). The Antiquarian Booksellers' Association, the major British association founded in 1906, requires professional knowledge and experience of its members (http://www.aba.org.uk, accessed June 1, 2003). The International League of Antiquarian Booksellers was founded in 1947 to uphold professional standards and integrity in the field of antiquarian book selling (http://www.ilab-lila.com, accessed June 1, 2003). Librarians can expect that dealers belonging to such organizations will abide by the organizations' codes. The websites of these associations include information about their members and standards; some associations also provide lists of books, manuscripts, and antiquarian print materials for sale by the members.

Web auctions and sales on such sites as eBay (http://www.ebay.com) and Amazon.com (http://www.amazon.com) (both accessed June 1, 2003) may offer bargains but some risks as well. Since the sellers on such services include nonprofessional individuals as well as dealers, the item descriptions may not be as detailed or accurate as librarians need. In cases where the library does not know the dealer, the library should strongly consider using one of the escrow services that hold payments until items are received and accepted.

Some major dealers and auction houses, such as Pacific Book Auction Galleries (http://www.pbagalleries.com) and Swann Auction Galleries, Inc. (http://www.swanngalleries.com) (both accessed June 1, 2003), offer online auctions, primarily for rare and antiquarian books, manuscripts, maps, and prints. Major auction houses such as Sotheby's and Christie's sometimes have sales of books as well; these sales usually contain more expensive items and collections.

RARE AND ANTIQUARIAN BOOKS

The world of rare and antiquarian books overlaps the world of out-of-print books. "Out-of-print becomes special collections materials becomes rare books along a continuum" (Overmier 2002, 3). On this continuum, rare books have a number of special characteristics. Rare books are generally much more expensive and more difficult to locate than items that have gone out of print relatively recently. Each library dealing with rare materials has its own definitions, but most identify rare items based on such factors as price, age, scarcity, physical characteristics, autographs, and regional interest. In nearly all cases, the condition of a rare book is the most important factor in determining its price.

The field of rare books has its own language to describe the size, physical condition, and history of the items. Terms exist to describe the printing history, any damage to the items, autographs, and other information about the condition or history of the books. Online glossaries of such terms are available at several sites, including Abebooks (http://www.abebooks.com) and the Digital Bibliophile Community (http://www.digibib.com) (both accessed June 1, 2003). Some of these sites also include lists of recommended readings that provide information about book dealers, authors, and collecting books. Other sources for such information are *ABC for Book Collectors* (Carter and Barker 2000) and *Book Collecting 2000* (Ahearn and Ahearn 2000).

The Rare Books and Manuscripts Section of the Association of College and Research Libraries division of the American Library Association holds conferences and provides information about rare books and special collections. The Out-of-Print Discussion Group of the Association for Library Collections and Technical Services division of the American Library Association meets at the American Library Association conferences and is a source of information for librarians seeking out-of-print items.

ExLibris is an electronic discussion list formed to discuss matters related to rare books, manuscripts, and special collections. It does not accept lists of items for sale, but it does accept notices from dealers announcing the release of new catalogs (http://palimpsest.stanford.edu/byform/mailing-lists/exlibris, accessed June 1, 2003).

Magazines for book collectors and dealers can provide useful information for librarians. Some examples are *Book Collector, Antiquarian Book Monthly,* and *Firsts.*

In dealing with rare materials, where prices may be extremely high, acquisitions librarians must work closely with the bibliographers who request the items and with specialized dealers. Since different editions and printings vary widely in price, librarians must verify the exact items desired. OCLC (the Online Computer Library Center, Inc.), national bibliographies, or bibliographies of an author's works may be useful resources when the librarian is attempting to locate this information. The dealer's reputation is vital; membership in the societies for antiquarian book dealers is one factor to consider when libraries are making major purchases. Librarians may also wish to consult with colleagues who have collections in related subject areas for recommendations.

Some specialized dealers issue catalogs or notify regular customers when new titles are available. Librarians must review these quickly; an item that has been desired for ages can be sold rapidly. Some dealers will notify libraries when they have items of potential interest before the items are listed in the dealers' catalogs. Librarians should respond to such inquiries whether or not they intend to purchase the items; telling a dealer why an item is not wanted can help the dealer tailor future inquiries more precisely.

Librarians who work in rare book collections and special collections areas may go on trips to review and purchase materials. Some institutions may provide such librarians with money in advance of the purchases; others will reimburse the personnel for the purchases. Acquisitions personnel must work closely with these specialists to process the purchases. The specialists may bring the items with them when they return from their trips or may arrange to have the materials shipped to the libraries. Rare book librarians may receive materials directly, rather than having them sent to the acquisitions department. Acquisitions personnel must verify that the materials have been received and get copies of the invoices before authorizing payment.

Some dealers will work on a library's want list, notifying the library when they locate specific items. The library and dealer should agree on guidelines, including the acceptable price range, the physical condition, and whether there is a time limit.

Determining reasonable prices for rare materials is complex; prices for an item may vary considerably. A major factor in pricing is the condition, and dealers may vary somewhat in their interpretations of what is "good" condition. Relatively minor differences in the physical condition of an item frequently result in major differences in the quoted price. Librarians can get some general ideas of the values of some titles by checking dealers' catalogs and Web listings. Some published guides to prices include the annual publications *American Book Prices Current* and *Book Auction Records*, which list prices from auctions. *Bookman's Price Index* lists prices from dealers' catalogs.

Rare book librarianship is a highly specialized area; acquisitions personnel must work closely with the librarians and dealers who are experts in this area.

ON-DEMAND PRINTING

A rapidly developing area of publishing, "on-demand" printing, may become an additional method of acquiring out-of-print materials. Although the Xerox/UMI Books on Demand service began in the 1960s, producing copies of items that were out of print, the process was rather expensive. New developments may mean that books remain in print longer or can be reprinted at a lower cost. Companies can strike agreements with publishers, such as the agreement between Lightning Print Inc. and Cambridge University Press, to provide copies on demand of titles that would otherwise become out of print. Some bookstore chains such as Borders and Barnes & Noble have done test projects in some of their stores to produce on-demand copies of items not on their shelves. Some authors are retaining or regaining the rights to issue their works electronically and are now publishing the items personally, either electronically or by printing on-demand copies. Creating books with this technology may seem easy when compared with the legal arguments concerning the rights of authors and publishers that are currently under way. Contracts written many years ago did not contain explicit clauses about electronic editions; the advances in technology have led to lawsuits over the rights to publish electronic versions. On-demand printing is still in the beginning stages, but the process has the potential to change the availability of out-of-print titles greatly. Some out-of-print dealers are concerned that on-demand printing will reduce their sales, just as some booksellers who deal in new books are concerned that the out-of-print market reduces their sales. On-demand printing is a rapidly developing area; it is too early to know if the fears of out-of-print dealers are justified, or if this process will become just another way of supplying information.

CONCLUSION

Perhaps more than most areas of librarianship, the field of out-of-print and rare book acquisitions has been transformed by the Internet. Items that once took years to find can now be searched for at several Internet sites and located in a few minutes. Librarians can immediately compare the descriptions and prices of items from several vendors. The acquisition of many out-of-print items can now be a routine part of the ordering process.

In spite of these changes, some things remain constant. The field still has dealers who are knowledgeable professionals ready to work with libraries to build collections just as their predecessors have done for generations. Libraries still need to find materials that are no longer readily available, and the process still requires careful attention. Rare books continue to require specialized knowledge; librarians continue to work closely with subject experts and specialized dealers. The goal of libraries is to acquire materials for their users. Out-of-print dealers, whether local stores or Internet dealers, are simply another means of fulfilling that goal.

REFERENCES

Ahearn, Allan, and Patricia Ahearn. 2000. *Book collecting 2000: A comprehensive guide*. New York: G. P. Putnam's Sons.

Book Industry Study Group. 1999. *The rest of us: The first study of America's 53,000 independent smaller book publishers*. New York: Book Industry Study Group.

Brunet, Patrick, and Lee Shiflett. 1992. Out-of-print and antiquarian books: Guides for reference librarians. *RQ* 32: 85–100.

Carter, John, and Nicholas Barker. 2000. *ABC for book collectors*. New Castle, DE: Oak Knoll Press.

Greco, Albert N. 1997. *The book publishing industry*. Boston: Allyn and Bacon.

Hilts, Paul. 1999. Dosing up on O-D. *Publishers Weekly* 246 (51): 46.

Landesman, Margaret. 1999. Out-of-print and antiquarian markets. In *Understanding the business of library acquisitions*. 2nd ed. Edited by Karen A. Schmidt. Chicago: American Library Association.

Overmier, Judith. 2002. Introduction. *Acquisitions Librarian* 27: 1–3.

Schiffrin, André. 2000. *The business of books: How international conglomerates took over publishing and changed the way we read*. London: Verso.

Chapter 9

Gifts and Exchange Programs

The mission of gifts and exchange programs is to acquire materials by means other than purchase, usually through donations of items or by trading items with other institutions. Nearly all types of libraries receive donations of materials; many people who donate materials are convinced that libraries will cherish the materials that they no longer want to keep. Many libraries have staff who are responsible for managing these donations. Although gifts programs and exchange programs have many similarities and are frequently run by one unit, they do have some distinct characteristics. There are more gifts units than exchange programs; exchange programs are more frequently found in research institutions and large academic libraries; and exchange programs often involve international partners (Leonhardt 1999, 52). Both gifts and exchange programs can be an effective method of enhancing libraries' collections by acquiring materials that cannot be purchased. However, sorting and processing the materials that are kept and disposing of the materials that libraries do not want and that must be discarded can absorb a great deal of staff time.

This chapter describes the advantages and disadvantages of these programs, the resources needed to operate effective programs, and some factors to consider when establishing and evaluating gifts or exchange programs.

ADVANTAGES AND DISADVANTAGES

Most people who have written about gifts and exchange programs have expressed strong opinions about their value. Supporters of such programs believe that libraries can acquire useful and valuable resources at minimal cost and can strengthen support for library programs. Clark (1990, 185) states, "Gifts and exchanges are a valuable and viable method for bringing unique material to the library." According to Johnson (1993, 11), "Gift materials are desirable because they can strengthen a library's holdings, fill gaps, supply replacements, and provide materials not available through purchase." Johnson also says that donations may "strengthen institutional relationships with individuals who may make additional donations." In addition, Leonhardt (1999, 54) comments that gifts may be one method for academic libraries to supplement the shrinking number of monographic purchases resulting from the combination of the lack of budget increases and rising serials prices.

Even those who advocate gifts and exchange programs acknowledge that the activities require staff time. Some critics feel that the benefits are not sufficient to justify the time and effort involved. Both Clark and Johnson caution that gifts are not free; libraries must sort and acknowledge the donations, process the desired materials, and dispose of the remaining items. Dickinson's view of unsolicited gifts is more negative than that of Clark, Johnson, or Leonhardt; he states that unsolicited gifts "comprise materials that libraries do not want, cannot use and that are encumbered by unacceptable conditions" (Dickinson 1997, 1).

Gifts and exchange programs can be valuable to libraries when the programs are carefully structured and staffed appropriately. Gifts and exchange programs must be well organized with clear collection policies describing the kinds of materials that the libraries need as well as the types of materials that will not be accepted. The staff must have the appropriate management, automation, and language skills.

ORGANIZATION OF GIFTS PROGRAMS

The administrative location of gifts and exchange programs varies among libraries. Some academic libraries include the gifts program in the collection management department. In many libraries, the gifts program is located in the acquisitions department because the purpose of the program is to acquire materials for the library collection. In libraries that do not have a specific unit to handle gifts, the acquisitions department frequently receives donations. The materials may be added to the collection; therefore, the processing can logically begin in acquisitions.

Gifts units process large amounts of material, handle correspondence, maintain records, deal with donors, and represent the institution to the public. They work with many areas of their organizations including collection management, processing, public relations, and development departments. They may deal with institutional legal and public relations departments when gifts involve bequests or publicity. In some large organizations, a development department may maintain information about all donations; gifts staff need to learn what information such departments wish to receive.

To accomplish these functions, personnel must be able to plan, organize, and manage the workflow; keep accurate, well-organized records; accept, receive, acknowledge, and sort donations; and arrange for the disposition of unwanted materials (Lane 1980, 4). Personnel need to know how to use computer programs; most gifts sections have streamlined their operations by using computer programs to maintain files of donations and acknowledgments. In addition to the management and organizational skills required to carry out these functions, personnel need initiative and tact. Gifts personnel frequently work with donors who are dealing with the stress involved in settling estates, are moving, or are hesitant about donating materials; the gifts staff must have the ability to assist donors with difficult choices as well as the patience and tact to work with these donors. In smaller libraries, the entire process may be a small portion of the assignment of one library staff member, and therefore it may be handled only when the pressure of other responsibilities allows. Larger libraries may have staff members and students who handle the gifts operations.

GIFTS OF MATERIALS

Gifts of materials are either solicited or unsolicited. Solicited donations are collections that the institution wants and works to acquire. Such collections are frequently valuable and require considerable time and effort to obtain; negotiations may continue for years. The process may involve the administration of the library and the institution as well as lawyers of all parties. The successful acquisition of major solicited gifts may result in publicity for the organization ranging from media coverage to large receptions honoring the donors. Unsolicited donations, which are the most frequent type of gifts, have not been requested by the institution, may arrive unexpectedly, and range greatly in usefulness.

Some libraries receive a large number of donations, while other more specialized libraries may not be given many materials. The quality of the donations varies as much as the size does. Some donations may include valuable first editions or scarce regional history materials; others will include outdated directories of telephone numbers or Internet sites. The majority of gifts are neither trash nor treasure; most donations are general materials that might be useful to libraries. Libraries may be able to replace missing items, add more copies of frequently used materials, or fill gaps in their collections.

Some publishers may send unsolicited items and include invoices, hoping that libraries will keep the materials and pay the invoices. These materials may be treated as gifts according to U.S. Postal Service regulations (http://www.usps.gov/websites/depart/inspect/merch.htm, accessed June 1, 2003). Libraries may develop a form letter to send to such companies that cites the USPS regulation and states that all such materials will be handled according to the institution's gift policies. In most cases the publisher will not send additional materials.

Accepting Gifts

Libraries need clear policies describing the types of materials they will and will not accept. Larger libraries may have collection development policies that describe the collecting priorities of the institution, and these are helpful to gifts personnel who deal with donors. Developing descriptions of the types of materials that are not wanted is equally important, if not more so, than describing the subject areas in which the library collects materials. For example, some libraries will not accept recent newspapers, popular magazines, paperback fiction, or textbooks, while other libraries want those types of materials. Some libraries may want donations of all types of paperback fiction; others only want novels that are about their geographic region. When libraries create policies that spell out what is needed and what is not wanted, the gifts staff can work with donors to the libraries' benefit.

Receiving Gifts

When the library receives donations, gifts personnel must count the materials and acknowledge the donation. Most libraries cannot list all the individual items in each donation; instead libraries frequently count the items in each category, such as magazines, paperback books, or maps. Gifts personnel send the donors an acknowledgment that includes the number of items received and a thank-you. They also create a record that includes the name and address of the donor, the number of items in the gift, the date it was received, and any special notes about the transaction. These records may be kept on paper in a file, or the information may be kept in a database created by the gifts personnel. Exceptional and valuable donations require special attention; see the section "Internal Revenue Service Regulations" later in this chapter for additional information. If the library or its institution has a development office, the gifts unit may need to inform it about donations. Each organization may need different information: while some departments may want lists of the individual donors, some may want only statistical information. Gifts staff must check with these departments and learn what information is needed.

Next, the donations are reviewed to determine which items will be added to the library collection. In larger libraries, collection development personnel may have worked with the gifts personnel to establish general guidelines for the initial review of materials. For example, selectors may have told the gifts personnel that materials such as how-to books, general magazines, paperback fiction, or textbooks may be designated for a sale or for immediate discarding without further review.

In some libraries, gifts personnel may search the library catalogs to determine whether the library already owns the items before selectors review the materials. In other libraries with limited staff or when few gifts are routinely added, items are not searched until the materials have been selected to be added to the collection.

After any initial sorting or searching, selectors or other library personnel review the remaining materials to determine what should be added to the library. Reviewers must evaluate them for both content and physical condition. They must remember that gifts do cost money to process and to house; gifts should not be added simply because money was not spent to purchase them. Items in poor physical condition must be evaluated to determine whether they are worth the time and money required to preserve. Libraries have received donations of materials that have been infested with bugs and with mold; unless these materials are extremely valuable, they should be discarded before they contaminate other materials. Selectors and gifts personnel should ask preservation consultants for advice about the options and potential costs involved in preserving or restoring rare items.

EVALUATION OF GIFTS PROGRAMS

Gifts programs provide libraries with some valuable material, some trash, and a great deal of material that falls in between the two extremes. Personnel must sort and process materials, discarding those items that are not added to the collection. When evaluating the value of gifts programs, libraries must consider what they gain and what the costs are to maintain the program. Many libraries find donations a valuable method of obtaining materials they had not purchased; others receive almost nothing that they need, leading them to stop accepting donations. When evaluating the cost of gifts programs, libraries must consider the salaries of those people accepting, sorting, and discarding the donations as well as the space required to store the materials.

The intangible factor in analyzing the value of a gifts program is the public relations benefit. Some individuals who donate some small collection may then donate more valuable collections or money in the future. Many people are reluctant to discard books; they may form very negative feelings toward a library that does not accept their donations.

Gifts programs can be very beneficial for some libraries but may not be appropriate for other libraries. Each institution must evaluate its needs and the potential benefits before deciding whether to establish such a program.

DISPOSING OF UNWANTED GIFTS

Libraries usually add only a small percentage of materials that are donated; some libraries add only about a fourth of the items received (Leonhardt 1997, 145). Getting rid of unneeded gifts can be a problem for many libraries because some organizations have regulations governing the disposition of institutional property. In some states, items donated to a public institution become state property when the items are accepted; libraries in those states may be required to follow state regulations designed to cover the disposition of furniture and equipment when they wish to dispose of books and magazines. The procedures vary greatly among the states, so librarians must learn what is required in their organization. They may need to consult with the institutional lawyers as well as the departments responsible for the management of physical property and of records.

Some libraries have official nonprofit Friends of the Library groups. In these libraries, all gifts may be donated to the Friends group and become library property only after the items have been accepted and processed for the library. With this arrangement, unwanted materials may be sold by the Friends or discarded without violating government or institutional regulations. Libraries must work closely with their institution to learn what policies must be followed and with their Friends groups to help the groups understand the institutional and Internal Revenue Service regulations.

Book Sales

Many libraries have book sales, either annual or year-round sales, which range from huge special events to a few shelves in the corner of the lobby. The book sales are a means of recycling materials, and they usually do make money for the libraries. A few libraries have made large amounts of money from the sales, while others have found that the staff time and the money required to hold large sales are not justified by the amount of money they make.

Book sales require people to sort and price the materials, space to display the items, and people to add up the totals and take the money. Some libraries price each item separately; others price materials by category, such as maps, tapes, or paperbacks. The sale must be advertised, which requires money to purchase ads or people to promote the sale. Depending on the size of the sale, space may have to be rented to house it. At the end of the sale, the remaining materials must be discarded, donated to other institutions, or stored until the next sale. Active Friends groups may have sufficient volunteers to manage sales; if not, library personnel may have to do the work. Friends of Libraries U.S.A. has information about managing book sales; see http://www.folusa.com (accessed June 1, 2003) for more information.

Some libraries have stores that sell unneeded gifts, withdrawn materials, cups, pencils, mouse pads, or other items. As with book sales, personnel must sort and price materials. Staff must remove any items that do not sell within a reasonable time; customers look for new stock regularly. These stores may be operated by library personnel or by volunteers. Libraries need to keep the stores open regularly scheduled hours, which can sometimes be difficult if the operations are completely run by volunteers.

Book sales can result in good publicity for libraries, giving the public an opportunity to find bargains. They can also cause problems if donors become upset when they discover their donations in the sale. All donors should be informed that the library may not add all their donations and that some materials may be included in a sale. Such information may not prevent a donor from becoming upset. Should this happen, library staff may be able to reassure the donor that all donations benefit the library whether the items are added to the collection, given to other institutions, or sold to bring money for other materials.

Libraries interested in having book sales or stores must discuss their plans with their institutions; some organizations may permit occasional sales but prohibit stores, or they may require that profits be reported systematically.

Sales to Dealers

Libraries or their Friends groups may be able to sell unneeded materials to used book stores or to dealers. Some dealers will offer cash for materials, while others will give the library credit that can be used for future purchases. Institutional regulations vary, so librarians must learn the policies of their organization. For example, some institutions allow the library to trade materials to dealers but prohibit direct sales of materials.

The price offered by dealers will be low, perhaps a third of the amount the dealer hopes to get when reselling the materials. Some dealers will offer a higher amount of credit than they will pay outright for materials. Some dealers will take materials on consignment and divide the profits with the library.

INTERNAL REVENUE SERVICE REGULATIONS

Donors may claim deductions on federal taxes for donations to libraries. Tax deductions for the donation of materials are governed by very specific Internal Revenue Service regulations. Donors valuing their donations at more than $250 must be able to provide the IRS with a written acknowledgment. Since libraries rarely know what value a donor is assigning to a donation, the library should acknowledge all donations in writing. The written acknowledgment must include the donor's name and address and the library or Friends group accepting the donation; the date it was accepted; and a description of the donation. This description should include the number of items in each format, such as magazines, paperbacks, or hardback books; it does not have to list each individual title.

The donor may assign a value to a donation greater than $250 and less than $5,000. According to IRS regulations, the library cannot do such appraisals when it is the party receiving the donation. Donors may consult sources such as *American Book Prices Current, Bookman's Price Index,* or Internet sites of out-of-print dealers to establish the value of their materials.

If a donor declares that a donation is worth $5,000 or more, the donor must file an official appraisal with his or her IRS tax return. Libraries may provide a list of potential appraisers to the donor. Dealers of used books often appraise collections and usually know of other qualified appraisers. The *American Book Trade Directory* contains a list of appraisers of books.

Donors may also need to file IRS Form 8283 for donations of property valued at more than $5,000. This form requires a description of the donation and the signature of the person in the institution responsible for receiving the donation. Librarians must learn who is authorized to sign such forms; in some organizations, the head of the gifts section may be authorized to sign them, while in other institutions the development officer or the institution's lawyer may be the only individual authorized to sign them.

If IRS Form 8283 was filed, and the library decides to dispose of items worth more than $500 from the donated collection within two years of receiving the materials, it must file IRS Form 8282. This step may result in a review of the donor's tax deduction. Most libraries are reluctant to deal with the paperwork and with the potential damage to their relationships with donors. To avoid such complications, libraries must review the materials carefully and accept only those items that they will add to the collection. If that is not feasible, libraries must find space to store the materials for the required two years or decline the donation.

Librarians should not attempt to provide advice about tax law. They should suggest that donors consult their lawyers or accountants. Librarians may also refer donors to the IRS's Internet site (http://www.irs.gov, accessed June 1, 2003) and keep copies of the appropriate forms and instructions in their files.

DONOR RELATIONSHIPS

Most donors want to help the library and are searching for an appropriate location for materials they can no longer keep. Most understand that the library may not need to keep all the items in a gift and are pleased when the library can use some items or suggest other options for disposing of the materials.

Gifts staff or subject selectors in larger libraries should review large gifts at the donor's home before accepting such a donation. The library personnel can evaluate the collection and determine the size of the potential donation. This information will help staff plan the physical aspects of packing, receiving, sorting, and processing the donation if it is accepted. In some cases, selectors may decide that much of the potential donation would not be useful and may ask the donor if the library can take only portions of the offered materials. After reviewing an offered collection, library personnel may decide that the materials are not needed or not appropriate for the library. They may then work with the donor to find alternatives to donating the materials to the library. Previewing offered gifts can prevent the arrival of a huge collection of unwanted materials at the library.

Some donors may ask the library to return to them any items that are not added to the collection. This requires that the items be identified so that they may be returned to the gifts section if they are rejected during processing; one of the simpler methods is to insert a colored piece of paper in each item that states, "[name of donor] collection; return to Gifts if not added." Any items that are returned to the unit can then be given back to the donor.

Libraries may be offered donations that are not appropriate for their collections, such as a collection of popular fiction offered to a specialized science library. Libraries that have book sales may use these donations for those sales. The gifts staff may be able to refer the donors to other area libraries that do collect the type of material being offered, to used book stores, or to charities that operate secondhand stores. If the library operates an exchange program, the materials might be useful for that operation. In addition to easing donors' feelings of rejection when their prized collections are not accepted, gifts personnel can help to ensure that the materials will be available to others who are interested in the subject.

Some donors, however, believe that the materials they plan to give to the library are extremely valuable and expect that the library will be deeply grateful and therefore willing to meet their every desire. Occasionally, but very rarely, this perception is accurate. Some donors will request special conditions before the materials are donated, such as having the materials located in a special room, having all items in the collection kept, having portions of the collection displayed continually, or otherwise creating many restrictions that govern how the materials may be used. Such requests and such donors are far more common than are the collections that justify the requests. Librarians must consult with their institutions to learn what requests can be granted; some organizations have very specific policies governing restrictive donation agreements. Personnel dealing with such individuals must be tactful in explaining what conditions are possible and what demands cannot be met. If the requests are unacceptable, the library must be prepared to reject the entire donation. The potential donation should be reviewed carefully to determine whether the library already has any of the materials, what condition the materials are in, and what the processing and preservation costs might be. The library will need to seek the advice of its institutional lawyers and development department in such negotiations since the conditions are usually legally binding on the organization.

The Rare Books and Manuscripts Section of the Association of College and Research Libraries issued a guide that addresses many of the frequently asked questions about old books. It includes information about the difference between old and rare books, book values, and appraisals; this information can help donors learn about their collections and the business of used and rare books. Libraries may wish to purchase copies of the brochure for distribution or refer donors to the Internet version (http://www.rbms.nd.edu/yob.html, accessed June 1, 2003).

EXCHANGE PROGRAMS

Most exchange programs are located in large academic or specialized research libraries. Because most exchange programs involve serials, they are frequently located in acquisitions or serials departments. Exchange programs are a form of barter among libraries; each party has materials that can be supplied in a trade. Most exchange programs are established to obtain items that cannot be purchased or to acquire items for less money than would be needed to purchase them. Programs may involve a balanced trade of serials in which each library provides a title published by its organization and receives a title published by its exchange partner. Exchange plans can include books and other materials; libraries may use unwanted gifts or publications of their institutions.

Many universities and scholarly associations publish journals in their areas of interest, such as regional literary or history journals. These serials are often the basis of an exchange program in which the libraries exchange these publications for similar publications from other organizations. Research libraries with area studies programs, especially those concentrated on international studies, often establish exchange programs with institutions in the relevant region.

Exchange programs are frequently the most effective, and sometimes the only, method of obtaining some international materials. Many governmental agency and departmental publications are not available for purchase but may be acquired through exchange agreements. Exchange programs eliminate the complicated questions of currency conversions, fluctuating currency values, billing, and government trade restrictions.

Exchange programs are also an opportunity for an institution to distribute its publications to a wide audience. The institution may wish to increase public awareness about it or to improve its public image. Having its publications available in libraries may be a portion of its public relations program.

Organization of Exchange Programs

Exchange programs, like gifts programs, are an alternative method to purchasing materials. They require careful organization and monitoring to be successful. In libraries with active exchange programs in international studies, personnel need the appropriate language skills.

Libraries may receive the materials that they use in their exchange programs from their institutions at no cost to the libraries. Many large universities have departments that publish serials; these departments may sell multiple copies of the serials that they publish to the library for a lower cost than subscribers are charged. Few university departments are willing to donate multiple copies of their serials to libraries. Even with the reduced cost, this expense must be budgeted. Exchange personnel must work with collection management and fiscal services to determine who will be responsible for authorizing the expenditures.

Materials that are to be distributed by exchange programs must be identified, purchased if necessary, and collected. Libraries must correspond with institutions in order to create a list of exchange partners; international programs will generally require staff with appropriate language skills. Sending materials to other libraries involves packing and postage; in addition, international shipping regulations dictate the weight of packages that are shipped outside the United States. The libraries must decide which portion of the budget will pay for the shipping costs; some libraries charge the acquisitions budget while others pay for these costs from the general operating budget. Records must be kept of what is sent and what is received to determine whether the exchange program is a fair and balanced one.

Evaluation of Exchange Programs

"Is the exchange program worth the time and expense? The answer will depend upon the size of the library and its exchange program, on the efficiency of the exchange operations and on the collecting needs and mission of the library. Moreover, it will ultimately depend on the ability of the library to maintain the cost-effectiveness of its exchange program" (Carrico 1999, 213). Each library must determine whether an exchange program is worth the money and time required to operate it. Institutions with strong international studies collections and programs may find them essential because they may provide materials that could not be purchased.

In evaluating an exchange program, libraries must determine the cost paid for the materials they provide and the postage and shipping costs. They must then compare those costs to what it would cost to subscribe to the materials. Libraries must also determine the value of the materials they receive that are not available for purchase. Intangible factors, such as public relations, international cultural relations, and the exchange of information will need to be evaluated in each situation before a library decides whether the exchange program is desirable. The cost analysis will be a basic portion of an evaluation, but it is not the only reason for continuing or dropping an exchange program.

U.S. FEDERAL DOCUMENTS EXCHANGE PROGRAM

The U.S. Government Printing Office is one of the world's largest publishers. Libraries may purchase individual materials or may receive materials automatically through depository programs operated by the Federal Library Depository Program. Many libraries are selective depository libraries; they receive specific titles or subject areas that they have selected. In libraries with departments responsible for federal government information, gifts staff should consult with the government information personnel about donated government publications. Federal depository libraries can list materials available for exchange on the Government Documents Exchange List (http://www.access.gpo.gov/su_docs/fdlp/index.html, accessed June 1, 2003). This list is available only to depository libraries. Notices of available materials are also sometimes posted on the electronic discussion list GOVDOC-L (listserv@lists.psu.edu). All states have federal depository libraries; libraries that are not part of the depository program may wish to consult depository libraries in their region for advice if they should receive large donations of government materials that they would like to share with other libraries. For more information about government publications, see chapter 5, "Acquiring Books and Media."

SOURCES OF ADDITIONAL INFORMATION

Internet resources have become very useful to gifts personnel. Electronic discussion lists allow personnel to communicate with colleagues, seek advice, locate needed materials, and dispose of materials libraries do not need. Some useful electronic discussion lists are BACKSERV (http://lists.swetsblackwell.com/mailman/listinfo/backserv, accessed June 1, 2003), which lists issues of serials available for exchange or sought by libraries, and Refex (listserv@listserv.arizona.edu), which lists reference materials available for exchange. Another resource is the Duplicates Exchange Union, operated by the Association for Library Collections and Technical Services division of the American Library Association; it facilitates exchanges of materials (http:/www.ala.org/content/Navigation Menu/alcts/Publications6/Duplicates_Exchange_Union1/Duplicates_Exchange_Union.htm, accessed June 1, 2003). Many subject areas have electronic discussion lists for librarians working in those subject areas; some of those also allow personnel to post messages asking for assistance in locating or disposing of unneeded materials.

Internet sites such as the Back Issues and Exchange Services (http://www.uvm.edu/~bmaclenn/backexch.html) and Gifts and Exchanges GiftXWeb (http://hubcap.clemson.edu/~johnsos/G&E/GEHome.html) (both accessed June 1, 2003) also provide information about gifts and exchange programs. Some libraries have created Internet pages describing their gifts or exchange programs.

The Gifts and Exchange Discussion Group of the Association for Library Collections and Technical Services division of the American Library Association provides information and assistance for those working in gifts and exchange programs.

CONCLUSION

Gifts and exchange programs can be "essential to most libraries" (Johnson 1993, 10) or "a significant, continuing and expensive problem" (Dickinson 1997, 1). Both opinions can be true, depending upon how libraries handle the programs. Well-organized, efficiently managed, and cost-effective programs clearly can benefit libraries. Such programs provide needed materials at a price far below what it would cost to purchase the materials. Careful and continuing evaluation of these programs will ensure that they provide appropriate materials at a reasonable cost.

REFERENCES

Carrico, Steven. 1999. Gifts and exchanges. In *Understanding the business of library acquisitions*. 2nd ed. Edited by Karen A. Schmidt. Chicago: American Library Association.

Clark, Mae. 1990. Gifts and exchanges. In *Understanding the business of library acquisitions*, edited by Karen A. Schmidt. Chicago: American Library Association.

Dickinson, Dennis W. 1997. Free books: Are they worth what they cost? *Library Issues: Briefings for Faculty and Administrators* 17 (5): 1–4.

Johnson, Peggy. 1993. Dollars and sense: When to look a gift horse in the mouth. *Technicalities* 13 (6): 10–13.

Lane, Alfred H. 1980. *Gifts and exchange manual*. Westport, CT: Greenwood Press.

Leonhardt, Thomas W. 1997. The gifts and exchange function in ARL libraries: Now and tomorrow. *Library Acquisitions: Practice and Theory* 21: 141–49.

———. 1999. A survey of gifts and exchanges activities in 85 non-ARL libraries. *Acquisitions Librarian* 22: 51–58.

Chapter 10

Bindery Operations

Libraries spend huge sums of money to purchase materials but comparatively small amounts to preserve those materials. "Conservation should start with the purchase decision (which ought to include consideration of how well the material will stand up to the expected use) and should end with the question of what to do about work, damaged materials and items identified in the weeding process" (Evans 2000, 498). Binding materials is an important component of preserving libraries' collections. Sales of the library binding industry were approximately $100 million in the late twentieth century (Orr 1996, 295). Members of the Association of Research Libraries spent more than $25 million on binding in 1997 (Association of Research Libraries 2001, 26). Bindery activities typically include mending and book repair and in-house binding procedures such as clipping and spiral binding, as well as using a commercial binder for binding periodicals and rebinding books.

In larger libraries binding operations are often part of technical services and located in acquisitions departments, especially when serials units are part of acquisitions. In the last decade, these operations have also begun to appear in preservation departments that may be part of either technical or public services. In large libraries with several branches, binding shipments may be handled by individual branches or centralized in one library. Some libraries may locate these operations in cataloging or even circulation departments. In smaller libraries, binding operations are usually part of technical services.

Binding has a long tradition dating back to the Romans (Campbell 1994, 6). For a long time it was a craft affordable to only rich collectors. Technological developments of the eighteenth and nineteenth centuries produced machinery that reduced the cost of binding drastically, making it affordable to libraries. Binding procedures like oversewing reduced the time and cost of rebinding, enabling libraries to bind materials easily.

The Library Binding Institute (LBI), established in 1935, is the principal trade association representing the library binding industry. It created standards "emphasizing quality of workmanship and materials and a discriminating approach to decision making" (NISO 2000, vii). As stated in its bylaws, it is committed "to raise and sustain standards of craftsmanship and quality, and to engage in research in methods of prolonging the useful life of the written word" (Rebsamen 1995, 19).

LBI standards were substantially revised in 1986, with the eighth edition, to acknowledge changing practices and technology in the industry. In the new standards, the ability to open volumes completely, allowing them to lie flat for photocopying, and conservative treatment of volumes with fragile binding became as important as the strengths of materials used to rebind materials. To address these redefined objectives, sewing through the fold, double-fan adhesive gluing, and recasing were incorporated as mainstream techniques.

In 2000, the first American National Standard for library binding, ANSI/NISO/LBI Z39.78-2000, was developed jointly by the National Information Standards Organization (NISO) and the LBI. Building on previous LBI standards, performance benchmarks were added to the materials specifications "to encourage suppliers to develop superior materials and for binders to accept them" (NISO 2000, vii). This revised standard recognizes that library bindings need to be flexible as well as strong and that they must meet preservation standards. The standard also recognizes that improved materials may become available between editions of the ANSI standards; therefore, binders and libraries may adopt new materials and techniques if those materials or techniques improve performance. Unlike previous LBI standards, this 2000 edition does not recommend specific products or procedures (Parisi 1999b, 7).

PRESERVATION

All libraries have some materials they want to preserve for the future whether they are large academic institutions with rare book collections or small public libraries with local history materials. All libraries want to ensure that the materials they acquire will survive long enough to meet the needs of their users. Preservation is a concern of all librarians regardless of whether the institution has a formal program dealing with all the issues related to preservation. "The main role of the acquisitions librarian in preservation is to help acquire materials in usable condition, and to refer newly received materials in poor condition for review or treatment before they are added to the collection. This role should be an integral part of the library's overall policy on preservation" (Hamilton 1993, 6).

Acquisitions personnel are usually the first library staff to see materials acquired by the library. Acquisitions, cataloging, and circulation staff are the only people who handle all the items. These staff must be trained to watch for materials that need preservation. Dealing with problems when the items arrive is easier and cheaper than repairing or replacing the materials later.

Acquisitions personnel should watch for items with loose pages or weak bindings, discs or media that accompany books, items that need to be tipped in, and items with paper in poor condition. Items needing repair or rebinding should be sent to the binding and repair section. Some publishers, especially those that issue paperbacks, use cheap paper and poor adhesive; libraries may have to rebind these materials when the items are received. If the binding is damaged or if sections of pages are loose, libraries may be able to acquire replacement copies from the publisher; however, sometimes better copies do not exist. Librarians must decide whether binding the existing copy is more cost efficient than attempting to replace the item. Acquisitions personnel should consult with the appropriate selectors to determine when the quality of paper or binding is indeed the standard that can be expected from a specific publisher or country.

Acquisitions personnel must be aware of basic preservation guidelines. They must not use potentially damaging materials, such as rubber bands that cut the edges of items or temporary sticky notes that leave residue on items.

LIFE SPANS OF MATERIALS

Some items created thousands of years ago still exist; some materials created a hundred years ago have crumbled away. The life span of materials varies widely and depends upon both the original material and the environment in which it is kept.

Books printed on alkaline paper are expected to last hundreds of years. Books printed on acid paper have a much shorter life span unless they are kept away from light, in an environment with moderate humidity, and are rarely handled. Some books printed on acid paper have become very brittle and fragile in less than a hundred years. The life span of paper and the appropriate treatment of brittle paper became a major debate in 2001 after Nicholson Baker wrote *Double Fold: Libraries and the Assault on Paper* (New York: Random House). Baker maintains that brittle paper does not disintegrate as rapidly as some librarians predicted. He criticizes the destruction of original materials after they have been reformatted and calls for the preservation of at least one archived original copy. Items with brittle paper may be preserved, but they do require special handling and appropriate storage.

The life span of videotapes and audiotapes also depends upon their storage. Tapes that are kept in dark areas, in plastic or other preservationally appropriate containers, and in areas with moderate humidity may last several decades. Frequently used tapes may wear out within a few years.

Compact discs are comparatively new, and their life span is still uncertain. The primary concern with compact discs, as with any technology, is technological obsolescence. Libraries must maintain the item and also the equipment required to read or to play the item. For example, few libraries still have the technology required to use 5 1/4–inch floppy disks. If the contents of such media are not transferred to current formats, the information can be lost. The lack of standards for digital information and the lack of consensus about archiving materials cause uncertainty about the preservation of electronic resources. Librarians must monitor technological developments and transfer materials from outdated formats to newer technologies as appropriate.

Microforms are generally considered one of the better means of preserving materials for archival purposes. When stored properly in containers that are preservationally sound and kept in moderate humidity, microforms can last for several decades. "Microfilm, if processed and stored in strict accordance with national standards, has an extremely long life and may be duplicated almost indefinitely with only minor loss of information. The technology itself is stable and the film produced may be read on any microfilm reader" (Kenney 1993, 3). Although patrons generally do not like to use microforms, they do acknowledge that this format does preserve the complete contents of the original items, unlike many electronic databases.

BASICS OF BOOK CONSTRUCTION

Books are created by printing the text on large sheets that are then folded into sections, called signatures, consisting of sixteen, thirty-two, or sixty-four pages. The signatures are folded, gathered, and collated into books on machines that sew each signature to the next one, creating the final printed item, known as the text block. The text block then receives a cover: either of stiff paper or of cloth or other material placed over a hard cover.

Some books are created by printing the text on individual sheets, rather than on signatures. The pages are collated and either sewn or glued together to create the text block, and then the covers are applied.

The quality of the construction of books and journals varies considerably among publishers. Many trade publishers use inexpensive techniques; some of their books cannot withstand the heavy use that many library books receive.

Binders that specialize in handling materials for libraries use materials and techniques that are designed to protect the materials and to withstand the use and abuse that many books receive from library patrons. These materials are usually stronger than those used by trade publishers (Parisi 1999a, 8–12).

The paper used in books has been made from many different plants and fabrics over the centuries. In the nineteenth century, manufacturers experimented with cheaper materials and techniques, many of which produced acid paper that eventually became brittle. Many books printed on such paper are too fragile to be re-bound; libraries must replace the content by purchasing reprinted editions; reformat the content by photocopying, microfilming, or digitizing the materials; or preserve the item by housing it in special boxes. In the late twentieth century, many publishers began using alkaline paper that is intended to last indefinitely.

Paper varies in the weight and in the coating. Some items have paper so thin that the printing on one side is clearly visible on the reverse side. Paper may be glossy with a thick coating that allows illustrations to reproduce well, or it may have very little coating, permitting ready absorption of ink. The publishers decide which type of paper is appropriate for each book or journal they publish.

MENDING AND REPAIR OF BOOKS

Many items may be slightly damaged when they are used; these materials may need minor repairs but do not need to be re-bound by a commercial binder. Library staff can extend the life of such items by performing minor repairs. The first step in mending is to review the item carefully. Only experts who specialize in conservation and restoration of items should mend items that are very valuable, such as very expensive books or books that are important as archival items. Many damaged items are trade books; the goal of the library is to extend the life of the items for a few more years rather than to conserve the physical items permanently.

In the past, many libraries used cellophane tape to repair torn pages or used household glue to repair loose bindings. Book-binding tapes were used to replace missing spines. These materials and techniques frequently caused extensive damage to the books. The cellophane tape became brittle and stained the paper. The glues stained pages and became hard. The book-binding tapes dried up and fell off, leaving residue on the pages. The repairs actually made the original damage to the items far worse. "In general, inexpert repairing of books accelerates their deterioration. They crack apart when opened, pages break away from bindings, and bindings break away from texts" (Merrill-Oldham and Schrock 2000, 227).

Techniques and materials have improved considerably in recent decades. Tapes, adhesives, and other materials are now created to preserve materials and minimize damage. Classes, Internet sites, and books are available to teach the appropriate techniques for repairing materials without harming them. Repairs and mending should be done carefully, and should be minimal; staff should try to do only repairs that can be undone if necessary. *Book Repair: A How-to-Do-It Manual* by Kenneth Lavender (New York: Neal-Schuman, 2001) describes methods for cleaning, treating, and mending books in detail.

Many items need repairs to the spine or the hinges that have become loose. The basic repairs for these problems involve applying glue along the inside of the hinges and spine, then allowing the book to dry under pressure. Repairing torn paper may be done by using pressure-sensitive paper-mending tapes or by using special types of paper and paste. Libraries must evaluate the item before deciding what technique is appropriate. Items that are not expected to be kept in the libraries' collections indefinitely may not require advanced conservation methods, while valuable items should receive more careful repairs.

Libraries sometimes receive indexes after serials have been bound or may receive errata sheets that are correction notices for material that was inadvertently omitted. This added information needs to be bound with the item. If these materials are thin, they can be included in the bound volume by a process known as "tipping in." The items to be added receive a thin coat of glue along one edge and are then inserted into the bound volume.

Items that cannot be repaired or re-bound can be placed in special acid-free boxes or folders intended to protect them. Most library supply companies and archival supply companies sell boxes in standard sizes, and some binderies will make boxes in any desired size. Many archival companies also sell materials that libraries can use to construct boxes in any size. These boxes help protect items from wear, allowing them to be used for a longer time.

IN-HOUSE BINDING PROCEDURES

Some libraries bind selected materials themselves rather than sending the items to commercial binders. Libraries use a variety of techniques and equipment for this in-house binding. The most common methods used are pam binding, spiral binding, thermal binding, VeloBinding, and pin binding. All of these methods except for pam binding require special equipment (Root 1989, 32–33). Following are some of the pros and cons of each technique.

Pam binding means putting materials in pamphlet cases that consist of sturdy covers with strips of material along the inside of the spine. The pamphlets are attached to the strips by sewing, stapling, or gluing. Sewing is the preferred technique because less damage to the pamphlets occurs; gluing and stapling may cause permanent damage to the pamphlets. Pam binding works only for items that are thin and light; items more than one-quarter inch thick cannot be pam bound.

Spiral binding uses a round plastic comb with teeth that forms the spine of the item; the teeth cut through the back margin of the item being bound. Volumes open flat, and the technique is comparatively inexpensive. Libraries must purchase the machines and a variety of sizes of the plastic combs. Most machines can bind materials that are up to two inches thick. The spines can break easily and paper can pull loose. If the items are damaged, rebinding them is difficult because much of the margin has been cut to allow the comb to be inserted.

Thermal binding involves heating adhesive, fixing it to the spine of the item, and applying a cover. Libraries must purchase the machines, the covers, and the adhesives or glue sticks. Some machines apply thin layers of adhesive that may be too weak for materials receiving heavy use. Some machines can bind materials that are up to three inches thick.

VeloBinding uses equipment that punches holes through the back margin of the items. Two plastic strips, one with teeth and the other with holes to accommodate the teeth, are inserted and pressed together, creating a rigid edge that holds the pages together. Materials may be up to three inches thick. Items bound in this manner cannot be opened completely. If the plastic breaks, the materials may not have enough paper strength to be rebound because much of the margin has been cut by the holes.

Pin, or tack, binding is similar to VeloBinding. Machines drill a few holes in the margin of the items and insert pins through the items. As with VeloBinding, the items do not open flat and must have large margins.

All of these methods require that the libraries purchase special supplies, and all except pam binding require that the libraries purchase equipment. Staff must learn how to operate the machinery, some of which involves chemicals and heat. Libraries must provide adequate space for the equipment. Most of these processes require that much of the margins of materials be destroyed, making rebinding nearly impossible. Some techniques prevent the items from opening completely, making photocopying difficult.

These techniques may be less expensive than commercial binding, but libraries must consider not only the initial cost but also the cost of supplies and staff time. Most of the methods are suitable for comparatively thin items; most cannot be used for items that are more than two inches thick. Libraries should also consider that most of these methods are appropriate for materials that will not receive heavy use and that will not be kept in the collections indefinitely.

COMMERCIAL BINDING

"What generally costs a fraction of a journal's price, requires little or no special equipment on the part of the library, helps preserve good order in your stacks, deters theft, extends a journal's shelf life, and helps library users with their citations? The answer is professional binding" (Stankus 1995, 1). Because binding is an activity that requires specialized knowledge and skills, expensive machinery, and a large work area, libraries consistently contract with companies for this service. Libraries partner with commercial binders to provide a service that would be cost prohibitive to perform in-house.

Libraries want to select the best commercial binder for their specific needs at a reasonable cost. Depending on the type of library, the process may be mandated by the state or directed by the parent institution. Institutions that are state funded generally must abide by their state procurement codes, while private institutions may have more flexibility in selecting commercial binders. Techniques for selecting a binder range from informal reviews of binders to highly structured request-for-proposal (RFP) procedures. The RFP document spells out the library's requirements for the binder and provides the factors by which the binder's responses will be evaluated including factors such as technical and material specifications, services, pricing, and references. The RFP puts the relationship between the library and the binder in a formal, legal framework that clearly states the expectations and responsibilities of both parties, giving each party the means to enforce its rights.

How to Find a Commercial Binder

Hundreds of bookbinders exist in the United States; some specialize in specific types of materials such as religious books, while others bind all types of materials. Librarians can locate binders by checking telephone directories to locate local companies, searching the Internet, or looking at the membership list of the Library Binding Institute (http://www.lbibinders.org, accessed June 1, 2003).

Services Provided by Commercial Binders

All commercial binders will bind books and serials and rebind materials that have been previously bound. Many binders make boxes that house materials needing special protection. Some binders do preservation services such as encapsulation, which is enclosing materials in transparent coverings.

Most binders do not have the ability to perform advanced conservation work such as deacidification or restoration. Libraries needing such specialized services should consult regional resources such as the Northeast Document Conservation Center (http://www.nedcc.org) or Conservation OnLine (CoOL) (http://palimpsest.stanford.edu) (both accessed June 1, 2003).

Factors to Consider When Selecting a Commercial Binder

Libraries selecting commercial binders must consider several factors involving both service and cost. The binders must be able to provide the libraries with a good product delivered in a reasonable time at a reasonable cost.

Libraries should ask if the binder is a member of the Library Binding Institute. While some reputable binders are not members, most of the larger binders do participate in this professional organization. The binder should use the ANSI/NISO/LBI standards for materials and procedures. These standards describe the quality of materials and the appropriate procedures that should be used to preserve library materials.

Binders should provide sturdy boxes for shipments of materials to and from the libraries. Libraries should be able to schedule the intervals between shipments and the timing of the pickups and deliveries of shipments. Many libraries that bind large amounts of materials request that binders pick up shipments from them every three to four weeks.

The turnaround time between the pickup and the delivery of shipments is crucial. Most commercial binders return shipments within three to four weeks. Many binders offer rush services for a small number of items, returning the materials within a week. This rush service may be more expensive and should be used judiciously.

Some binders pick up and deliver shipments themselves, while others use commercial shipping companies. Whichever method is used, the service must be reliable. The shipments must be picked up and delivered according to the established schedule and the materials must not be damaged in shipping.

Some binders offer a wide choice in the quality and colors of the cloth used for binding, while others offer only a few choices. Some binders provide a few colors they use as the default colors for most binding but offer other colors for a higher cost.

Most large binders have computerized systems that record the instructions previously used to bind volumes of serials. These binders provide libraries with software that is installed on the libraries' computers allowing data to be exchanged over the Internet. Many of these systems can produce binding instruction slips or lists of items included in specific shipments; libraries can include this information with the shipments as well as transmit the information to the binderies electronically. Some of these automated systems also can interface with the libraries' integrated library systems. These bindery databases may allow libraries to compile lists of shipments and track expenditures. Libraries with large amounts of binding should ask about the binder's automated services; these systems can eliminate the need to enter data about each title annually when another volume is bound.

Binders vary not only in their fees but also in how the charges are calculated. Some binders charge a flat fee for binding and labeling any item that is within a specified size range. Other binders charge separate fees for each line of lettering. Most binders charge more for items that are very large. The cost for gluing items is usually lower than the cost of sewing an item. Librarians must review the complete list of fees carefully.

Even the most skilled binders may occasionally damage or lose an item. Librarians must ask whether the binder will pay for the item or replace it.

Libraries must consider what types of services they will use most frequently, review the fees for those services, and evaluate the services offered by the binders when selecting the company for their organization.

Preparing Materials for Binding

Staff frequently identify items that need to be bound when the books are returned after being circulated. Some libraries bind journals as soon as the last issue in a volume arrives. Bindery staff may review the shelves to find serials that are ready to be bound. Automated systems can generate lists of serials that are usually bound at a specific time of the year; bindery personnel can then verify that the volumes are complete.

Items that are received in the bindery section should be checked out to the bindery as soon as possible. The records should show that the items are in the bindery and show the dates when the items are expected to be returned to the shelves. Inevitably, a patron will be looking for an item that has just gone to the bindery, and public services personnel need to be able to tell the patron when the item will return. In some cases, the patron may be able to use the material if it has not yet left the building; if that is not possible, and the item will not be available for weeks, the patron should be encouraged to obtain the item through interlibrary loan.

In larger libraries, personnel may review the books and new journals before the items are sent to the bindery. In some cases, purchasing a new edition or a reprint of a book may be preferable to rebinding a heavily used title because the newer printing may last longer than a re-bound version if the paper is of better quality. Some books may no longer be needed or may not be worth the cost of rebinding, and personnel may decide to discard them rather than rebinding the items. Selectors may decide that fragile items that cannot be bound may be replaced, reformatted, discarded, or boxed.

Staff should put serial issues in order, including the index, and verify that all issues are present. If any issues are missing, staff may attempt to replace the missing issues or may tell the binder to bind the volume even though issues are missing. Acquisitions may attempt to replace issues from the publisher or from dealers specializing in missing issues. The incomplete volume may be held in the bindery section or returned to the circulating shelves. If the issues are held in the bindery, patrons must be allowed to use them and then return them to the bindery. Issues that are returned to the circulating shelves may receive more damage, and other issues may become missing; libraries must decide which approach works best for their patrons. If volumes are bound incomplete, the bindery must insert a page in place of the missing issue that states the issue was missing when the volume was bound; this step eliminates questions from frustrated readers about apparent binding mistakes.

Staff must decide how many issues of periodicals should be bound in one physical item, which color of binding should be used, and how the title and call number should appear on the spine of the volume. After these decisions are made, the library staff and the binderies will retain this information in order to follow the same pattern when later volumes of the titles are to be bound.

Commercial binders will also collate the serials issues when the issues are received. Some binders will check each item page by page, but this step often costs an additional fee. Binders will return incomplete materials to the libraries. Libraries should check materials before they ship them to their binders to minimize such returns.

If any items require special handling, the library staff must identify them for the binder and include special instructions. Staff should point out any items that need pockets made in the bound volume or folded illustrations that will require special attention.

The library should list all items in the shipment, and the library's circulation system should show that the items are checked out to the bindery to verify what was included in each shipment.

Most binders provide sturdy boxes that are reused for each shipment. Staff should pack the boxes carefully to avoid damaging the materials. The boxes should be full, with packing materials around the edges if needed, to minimize shifting.

Receiving Bindery Shipments

When boxes return from the bindery, library staff should open them carefully. Because boxes are usually full, staff must be careful to cut through the tape but not into the contents.

The items must be matched against the list of items sent to the bindery to determine that all items have been returned. The invoice must be checked to ensure that all items are listed and that the prices are correct. When the invoice has been approved, staff should forward that bill to fiscal services for payment. If any items are missing, or any price is incorrect, bindery personnel must communicate with the binder immediately.

Personnel should review the quality of the work when the items are unpacked. The items should not have any glue spots, the fabric and paper should be smooth, all pages should be secure, the hinges should be tight, and the lettering should be correct. Personnel should report any problems to the binder immediately.

After the items are examined, the circulation records should be changed to indicate the items have been checked in, and the items must be returned to the shelves as quickly as possible.

Specifications for Binding Books

For many years, library binders dealt primarily with serials. As a result of serials cancellations and the growth in the number of serials available digitally, many libraries have reduced the number of serials subscriptions. Many libraries are now sending an increasing number of books to be bound or re-bound. Some libraries have all paperbacks bound when they are received. Many libraries are finding that heavily used books need to be re-bound to extend the life of the items for future readers. Some paperbacks published in foreign countries are published in bindings that will not withstand library use and must be bound to preserve the items.

Specifications for binding books should conform to the ANSI/NISO/LBI standard for library binding. A book or monograph, as defined by the standard, is "a single text block that can be bound without requiring the binder to match the spine lettering and/or color of cover to that of another volume" (NISO 2000, 2). If the book being re-bound is part of a set and the library wants it bound in a specific color to match the other volumes, that information must be included in the instructions to the binder.

When binding a book, the text block, which is the grouping together of the pages to be bound, is generally trimmed squarely and as little as possible to preserve the margin in case the book needs to be rebound at a later date. Libraries may specify that the edges not be trimmed at all; this no-trim option may result in slightly uneven edges but will preserve the margins and any information that is near the edges.

The width of the book may determine which binding method can be used. Double-fan adhesive binding cannot be used on items more than two inches thick. When very thick items need to be re-bound, the staff may request that the items be bound in two or more parts.

When a book is being bound, a case, which is the outside covering, is created separately. Cases consist of boards, the two firm pieces that form the front and back covers, the outside fabric covering, the inside lining, and the spine. The boards, spine, and fabric are cut to the appropriate sizes. The text block is attached to the case, and the lining papers are added. When the book is completed, all corners are neatly folded and covered by the lining. All edges should be even, the fabric should be smooth, and no glue should show.

Many spines are formed into a slightly rounded shape to provide space for the threads that are sewn through the spine and to allow the item to open flat. Books that have flat text blocks and spines, such as most paperbacks, may be re-bound with flat spines. Librarians should discuss the options of flat and rounded spines with their binders, as the different procedures may also dictate different costs.

Spines are lined in order to strengthen the spine and to preserve the volumes. The spine linings of volumes more than two and one-half inches thick and of items that have been sewn through the fold and are more than one and one-half inches thick should be reinforced with spine lining cloth or thick alkaline paper.

Most books are bound with the covers between one-sixteenth and three-sixteenths of an inch wider than the text block on all sides. Text blocks that are very heavy may be bound without this additional edge, binding the text block flush with the bottom of the covers. This method prevents the text block from sagging and pulling away from the spine when the items are properly shelved in an upright position. Librarians should ask binders about the options and costs of this technique of binding materials flush to the bottom.

Many varieties of fabric, boards, glues, and threads are available to bind materials, and new products continually emerge. The ANSI/NISO/LBI standard for library binding lists the technical specifications for materials that are currently approved for use and describes the process required to approve new materials.

Specifications for Binding Serials

Specifications for binding serials should conform to the ANSI/NISO/LBI standard for library binding. A serial or periodical, as defined by this standard, "is one or more serials issues that must be bound as a single unit. It requires the binder to match the spine-lettering pattern, color of cover, and color of stamping foil to other volumes having the same title. For the purpose of this standard, multi-volume monographs are considered to be periodicals" (NISO 2000, 2).

Binding of serials falls into two categories: first-time hardcover binding of paper-covered serials issues for library use, and rebinding of hardcover serials volumes for library use. Libraries bind serials in order to prevent the loss of individual issues since thieves have more problems stealing bound volumes than individual issues, to protect the issues from wear, to keep the shelves more organized, and to help patrons find the issues more easily.

Based on the library's specifications, the binder will use one of the five methods of leaf attachment: recasing, sewing through the fold, double-fan adhesive gluing, oversewing, or side sewing, all described below in the "Methods of Commercial Binding" section.

The basic procedures for binding serials are the same as those used for binding books; see the earlier sections "Preparing Materials for Binding" and "Specifications for Binding Books" for more information.

Methods of Commercial Binding

Once books arrive at the commercial binder, the bindery staff will inspect them for completeness and defects. Based on the library's specifications, the first step is to use one of five methods for attaching the pages, or "leaves," of a volume to each other. These methods include recasing, sewing through the fold, double-fan adhesive gluing, oversewing, and side-sewing. Some binders also offer a cheaper and less durable method known as economy binding. Deciding which method is best depends on the condition, size, paper, and original construction of the item, as well as the type of use that the item may receive. Libraries should specify what methods of binding are acceptable and ask their binders to inform them when the methods selected by the libraries are not appropriate for the items.

Recasing

Recasing is usually done when the text block is relatively undamaged and the original sewing thread is not broken. The old covers, spine lining, and adhesive are removed, new covers are created, and the new covers are then sewn onto the original text block.

Sewing Through the Fold

Items can be bound by sewing the signatures together one at a time. Each signature is sewn to the next signature, one at a time, to create the text block. This method is very strong and allows the bound volume to open well. Sewing through the fold may be done by hand or by special machines. This traditional method of binding is usually more expensive than other commercial binding techniques.

Double-Fan Adhesive

Double-fan adhesive binding uses adhesive to glue the pages together, creating the text block. The glue is applied to the pages, which are then fanned back and forth in order to spread the glue evenly on the edges to attach the pages to the adjacent pages. Some items with heavily coated or heavy paper may not be appropriate for this technique because the adhesive may not adhere properly. The method results in items that open flat, making photocopying easier. Because the margins do not have to be cut away or sewn, the items suffer less damage.

Oversewing

Materials that are bound using the oversewing technique are sewn through the inner margin. Unlike the method of sewing through the fold, oversewing is used to bind single pages rather than items created in signatures. This method reduces the margin and does not allow the items to open flat. Because the items are tightly bound, photocopying is difficult. This method works best for items that have wide margins, at least one-half inch, and flexible paper since stiff paper can be torn by sewing.

Sidesewing

Sidesewing can be done on items that are less than one-half inch thick. The items are stitched through the entire book rather than in sections. This method also requires that the items have wide margins and flexible paper.

Economy Binding

Some binders offer less expensive alternatives to the standard methods approved by the Library Binding Institute. These alternatives may include building covers directly on the text block; putting a plastic coating, such as Mylar, on the book covers; or using a lower grade of cloth for the covers. These methods may be appropriate for materials that will not be heavily used or will not be kept in a library's collection indefinitely.

Evaluating Binderies

Librarians should monitor the work of their binders to ensure that the companies are performing at an acceptable level. When shipments are returned from the binder, staff should examine the volumes for errors in labeling or mistakes in the binding. Librarians should track the turnaround time and the promptness of the deliveries. Any errors should be documented; while occasional mistakes will happen, any pattern of errors should be discussed with the binder and evaluated when contracts are being reviewed. Staff should monitor the invoices in order to identify any unexpected charges or changes in costs. The binder should follow the instructions of the library and adhere to the terms of the contract. If the binder uses automated software to manage the shipments, the program should be easy to install and to use. A more intangible factor is customer service; this may include responsiveness to questions, assistance in training staff, or provision of special services such as rush binding.

COMMUNICATION

Communication between library and binder is crucial. Librarians must make their expectations clear and work closely with binderies to ensure that the expectations can be met. If at all possible, staff should tour their bindery to learn how the work is done. Librarians must discuss any concerns with their binder to resolve potential problems quickly.

Librarians should provide clear records that show when items have been sent to the bindery and when they are expected to return. Patrons and public services will inevitably need a volume that has just gone to the bindery; they need to know when it will return. Staff responsible for sending materials to the bindery should discuss the schedule with public services staff. Some academic libraries send many journals to be bound at the beginning of a semester or quarter; this schedule allows materials to be available later when term papers are being written. Staff should also ask if any special programs will be held, such as a summer institute focusing on a topic such as linguistics; journals supporting such programs should not be sent to the bindery during that time.

TRAINING

Staff responsible for binding and mending operations have a number of resources available. If a commercial bindery is nearby, the staff should tour the operation. Information is available from several Internet sites, including LBI (http://www.lbibinders.org), the Northeast Document Conservation Center (http://www.nedcc.org), and Conservation OnLine (http://palimpsest.stanford.edu) (all accessed June 1, 2003).

CONCLUSION

"It is evident that the current level of expenditures by libraries on commercial library binding indicates the importance of binding as a preservation activity and a legitimate area for considered resource management. Unfortunately, this importance is not reflected in the managerial structure of most libraries, and decisions affecting the long-term stability of the collections and many thousands of dollars are still made by clerical staff with little knowledge of the needs of the user and only a perfunctory acquaintance with binding structures" (Dean 2000, 263–64). Binding operations that function well can preserve collections, improve the accuracy of shelving, help users find materials, and even reduce costs by reducing the number of replacement copies that must be purchased. Well-organized bindery and repair programs are a vital part of libraries' preservation and service operations.

REFERENCES

Association of Research Libraries. 2001. *ARL preservation statistics, 1997–98.* Washington, DC: Association of Research Libraries.

Campbell, Gregor R. 1994. Preservation. *The New Library Scene* 13 (October): 6.

Dean, John F. 2000. Commercial library binding. In *Preservation: Issues and planning,* edited by Paul N. Banks and Roberta Pilette. Chicago: American Library Association.

Evans, G. Edward. 2000. *Developing library and information center collections.* 4th ed. Englewood, CO: Libraries Unlimited.

Hamilton, Marsha J. 1993. *Guide to preservation in acquisitions processing.* Chicago: American Library Association.

Kenney, Anne R. 1993. The role of digital technology in the preservation of research library materials. In *Preservation of electronic formats and electronic formats for preservation,* edited by Janice Mohlhenrick. Fort Atkinson, WI: Highsmith Press.

Merrill-Oldham, Jan, and Nancy Carlson Schrock. 2000. The conservation of general collections. In *Preservation: Issues and planning,* edited by Paul N. Banks and Roberta Pilette. Chicago: American Library Association.

National Information Standards Organization (NISO). 2000. *Library binding.* Bethesda, MD: NISO Press.

Orr, James. 1996. Combining old world craftsmanship with new world technology: A quarter century of library binding in review, 1965–1900. In *Technical services management, 1965–1990: A quarter century of change and a look to the future: Festschrift for Kathryn Luther Henderson,* edited by Linda C. Smith and Ruth C. Carter. New York: Haworth Press.

Parisi, Paul A. 1999a. The making of the modern book. *The New Library Scene* 18 (2): 8–12, 17.

———. 1999b. Weighing the technical options. *The New Library Scene* 18 (3): 6–12.

Rebsamen, Werner. 1995. New directions for library binders. *The New Library Scene* 14 (1): 19–22.

Root, Trudie A. 1989. Inhouse binding in academic libraries. *Serials Review* 15 (3): 31–40.

Stankus, Tony. 1995. Binding is still good discipline. *Technicalities* 15: 1, 18–19.

Chapter 11

Outsourcing Acquisitions

Outsourcing became an extremely controversial topic among librarians in the late twentieth century. Numerous books, articles, and meetings describe outsourcing as either the salvation or the destruction of libraries. This chapter discusses what outsourcing is; why it is so controversial; how libraries can decide whether it is appropriate for them; and how to plan, implement, monitor, and evaluate outsourcing projects.

DEFINING OUTSOURCING

When the term "outsourcing" began to be used in the manufacturing and business arenas, it referred to the practice of hiring individuals to do specific tasks such as manufacturing parts used in automobiles or to do temporary clerical jobs outside the physical plant. The outsourced employees were not on the permanent payroll of the companies that contracted for their services. Hirshon and Winters (1996, 15) define outsourcing as "a method employed by an organization to hire or contract with an outside individual, vendor or agency to perform an operation or process rather than using in-house staff to accomplish the task." Outsourcing may also include privatization, which has been defined as "contracting out for services in a way that shifts control over policies for library collections and services from the public to the private sector" (Hill 2001, 220). When libraries outsource some functions, they retain control over the policies concerning the functions. When libraries are privatized, the outside companies control the policies and management.

Although the term "outsourcing" did not appear frequently in the library science literature until the 1990s, libraries have been outsourcing some operations for many years. Libraries have traditionally outsourced functions such as binding, security, or janitorial services. Libraries have purchased bibliographic information for about a hundred years, first purchasing cards from the Library of Congress and later purchasing electronic records from vendors. When vendors began producing indexes to periodicals in the late 1800s, libraries stopped indexing those periodicals. Many libraries began using approval plans in the 1970s, effectively outsourcing portions of their selection activities. Libraries that purchased large microform sets also purchased the bibliographic records for those titles, outsourcing the cataloging. Many libraries consolidated nearly all orders for serials or books with a few vendors, sending most orders to vendors that handled ordering, invoicing, and claiming for the libraries.

The use of outsourcing grew rapidly in the late twentieth century. Currently, the most common outsourcing programs are approval plans, which consolidate ordering of materials and cataloging. Library vendors have expanded their services from their traditional role of providing materials; many now provide a variety of outsourced services that include physical processing and cataloging.

All types of libraries have experimented with outsourcing of some type. In the 1980s and 1990s some entire libraries in federal agencies were privatized, turned over to commercial companies that operated the libraries for the government. This trend of privatization led to grave concerns among librarians who believed that the quality of service would decline and that the professionalism of librarianship would be compromised (Boss 1998, 565). Some federal libraries continue to be privatized, while the government once more operates others. Many public libraries purchase bibliographic records for their catalogs or use approval plans for portions of their collections. The major controversy in the public library community occurred in 1997 when the Hawaii State Library outsourced selection and processing activities in its public libraries. The Hawaii experiment failed disastrously for a number of reasons, many of which were unrelated to the usefulness of outsourcing; for more information on the Hawaiian experience, see the section later in this chapter. Some companies have outsourced their special libraries, hiring organizations to operate them; many other companies have outsourced specific functions such as acquiring and receiving their serials. Academic libraries have outsourced many functions ranging from approval plans to cataloging; some have outsourced entire departments, while others have outsourced selected functions.

THE CONTROVERSY ABOUT OUTSOURCING

Outsourcing became quite controversial in the late twentieth century, when entire library departments or functions were outsourced and when entire libraries or library systems were privatized. Some librarians believe that outsourcing can improve efficiency and save money. Others believe that outsourcing removes core functions from the library's control, destroys morale, and may actually increase costs. Still other librarians believe that outsourcing is an effective tool that may be appropriate in some cases. The disagreement has been apparent in discussions at the conferences of the American Library Association.

American Library Association's Statements

In 1997, the American Library Association (ALA) established the Outsourcing Task Force, charging it to gather data about outsourcing and to advise the ALA about outsourcing and related issues. In 1999, the Outsourcing Task Force recommended that a formal study be conducted on the impact of outsourcing and privatization on library services and management. The report was prepared by the School of Library and Information Studies of the Texas Woman's University (Martin 2000, 1). The report concluded, "We found no evidence that outsourcing *per se* represents a threat to library governance, or to the role of the library in protecting the First Amendment rights of the public.... In general, we found no evidence that outsourcing *per se* has had a negative impact on library services and management. On the contrary, the evidence supports the conclusion that outsourcing has been an effective managerial tool, and when used carefully and judiciously it has resulted in enhanced library services and improved library management. Instances where problems have arisen subsequent to decisions to outsource aspects of library operations and functions appear to be attributable to inadequate planning, poor contracting processes, or ineffective management of contracts" (Martin 2000, Executive Summary). The report recommends that the American Library Association should encourage the regular gathering of data that would document the extent of outsourcing, increase the regular discussion of outsourcing issues and trends in the ALA's journals, foster the development of guidelines and model contracts related to outsourcing, and encourage further research about the impact of outsourcing on library services and management (Martin 2000, 55).

The report was presented to the Council of the American Library Association in 2000. Those who viewed outsourcing and privatization as threats to the core values of professionalism and free access to service attacked the report. The Council received the report and agreed to ask the president of the ALA to identify methods of developing definitions that would clarify the difference between outsourcing and privatization and to bring together guidelines related to outsourcing that had been developed by groups within the ALA (Flagg 2000, 81–82).

In 2001, the ALA Council passed a policy that denounced privatization, affirming that "publicly funded libraries should remain directly account-able to the publics they serve" and that the ALA "opposes the shifting of policy-making and management oversight of library services from the pub-lic to the private, for-profit sector." People opposed to the policy said that such statements interfere with the right of libraries to decide what man-agement structures meet the needs of the individual libraries (American Library Association Council 2001).

The American Library Association continues to discuss and debate out-sourcing and privatization; no immediate resolution seems likely.

In Favor of Outsourcing

Supporters of outsourcing state that successful outsourcing projects save money by reducing personnel costs, increase flexibility by allowing personnel to be moved into more crucial areas of the organization, improve the efficiency of processing materials, and accomplish projects that cannot be done with existing staff. Supporters believe that outsourcing can help libraries operate more effectively by allowing them to focus on their pri-mary responsibilities.

Businesses and organizations in all areas are dealing with uncertain economic futures. The rapid economic growth of the twentieth century has faded, leaving most libraries facing budgets that receive small, if any, annual increases, while many other libraries must deal with budget reduc-tions. At the same time, libraries are being asked to provide more resources and services. Libraries must identify ways to work more effi-ciently, and many librarians believe that outsourcing is one solution.

Libraries needing to increase staff in public services areas or to reduce their personnel budgets often consider outsourcing as an alternative to maintaining their existing level of staffing in technical services. If vendors can do some functions, the library personnel responsible for those tasks might be retrained and transferred to other areas, or perhaps fired in order to reengineer the libraries' staffing. If the number of personnel is reduced, money paid for salaries, benefits, supplies, and computer access can be saved. "Outsourcing has earned a reputation for being cost efficient and has become an important as well as a necessary business strategy for reengineering the workplace" (Alvin 1999, 262).

Many libraries outsource tasks that they are unable to do. Libraries frequently hire vendors to convert card catalog records into machine-readable records for their online catalogs when the libraries do not have enough staff or time to do the project. If the libraries' personnel do not have specialized language skills needed to process some materials, libraries may hire vendors to process those materials. Libraries with very few personnel may decide to hire vendors to do the cataloging or to create lists of their electronic journals so that they may use their own personnel in public services.

Companies may be able to supply some services at less cost than what the libraries are spending to do the work; they also may be able to do the tasks more rapidly than the libraries are able to do them. In processing materials, libraries create bibliographic records for every title that is added. Vendors also create similar records; they can then sell those records to several libraries. Selling the records to multiple libraries allows vendors to distribute the costs, selling each record at a lower price than the amount that each library would spend to create the same record.

Some vendors operate large approval plan programs and also provide cataloging records; such companies can deliver current materials that are completely cataloged, marked, and labeled. In many cases, these materials can be received by libraries and sent directly to their shelves in a very short time. The process may take far less time than the libraries formerly required to order the materials, receive them, catalog them, and mark them.

Vendors may be able to perform tasks for a lower per-item cost than many libraries can because the vendors can save money on personnel costs. Vendors can employ staff without the restrictive civil service, union, or academic personnel policies that govern many libraries. They can demand higher levels of productivity and deal with personnel problems more readily than most libraries are capable of doing. Montgomery (1995, 66) writes that "outsourcing is a way of circumventing the difficult process of transforming an often resistant, entrenched and tradition-bound workforce into a more economically cost effective work unit."

Supporters believe that by outsourcing some functions, libraries can focus more attention on areas they have identified as priorities, save money, and provide better service.

Opposed to Outsourcing

Many librarians strongly oppose outsourcing because they believe it attacks the core foundations of library science, including public service and professional knowledge. Opponents say that the cost savings have not been proven and that the impact upon staff morale can be devastating.

They maintain that the statistics about improved productivity are inconclusive and contradictory. They feel that the quality of the product created by vendors is not as good as that produced by libraries. Opponents think that libraries that outsource major functions can no longer meet the special needs of their local patrons because those libraries surrender control over the process and products. They believe that extensive outsourcing leads to the loss of professional expertise and the abandonment of the responsibilities that form the philosophical basis of librarianship.

All vendors supply lists of their charges for physical processing and cataloging as well as of related costs. While establishing the costs vendors charge for processing is relatively simple, establishing the costs in libraries is more complicated. Some libraries determine costs by having staff keep diaries that show the time spent on each task. Others estimate costs per task by compiling the total personnel, supply, and computer costs for a function; this total is compared to the numbers of units produced to obtain a figure for processing each item. The figures vary widely among libraries, both because few standard methods of cost accounting exist and because cost analysis is not a strength of most librarians. "Cost management principles and techniques available for economic library management are among the weakest in the repertoire of library management" (Lawrence, Connaway, and Brigham 2001, 541). Most figures of cost savings resulting from outsourcing are estimates, and comparing them among libraries is meaningless.

Personnel who work in areas that are being outsourced are fearful that they will be fired or that they will not be able to deal with new responsibilities in other areas. Many businesses have used outsourcing as a method of closing units and firing employees. While this result is less common in libraries, many do use outsourcing as a method of reengineering in order to transfer technical services personnel into public services areas, or to maintain the same level of staffing in technical services while increasing staff in other areas of the libraries. Some libraries use outsourcing as a means of removing personnel or eliminating departments that refuse to change, are unproductive, or that the administration considers difficult to manage. This action should occur as a last resort; by using outsourcing to avoid dealing with difficult situations, the administration is abandoning its responsibilities to manage its organization. Personnel concerns about firing and reassignments are legitimate and must be acknowledged and addressed. Stress is an inevitable part of change, and restructuring assignments, transferring positions, and laying off personnel will cause a great deal of stress regardless of how well any outsourcing project may be managed.

When functions such as acquisitions or cataloging are turned over to vendors, libraries have less control of the procedures; other institutions now select materials and create the bibliographic records in the catalogs. If libraries do not retain experts in the areas being outsourced, they cannot evaluate the results of the outsourcing projects satisfactorily, and they cannot resume the activities easily if the projects should fail unexpectedly. The institutional memory of local practices and history vanishes.

The debate over the impact of outsourcing on the profession of librarianship is emotionally charged because it involves disagreement about the core values of librarianship. The most intense opposition is to the outsourcing of entire library systems or major functions. Outsourcing may turn some library operations into "generic commodities" that can be easily purchased (Schneider 1998, 66). "When libraries outsource functions that are core to the essence of librarianship, they send a message about the field itself, and contribute to a spiral of lessened expectations for the profession, for those who practice it, and those they serve" (Hill 2001, 229). In discussing the possibility of outsourcing all selection activities, Cassell states, "Outsourcing all your selection really is abdicating your role as a librarian" (Flagg 2000, 82).

Outsourcing as a Tool

As the denunciations and praises of outsourcing continue, a third opinion has gradually developed. Some librarians maintain that outsourcing is neither the destruction nor the salvation of libraries, but a tool; when properly managed, outsourcing can help librarians improve their productivity and their services. "Outsourcing should be viewed like any other strategic business move: as a way to lower costs while improving (or at least not sacrificing) quality, and as a means to better concentrate and support core services" (Ogburn 1994, 364). Outsourcing cannot solve every problem; it is one possible solution that should be considered as an option when libraries evaluate their missions and services. "Part of the problem seems to be a continuing tendency to rely more on feelings than on solid data, and a consistent talking at cross-purposes: those in favour of outsourcing tend to look at cost and efficiency, while those opposed tend to discuss quality issues. Perhaps if some more rigorous study of the former could be combined with similar analysis of the later, the profession would be in a better position to decide when, if ever, and what, if anything, to outsource" (Sweetland 2001, 173).

Outsourcing is a complex process that requires a great deal of planning; the projects must be monitored and evaluated by libraries. When outsourcing is a means to improve services and when it is planned and managed effectively, libraries can carry out their missions more effectively, using outsourcing as one of many management resources.

WHY SHOULD LIBRARIES OUTSOURCE?

If outsourcing can be complex and controversial, why are many libraries doing it? Some libraries use outsourcing as a way to deal with major changes in their budgets, while others use it as a means of improving services. Many libraries face the need to provide more services without budget increases; many others are dealing with reductions in their budgets. A few libraries are receiving funding increases or are receiving support to establish new branch libraries in their systems. Libraries that must try to do more things with fewer resources, as well as those libraries dealing with major expansions, must examine their operations and search for ways to improve their efficiency. Institutions opening new libraries may hire vendors to provide "opening day collections," by which is meant that vendors supply all the materials, completely processed and ready for shelving. Libraries that have reduced their staff may investigate outsourcing as a means to accomplish the work they can no longer afford to do. New administrators and new personnel frequently review the existing structure and procedures; they may propose outsourcing for some functions. When libraries acquire new integrated library systems, all procedures may be reviewed, and outsourcing some functions may be considered. All types of libraries desire to be efficient; they must provide the best service possible when many people believe that all materials are available for free over the Internet. Outsourcing can be a tool that helps improve the efficiency of libraries.

Outsourcing may enable libraries to hire companies to do some tasks at lower costs than the libraries were paying. Outsourcing can result in greater flexibility in the way libraries use their personnel by allowing them to transfer the staff whose work was outsourced into other areas. Outsourcing limited or one-time projects can eliminate backlogs and improve service by making materials available to the libraries' users. Vendors can catalog large backlogs of materials that libraries have been unable to process.

Outsourcing can allow libraries to focus on their mission and core functions while contracting with vendors to do those tasks that are necessary but not central to the identity of the library. A major challenge for libraries considering outsourcing is defining what their core functions actually are.

WHAT FUNCTIONS MIGHT BE OUTSOURCED?

Organizations are defined by their functions; each institution performs some basic role that identifies its character. Such primary functions are referred to as "core competencies" in the business literature. "These activities, called core competencies, are essential to the identity of the organization and if taken away would eliminate the need for the company to be in business" (Bénaud and Bordeianu 1998, 6). Core activities are directly related to the mission and priorities of the organizations and are generally not outsourced, or are at most partly outsourced. For example, selection may be a core activity, but a library may outsource portions of selection by using an approval plan while maintaining other selection activities in the library.

Outsourcing is common in many areas of technical services. Examples of outsourcing include approval plans and consolidating orders with vendors in acquisitions; shelf-ready processing and retrospective conversion in cataloging; and microfilming and digitization in preservation. Some special libraries outsource their serials collections: vendors receive the serials issues, enter the libraries' databases, check in the issues, mark them, and send them to the libraries. Outsourcing of the cataloging functions is frequently proposed because the costs of cataloging are perceived as very high, the processing of materials is believed to be too slow, and the cataloging standards are seen as too rigid and too removed from public services (Bénaud and Bordeianu 1998, 91). Outsourcing in acquisitions frequently involves approval plans, cataloging purchased from approval vendors, and consolidation of orders with vendors.

Libraries must examine their mission and goals to identify which functions they must do themselves and which ones might be candidates for outsourcing. Activities they identify as secondary to the organization's main purpose may be candidates for outsourcing. "Many libraries have realized that after years of trying to be all things to all people, they can serve their community and patrons better if they focus their energies on a service-oriented agenda" (Alvin 1999, 266). If secondary functions are outsourced, libraries can concentrate their resources on core functions.

The problems begin to arise when libraries start to identify which activities are core and which are secondary. Some librarians assert that the core activities of most libraries are reference, circulation, interlibrary loan, and collection development (Boss 1998, 566–67). These activities require knowledge of the library's users and collection at a depth that cannot be expected of most vendors. Others believe that cataloging should be considered a core function because it is central to the mission of providing access to materials. Core functions vary among libraries; cataloging unique materials is frequently a core function of research collections, but smaller libraries may be able to outsource their cataloging in order to concentrate on the functions that are central to their mission. "In essence, the business of technical services is to enable library users to locate and obtain the information they need quickly and easily. Viewed in this way, it becomes clearer that our functions are not the same as our purpose, and that some of our functions are not truly core services" (Hirshon and Winters 1996, 6). Each library must identify its mission and its core functions before deciding which functions it can evaluate for outsourcing.

WHEN SHOULD OUTSOURCING BE CONSIDERED?

Outsourcing should be a management tool, not a goal. The starting point is a review of existing procedures; personnel should evaluate what is being done and ask whether the procedures meet the goals of the units. Libraries should review all procedures frequently to ensure that the processes are still necessary. Procedures can take on a life of their own; an operation may be done because the process was needed in the past or because a former staff member wanted it. Personnel must examine such procedures to see whether they are still useful or necessary. This type of ongoing evaluation differs in scope from the examination that may lead to outsourcing.

Libraries considering outsourcing usually are conducting a major review of their processing operations. The process may be part of an evaluation of all operations, or it may be part of a reengineering review of technical services. Reengineering is a method of analyzing all procedures to identify ways of improving operations; the review frequently examines all processes from the beginning of the selection process through the final cataloging and marking steps. The personnel conducting the review must start with the goals and mission of the library as the foundation of their work. They must then look at the operations in order to decide which functions are organizational priorities. Personnel may discover ways to improve operations considerably by eliminating some procedures or by revising the flow of materials. A thorough review may lead to improvements in efficiency, eliminating the need to outsource functions, or may lead to the proposal to outsource some functions. Outsourcing projects frequently involve many different areas of an institution; libraries must plan, implement, and evaluate the projects carefully.

PLANNING OUTSOURCING PROJECTS

After libraries have decided to outsource some operations, they must decide exactly what functions will be outsourced and how the process will be implemented. The most important factor in the process is communication. Inadequate communication will lead to delays, unsatisfactory results, or complete failure. The libraries must review their decisions as the process develops and revise the decisions as necessary. Libraries must establish their expectations of the outsourcing process and identify the criteria that will be used to evaluate the results. Librarians should have a clear understanding of the objectives of the project; these objectives should be the basis of the implementation and evaluation of the project.

Planning major projects requires considerable time; libraries must assign staff to do the planning and must allow sufficient time for the process. Libraries must identify the people who will have the authority to decide whether to implement an outsourcing project. The libraries must also identify the people who will be responsible for managing the project. The library and the institutional administration must support the outsourcing project and be prepared to commit the staff, time, and money required to make it successful.

Who Must Be Involved in Planning Outsourcing Projects?

All areas involved in the tasks being outsourced should be involved in the planning process. The challenge to those organizing the project is to identify all the areas that are affected. Outsourcing involves far more areas than the units doing the tasks being considered for outsourcing.

The administration of the library and its institution must be fully informed of the proposal to outsource some functions if the decision to outsource was not an administrative directive. Outsourcing frequently results in changes in personnel assignments, legal contracts with companies, and changes in the manner in which expenses are charged. The administration must know what results are expected in order to plan for the implementation of outsourcing. Outsourcing frequently requires additional money at the beginning of the process. Although cost savings might be realized after outsourcing is fully operational, that may not happen for many months; the administration must find the funds to pay for the expenses from the start of the process.

Outsourcing may result in the transfer of personnel among departments and change in job assignments. The personnel and human resources departments of the libraries and their institutions must be closely involved, especially in organizations that have civil service, union, or personnel structures that restrict reorganization. When job reassignments are proposed, the impact upon salaries must be reviewed. In some organizations it will be impossible to reassign personnel without the approval of the human resources department. Libraries should develop a preliminary plan describing what personnel changes are under consideration and work with their respective human resources departments to achieve proposals that are acceptable to the library management, the personnel involved, and the human resources departments.

Libraries may select companies that were not previously under contract to the library. Outsourcing will change financial procedures because the methods in which some services are charged may be changed. Libraries may be required to request proposals or bids for the services that will be outsourced. These possibilities require that the fiscal services and purchasing units of the libraries and the institutions participate in planning outsourcing projects. The fiscal services units may need to establish new companies as institutional vendors or to create new categories in the budget in order to track the expenses for outsourcing. A formal bid process may involve the organizations' purchasing and legal departments and may take months to complete.

Few library processes are completely independent; materials progress through a series of steps. The operations of each unit depend on the information provided in prior steps. When libraries consider outsourcing an operation, they must determine what impact the outsourcing will have on the steps taken both before and after the activities being considered for outsourcing. For example, if a library plans to change an approval plan into an automatic purchase plan that supplies shelf-ready materials, it must consider that the collections budget must pay for items that would have been rejected on approval. Although some implications are obvious, others will not be identified without the involvement of personnel in all areas working with the materials. Involving personnel from a wide range of departments in the planning will reduce the number of unanticipated problems when outsourcing begins.

The units currently doing the processes that are to be outsourced must be actively involved in the planning. The personnel in those areas are the experts who can describe what steps are being done and why they are necessary. Such personnel have the technical knowledge needed to define the requirements that will be supplied to the vendor; they must be involved in the process from the beginning to ensure that all crucial elements are included.

If the personnel in the units being outsourced are not involved in the planning, they may become concerned about the possibility of firings, layoffs, and job transfers. The increased stress can damage morale and reduce productivity. Managers must include these personnel in the planning and communicate continuously with them; if managers fail to communicate well, any project may fail rapidly. "One of the most common reasons for the failure of outsourcing ventures is the failure to manage change, to recognize that time must be allowed for staff to understand what will occur and why, to build strong lines of communications between all players (vendors, managers, and staff), and to offer empathy and respect to those caught in the throes of rapid change" (Wallace 1997, 163).

Creating an Outsourcing Committee

Libraries planning to outsource a function generally establish a group to create the plan and implement the decisions. The committee must include representatives from the major areas involved. The group needs a leader who can encourage all members to participate and also can ensure that work does not get stalled. When a planning process degenerates into endless meetings without any results, the process fails. Some personnel may see the group discussions as a way to delay or stop outsourcing; the chair and other members of the committee must ensure that the committee continues to make progress. The chair of the committee must invite communication, set timelines, and guide the group to a conclusion. The committee should set the criteria that will be used to evaluate the success of the project; those criteria should be established at the beginning of the project so that the personnel can gather the necessary data throughout the process. The committee is responsible for planning the project and leading the implementation process; its members must be willing to make decisions and take risks.

Gathering Information

Personnel must begin the process of outsourcing by learning what procedures exist in their library. It may be helpful to diagram the flow of materials through the entire process from ordering through cataloging and marking. The procedures of the unit that may be outsourced should be analyzed in detail. As libraries identify existing procedures, personnel must evaluate what steps could be taken to make the processes more efficient, less expensive, or more effective. While reviewing the workflow, libraries may identify ways to streamline operations and improve efficiency. At this point, libraries may decide that sufficient improvements may be made within the library, making outsourcing unnecessary. Libraries considering outsourcing must investigate their options and the processes involved. In addition to consulting the numerous articles and books written about outsourcing, librarians can consult with their colleagues and attend meetings held by library associations. The electronic discussion lists dealing with acquisitions, serials, and cataloging frequently include questions and information that can help librarians investigating outsourcing. Vendors can provide information about their services as well as references from libraries using the vendors' services. Services and options change rapidly; librarians must work closely with colleagues and vendors to gather and analyze current data.

Analyzing Costs

Libraries considering outsourcing as a way of reducing costs must analyze their current costs and the costs involved in outsourcing. "There is no guarantee that outsourcing will reduce costs. If a library is highly efficient, or if the outsourcing vendor is inefficient, it is possible that outsourcing will increase costs. The problem for most libraries is that they do not know their costs. The only way to determine whether cost savings can be realized is to undertake a cost study of the in-house activity" (Boss 1998, 567).

The two primary methods of analyzing libraries' costs are cost analysis and cost allocation. The cost analysis method tries to measure the time required to accomplish specific tasks. Staff may be asked to keep track of their time by recording what they do in segments that may range from fifteen minutes to an hour. The data are analyzed to determine how much time is required for specific tasks. This method is only as accurate as the data provided by the staff; when people are required to track their activities closely, they may minimize time spent on breaks or in conversation and maximize time spent working. Personnel who have multiple assignments, such as acquisitions personnel who also work at a reference station, must track their time carefully. Tracking takes time, and may be resented by employees who are already overworked, as well as by those who feel that such tracking is part of a management plan to assign additional work to the employees. The cost allocation method takes all costs spent on a task and compares that figure to the number of items produced (Lawrence, Connaway, and Brigham 2001, 542–43). The cost figures may include salaries, fringe benefits, supplies, and computing costs. Some libraries may be able to identify costs for telephone lines and for space as well. After gathering the data and determining what their cost to process each item is, libraries can compare their costs with the costs charged by vendors for the same procedures. Hirshon and Winters (1996, 42–47) provide examples of spreadsheets that can be used to compare the costs of outsourcing with the costs of processing materials by the libraries.

Most figures used in analyzing costs are estimates; they are useful for comparison purposes, but they are not absolute figures that can be used for budgeting the precise expenses of outsourcing. Vendors may change prices between the initial request for information and the final bid. Libraries may discover some added steps that need to be included in the outsourcing work, which may increase the price. Libraries may decide that they should overestimate the costs of outsourcing slightly when doing the initial cost analysis in order to avoid unfortunate surprises at a later time when costs increase unexpectedly. All these considerations tend to make the estimates less concrete, making precise budgeting very difficult.

REQUESTS FOR PROPOSALS

Some libraries may be required to issue requests for proposals (RFPs) for outsourcing projects. RFPs are sometimes generically called "bids"; however, bids may also refer to the request-for-quote process in which only the price, not the service, is considered. RFPs are documents that describe the services needed by the institution; the documents are sent to companies capable of providing the desired services. Companies send their proposals to the institutions, which then award legal contracts to the companies presenting the best proposals.

Institutional Requirements

Librarians must learn the requirements of their governing institution. Some organizations require that RFPs be sent out for any products and services costing more than a specific amount, such as $5,000, while others may not require them for services at all. Librarians must work with their organization's legal and purchasing offices to learn what the regulations are. Some organizations will assign personnel from their purchasing office to work with the libraries when RFPs are required.

Identifying Vendors

Librarians can identify vendors by asking colleagues for recommendations and by consulting reference lists such as AcqWeb (http:// acqweb.library.vanderbilt.edu, accessed June 1, 2003). Libraries may wish to invite some vendors to give presentations to the staff in order to gain more knowledge of what services are available. Vendors should have experience and knowledge of their fields, strong customer service, reasonable costs, quality control, and the willingness to improve their services as new technology becomes available.

Writing RFPs

Libraries frequently create a committee or task force to write the RFP, work with the institutional purchasing office, and evaluate the proposals. Librarians writing the RFP must identify which factors they require the vendors to supply and which factors would be desirable but not absolutely required. The group writing the RFP must establish a time line that specifies when the requests will be sent to the potential vendors, when the responses are to be sent to the libraries, and when the decisions will be made. The review process must be confidential and unbiased; all responses must be evaluated fairly.

Contents of the RFP

Most bids contain two types of information: one, legally required statements describing what financial information must be supplied and clauses about termination and payment (sometimes this standardized information is called a "boilerplate"), and two, a description of the actual service or services being requested by the library. Librarians must describe their specific needs in the RFP. Many vendors have created packages of services, but these may not meet the needs of libraries.

The specific description included in the RFP will vary with the type of service being requested. If libraries are requesting proposals for an approval plan, they will request information about such factors as pricing, invoicing, coverage of publications, automated services, and the time required to provide materials. When libraries are requesting proposals for specialized services such as microfilming or digitization, they will ask about such factors as the vendors' equipment and staffing. Libraries requesting proposals for cataloging services will want to know what level of cataloging can be provided, what types of materials will be cataloged, whether the vendors' systems are compatible with those of the libraries, and what the costs will be for all steps in the process. Libraries requesting proposals to consolidate their serials subscriptions or monographic purchases will ask for information about service charges or discounts, the types of materials that can be supplied, the types of materials that the vendors cannot provide, and the automated services available.

Criteria for Evaluating the Proposals

Libraries must establish the criteria they will use to award the contract. The task force should establish specific factors that can be evaluated, such as the vendors' ability to work with the library's automated systems or the vendors' costs for each desired service. All personnel reviewing the bid responses should evaluate the vendors fairly. The task force may ask library personnel who are not task force members to review the responses; diverse views can help identify strengths or weaknesses of the proposals.

References

Libraries should request that vendors supply references; the organizations providing the references should be similar in size, budget, and mission to the libraries requesting the proposals. Librarians should ask for references that use the same type of integrated library system; network compatibility is a crucial factor in the success of any project involving automation.

Legal Requirements

Requests for proposals are legal agreements. The documents should include definitions of key terms, the responsibilities of the vendors and the libraries, and a description of what is being supplied. Libraries must include clauses that allow for termination if a vendor's performance falls below criteria that are detailed in the bids or if the library's needs change considerably. The contracts should also include enough flexibility to allow some mutually agreed-upon changes without having to rewrite the entire document. Many institutions issue contracts that cover one year, with an option of renewing the contract for additional years if both parties are satisfied with the arrangement. Librarians must be aware of the length of the contract period and of the number of renewals that are allowed. Most organizations expect that libraries will initiate the procedures to renew a contract or the process of issuing a new RFP. For more information about the bid process, please see chapter 4, "Domestic and Foreign Vendor Selection and Evaluation."

IMPLEMENTING OUTSOURCING PROJECTS

Outsourcing will cause changes in procedures, workflow, and staffing assignments. While many changes can be anticipated, unexpected results are inevitable. Personnel must remain flexible and must work with their colleagues and with vendors to resolve any problems. Outsourcing will result in some loss of control; vendors will not handle all materials exactly as the library might have done. The library must decide which differences are acceptable and which must be corrected. Frequent communication between library and vendor is crucial to the success of an outsourcing project.

As with any new operation, training is essential, and outsourcing requires training on a variety of levels. Procedures will need to be adjusted as outsourcing is integrated into a library's workflow. Library staff working on the outsourced project must be trained, of course. Vendors may supply training materials or may send representatives to the library to train the staff. The library must teach the vendors what it expects of them. If staff are being reassigned, they must be trained for their new assignments. As procedures are revised and the outsourcing project is refined, training must continue. Training, like communications, must be continual and systemwide.

EVALUATING OUTSOURCING PROJECTS

To evaluate the success of an outsourcing project, librarians must have a clear understanding of the original purposes of the project and must identify how success will be identified. Defining at the beginning of the process the criteria they will eventually use to evaluate the project identifies the data that will be needed for the evaluation. If the criteria are identified at the end of the process, the library may discover that the necessary data were not collected, making evaluation difficult, if not impossible. Librarians must evaluate the project using specific data and criteria, not by considering personal preferences.

If cost reductions were a major goal of outsourcing, the library must update its spreadsheets to determine whether the expected savings were achieved. Other criteria might include improved service, which could be demonstrated by reducing the time required to process materials, or a reduction in staffing.

The library must evaluate the quality of the vendors' work. If the work is not acceptable and must be redone by the library, the library does not save money or time. Librarians must identify and document errors. Librarians and the vendors must agree on what constitutes errors and what are differences of interpretations of procedures or cataloging rules. The library should track delivery times and the time required to process materials. "Professional librarians must continue to be the liaison between the vendor and the library. This is a crucial component for the ongoing success of our current outsourcing operations, and librarian expertise will be required in the consideration and planning of further outsourcing projects" (Propas and Johnson 1998, 285).

Librarians should gather information from personnel working on the outsourcing project, from personnel who deal with the vendors, and from those who work with the materials processed by the vendors.

COMMUNICATION

The importance of communication cannot be overstated. The committee responsible for implementing the project must keep all involved personnel informed at all stages. The committee should also apprise the entire library of the general progress and results of the implementation.

Because acquisitions obtains materials and delivers them to other units, any outsourcing done by acquisitions affects other departments, and outsourcing done by other departments affects acquisitions. "Because of this double impact, close communication, cooperation and collaboration must be maintained among all the departments involved" (Bénaud and Bordeianu 1998, 89).

Communication between the library and the vendor is equally vital. The library may wish to identify one or two people to be official spokespeople with the vendors. These individuals should consult with vendors about any problems or concerns as they occur. A vendor cannot work with the library to correct problems if the library has not informed it that problems exist.

IMPACT ON STAFF

Outsourcing may affect staff in many ways ranging from enthusiasm to despair. Librarians must work closely with personnel, involve them in the planning process, and keep them informed of progress. Many personnel find change difficult to cope with, and managers must try to help people deal with the rapid and dramatic changes that may result from outsourcing. Personnel management is always complex, and outsourcing may increase the level of difficulty for managers. "People whose jobs are outsourced often feel displaced, disoriented, fearful, and quite possibly very angry. Other employees whose jobs may not be directly affected may become fearful that their jobs will be next" (Hirshon and Winters 1996, 143). In other libraries, outsourcing may have a more positive impact. "Outsourcing may break organizational bottlenecks and may eliminate barriers between library departments" (Bénaud and Bordeianu 1998, 28). Some staff may find that outsourcing provides a welcome opportunity to learn new skills and expand their responsibilities (Carter 1997, 13). The impact of outsourcing will depend on the skill of the library's management, the size and nature of the work being outsourced, and the ability of the staff to deal with challenges (Hirshon and Winters 1996, 144).

CONSIDERATIONS AND CAUTIONS

Unexpected events occur regardless of the experience of the vendors or the libraries; no one anticipates every possibility. Excellent communication will minimize problems, but unforeseen things will happen. To deal with such possibilities, libraries need to maintain the expertise in the library to resolve concerns and to evaluate the project. For example, if all cataloging is being outsourced, the library will still need catalogers who can evaluate the quality of the work provided by the vendor. When acquisitions is being outsourced, some funds will need to be retained for discretionary purchases; no bookseller can provide all materials in all areas.

The library must monitor the project carefully. The quality of work may vary between vendors; the outsourced work must meet the standards set by the library. Vendors merge or disappear; changes in corporate ownership can result in differences in service. As budgets change, the library may need to revise the amount of materials received. When a library begins an outsourcing project, it needs to monitor the project carefully; after the project is well established, the library may be able to evaluate it by doing occasional random checks.

SUCCESSFUL AND UNSUCCESSFUL OUTSOURCING PROJECTS

Outsourcing acquisitions began to increase in the 1970s with the development of approval plans; outsourcing cataloging in academic libraries began to develop rapidly in the 1990s when Wright State University outsourced its entire cataloging department. Many libraries have begun outsourcing since then. The success or failure of an outsourcing project depends upon the goals of the project; no universally accepted standards can be used to evaluate projects and compare them against each other.

Wilson and Colver (1997, ix) invited librarians to present case studies of successful outsourcing programs. The libraries included academic, special, and public libraries; the projects ranged from very small ones to large ones. Many of these libraries reported that they saw considerable savings in costs or in processing time; others gained increased flexibility in staffing. All the successful projects shared two factors: librarians or the library staff realized that outsourcing is a complex process, and they saw the relationship between the library and its vendor become much closer than it had been in the past (x–xi). Successful projects depend on the desire of the library staff to make the project work and on the working relationship between the library and its vendor. Such successful projects may reduce costs considerably, improve processing time, improve service to patrons, and increase the flexibility in personnel staffing.

When planning, communication, and management are inadequate, any project will almost certainly fail. The failure of the Hawaii outsourcing project serves as a classic example of a project inevitably headed toward failure. "Too many changes within a relatively short time, with insufficient planning and poor internal communication, spelled doom." (Alvin 1999, 279). In the late 1990s, the state librarian of the Hawaii public library system was faced with a 25% reduction in the budget. As part of the solution, he decided to outsource acquisitions and processing. The staff of the library system were not significantly involved in the planning of the project, the selection of the vendor, or the implementation of the project. The vendor awarded the contract to select, acquire, and process materials did not have access to the system's catalog, and consequently it delivered materials that duplicated some items already owned by the libraries. The vendor was unable to deliver materials within the time specified in the original contract and failed to deliver sufficient materials about the region. The state librarian also arranged for new contracts with new vendors for a serials catalog and an online catalog. The acquisitions vendor and the library's staff were unable to communicate. The personnel of entire processing units were reassigned. The libraries continued to accept gifts but no longer had sufficient staff to process the materials. Numerous lawsuits were filed; the legislature investigated, the publicity reached the national press, and the project was canceled (Martin 2000, 29–31). The Hawaii project wasted time and money, resulted in poor publicity, and damaged reputations. The lack of intensive communication and planning, of careful review of an unbiased proposal process, and of realistic implementation plans all combined to turn the Hawaii experience into an excellent example of what to avoid in any project.

CONCLUSION

Outsourcing remains controversial for many librarians. The data documenting the success, or even the extent, of outsourcing projects remain inconclusive or nonexistent (Martin 2000, 19). Since the early 1990s, outsourcing has increased dramatically as many libraries have contracted with vendors to outsource some functions so as to save money, improve services, or allow the libraries to focus on core functions. Outsourcing is appropriate for some functions in some libraries; it is not a universal solution. Libraries should not look at outsourcing as a goal; it is a tool that may be useful in some instances. Outsourcing projects require thoughtful leadership, careful planning, extensive communication, continuous monitoring, and evaluation. Libraries considering outsourcing must discuss the issues existing at the core of the controversies about outsourcing. Underlying tensions caused by disagreements about the mission of the library, the identification of core functions, and the role of outsourcing can doom an outsourcing project from the very beginning.

Libraries must consider their needs, budgets, personnel, and vendors before initiating any outsourcing projects. Outsourcing can change the workflow, organizational structure, and roles of staff. Management must care about how outsourcing will affect personnel. Personnel must be flexible and willing to explore options created by outsourcing. Libraries must consider their responsibilities to other libraries and to the profession as well as their need to provide rapid service at the lowest possible costs.

The services offered by vendors continue to develop; librarians must learn about new possibilities by reading, monitoring electronic discussion lists, and talking with library colleagues and vendors. The relationship between librarians and vendors may not be an equal partnership since outsourcing involves the purchase of services, but outsourcing does require that librarians and vendors work very closely together.

When outsourcing is used as a means of improving services and managing budgets, it can be a useful tool. As with all complex procedures, librarians must plan, implement, and monitor outsourcing projects carefully. Outsourcing presents opportunities as well as challenges; successful outsourcing may improve service and reduce costs.

REFERENCES

American Library Association Council. 2001. 2001 Annual Conference. <http://www.ala.org> (accessed June 1, 2003).

Alvin, Glenda. 1999. Outsourcing acquisitions: Methods and models. In *Understanding the business of library acquisitions*. 2nd ed. Edited by Karen A. Schmidt. Chicago: American Library Association.

Bénaud, Claire-Lise, and Sever Bordeianu. 1998. *Outsourcing library operations in academic libraries: An overview of issues and outcomes.* Englewood, CO: Libraries Unlimited.

Boss, Richard W. 1998. Guide to outsourcing in libraries. *Library Technology Reports* 34: 557–680.

Carter, Kathy. 1997. Outsourced cataloging and physical processing at the University of Alberta Library. In *Outsourcing library technical services operations: Practices in academic, public, and special libraries*, edited by Karen A. Wilson and Marylou Colver. Chicago: American Library Association.

Flagg, Gordon. 2000. ALA Council: Core values, outsourcing dominate agenda. *American Libraries* 31 (8): 81–83.

Hill, Janet Swan. 2001. Outsourcing: Understanding the fuss. In *The Bowker annual: Library and book trade almanac.* 46th ed. 218–32. New Providence, NJ: R. R. Bowker.

Hirshon, Arnold, and Barbara Winters. 1996. *Outsourcing library technical services: A how-to-do-it manual for libraries.* New York: Neal-Schuman.

Lawrence, Stephen R., Lynn Silipigne Connaway, and Keith H. Brigham. 2001. Life cycle costs of library collections: Creation of effective performance and cost metrics for library resources. *College and Research Libraries* 62: 541–52.

Martin, Robert S. 2000. *The impact of outsourcing and privatization on library services and management: A study for the American Library Association.* Denton: Texas Woman's University School of Library and Information Studies.

Montgomery, Jack. 1995. Biz of acq: Outsourced acquisitions?—Let's meet the challenge. *Against the Grain* 7 (2): 66–68.

Ogburn, Joyce L. 1994. An introduction to outsourcing. *Library Acquisitions: Practice and Theory* 18: 363–66.

Propas, Sharon W., and Sue-Ellen Johnson. 1998. Outsourcing, quality control, and the acquisitions professional. *Library Acquisitions: Practice and Theory* 22: 279–85.

Schneider, Karen G. 1998. The McLibrary Syndrome. *American Libraries* 29 (1): 66–67.

Sweetland, James H. 2001. Outsourcing library technical services—What we think we know, and don't know. *Bottom Line: Managing Library Finances* 14 (3): 164–75.

Wallace, Pamela. 1997. Outsourcing book selection in public and school libraries. *Collection Building* 16: 160–66.

Wilson, Karen A., and Marylou Colver. 1997. *Outsourcing library technical services operations: Practices in academic, public, and special libraries.* Chicago: American Library Association.

Chapter 12

Professional Ethics

The terms "ethics," "values," and "morality" all refer to standards of behavior, but each has a slightly different meaning. Ethics has been defined as "the moral principles of right and wrong, good and bad, to which we as a profession have subscribed as a covenant between us as professionals and our clients, peers and society" (Zipkowitz 1996, 2). Robert Hauptman defines the term as "that branch of philosophy that deals axiologically with the interrelationship of human beings to each other, animals, the environment, and indeed all that exists in the universe" (Hauptman 1999, 1). Many other similar definitions exist, just as there are many definitions of values, morality, and professionalism, but for the purposes of this chapter, we will use Zipkowitz's definition of ethics. Gorman defines a value as "something that is of deep interest (often and quite reasonably self-interest) to an individual or a group" (Gorman 2000, 5). Morality implies "the sense of conscience and right and wrong that we derive from our upbringing. Morality is highly personal and functions instinctively" (Severson 1997, 7). This chapter does not discuss issues of ethics, morality, or values related to public services, reference, or censorship; those topics are not in the scope of the book, but the literature in those areas is extensive. The chapter focuses on the ethics and values that form the foundations of professional behavior among acquisitions personnel.

Why should a discussion of ethics or values matter in this book, or in the profession? Ethics affect our personal and professional decisions. Without consideration of the principles that guide one's behavior, an individual may not have an understanding of acceptable actions or be able to recognize when one is moving incrementally away from acceptable behavior. The topics of ethics and values have received increased attention in the late twentieth and early twenty-first centuries. The media continually bombard their audience with stories of corruption and serious ethical lapses, even at top levels of business and government. Discussions of values are useful because values are the "standards by which we can assess what we do; measure how near we are to, or how far we are from, an objective; and compare our actions and our state of being to those of others and to the ideals represented by our values" (Gorman 2000, 7). Such discussions may help teach those new to the field about the core philosophy of the profession and may illuminate values for those who are more experienced (Richards 2000, 88).

Individuals have many values and may hold differing standards of moral and ethical behavior. Explorations of ethical behavior in the profession of librarianship can help all personnel learn what behavior is expected of librarians by their colleagues and those who work with them. Most discussions of ethical lapses blame many of the failures on ignorance, thoughtlessness, and lack of organizational guidelines, with far fewer problems arising from egotism or deliberate misconduct (Goehner 1991, 81). Exploring ethical questions can reduce problems and improve relationships among colleagues and business associates. "The value of values...is that they point us toward what is important and worthy in the long run, and lift us out of our preoccupations with the mundane and the bureaucratic. They remind us that there is more to our work than this week's statistics, and that each day's decisions should advance our professional mission and not just help us get through our current heap of quandaries and hassles" (Finks 1989, 352).

THEORIES OF ETHICS AND VALUES IN LIBRARIANSHIP

Most research about librarianship has dealt with practical solutions to specific problems; however, some philosophical and theoretical studies have been done as well. One of the first major contributions to an ethical theory of librarianship was written by S. R. Ranganathan, who formulated five "laws" of librarianship in 1931: books are for use; every reader his or her book; every book its reader; save the time of the reader; and a library is a growing organism. These concepts still serve as a foundation for the philosophy that libraries exist to provide materials to all their users, guiding libraries more than seventy years after they were published (Ranganathan 1963, 9).

In the mid-twentieth century, Jesse Hauck Shera wrote about the nature and history of knowledge and about how library systems meet the needs of individuals and of societies. "The values that we can derive by inference from Shera's social epistemology are scholarship, stewardship, literacy and learning, service, and the good of society" (Gorman 2000, 21). Shera's emphasis on literacy and on improving the social environment became major themes in the philosophy of librarianship in the late twentieth century.

In 1967, Samuel Rothstein stated that librarians needed a "declaration of principles" that would include a statement of beliefs, values, and goals; a description of the skills that are special to librarianship; and an identification of the major issues facing librarians. His list of core values included the belief that reading is important; the belief that librarians can and should educate users and elevate the taste of the community by providing appropriate materials; a commitment to intellectual freedom; and a belief that libraries play an important role in providing users with all types of information. Rothstein identified the special skills of librarians as the abilities to develop and arrange collections, to find information for users, and to manage library operations effectively (Rothstein 1968, 157).

In 1989, Finks urged librarians to reexamine their values. His description of professional values as those values that are "inherent in librarianship" included service to the public, stewardship of collections and information, and a belief in the value of knowledge. Finks stated that values affect the way libraries function on a daily basis. "If, for example, we consistently apply the value of service, there are certain predictable outcomes—a more satisfied clientele and a higher efficiency in the use of our resources—that we may believe to be better than the outcomes of other decisions we could make" (Finks 1989, 356).

A decade later, Gorman (2000, 26–27) used the work of Ranganathan, Shera, Rothstein, and Finks to identify eight central values of librarianship: stewardship of information and of libraries; service to all individuals, communities, societies, and posterity; intellectual freedom; rational organization and management of libraries; literacy and learning; equitable access to knowledge, information, and services; privacy; and supporting the values of a democratic society. These values, according to Gorman, should form the foundation of library services.

CODES OF ETHICS

Many groups in the information sciences, such as the American Association of Law Libraries, the Society of American Archivists, and the American Society for Information Science, have published professional guidelines and ethical codes. Most such codes include a core group of professional values, such as intellectual freedom, protecting the privacy of users, intellectual property rights, professional neutrality, equity of access, preservation of the cultural record, patron service, and information literacy (Dole, Hurych, and Koehler 2000, 289). The American Library Association has adopted two major statements related to ethics, its *Code of Ethics* and its *Library Bill of Rights*.

American Library Association
Code of Ethics

First discussed in the 1920s, the *American Library Association Code of Ethics* has been revised regularly since then. The American Library Association Council adopted the latest revision in 1995. Jonathan A. Lindsey and Ann E. Prentice describe the history, development, and revisions of the code in *Professional Ethics and Librarians* (1985). The *ALA Code of Ethics* has always been a broad statement of ethical beliefs, which has led to considerable criticism by those who have wanted the code to be more specific. The code in use in the 1960s was criticized for being too general and for its lack of a statement describing the core values of librarianship (Rothstein 1968, 156–57). Although later versions of the code have included some more specific values, some librarians maintain that the code is still much too general. The eight principles of the *ALA Code of Ethics* issued in 1995 are as follows:

- We provide the highest level of service to all library users through appropriate and usefully organized resources; equitable service policies; equitable access; and accurate, unbiased and courteous responses to all requests.

- We uphold the principles of intellectual freedom and resist all efforts to censor library resources.

- We protect each library user's right to privacy and confidentiality with respect to information sought or received and resources consulted, borrowed, acquired or transmitted.

- We recognize and respect intellectual property rights.

- We treat co-workers and other colleagues with respect, fairness and good faith, and advocate conditions of employment that safeguard the rights and welfare of all employees of our institutions.

- We do not advance private interests at the expense of library users, colleagues, or our employing institutions.

- We distinguish between our personal convictions and professional duties and do not allow our personal beliefs to interfere with fair representation of the aims of our institutions or the provision of access to their information resources.

- We strive for excellence in the profession by maintaining and enhancing our own knowledge and aspirations of potential members of the profession. (American Library Association 1995)

As with previous versions, this code has been criticized for being very general, for not including a definition or a mission statement of librarianship, and for lacking any means of enforcement (Zipkowitz 1996, 4). During the discussions of the 1995 revision, the chair of the American Library Association's Committee on Professional Ethics stated that the code was intended to be the "broadest statement of those beliefs that are held in common" and that the committee believed the code should be voluntary. Since there is no national licensing board for librarians, enforcement of ethical standards becomes impossible (ALA Council actions 1995, 676).

The *Library Bill of Rights*

The *Library Bill of Rights*, first adopted by the American Library Association in 1948 and revised most recently in 1996, states the rights of library users and the obligations of librarians to their users. It reads as follows:

+ Books and other library resources should be provided for the interest, information, and enlightenment of all people of the community the library serves. Materials should not be excluded because of the origin, background, or views of those contributing to their creation.

+ Libraries should provide materials and information presenting all points of view on current and historical issues. Materials should not be proscribed or removed because of partisan or doctrinal disapproval.

+ Libraries should challenge censorship in the fulfillment of their responsibility to provide information and enlightenment.

+ Libraries should cooperate with all persons and groups concerned with resisting abridgment of free expression and free access to ideas.

+ A person's right to use a library should not be denied or abridged because of origin, age, background, or views.

+ Libraries which make exhibit spaces and meeting rooms available to the pubic they serve should make such facilities available on an equitable basis, regardless of the beliefs or affiliations of individuals or groups requesting their use. (American Library Association 1996)

American Library Association's Core Values

In 1999, the American Library Association's Core Values Task Force issued a draft statement titled "Librarianship: Core Values" and intended to supplement the *ALA Code of Ethics* and the *Library Bill of Rights.* Following are the proposed core values:

- The connection of people to ideas.
- Unfettered access to ideas.
- Learning in all of its contexts.
- Freedom for all people to form, to hold, and to express their own beliefs.
- Respect for the individual person.
- Preservation of the human record.
- Interdependence among information professionals and agencies.
- Professionalism in service to these values. (American Library Association 1999)

This draft was presented at the annual conference of the American Library Association in 2000. Some ALA Council members criticized the draft for being too brief; others questioned the need for such a document at all (Sager 2001, 149). The Council appointed a new task force to address the need for and content of a statement of core values. A report from the Core Values Task Force II is expected in 2003 (American Library Association Council 2001).

ETHICS IN ACQUISITIONS

Ethical behavior may involve four standards, according to Bushing (1993, 48): honesty, respect for people, professional integrity, and good business practices. These standards form the foundation for ethical behavior in acquisitions work. Initial discussions of ethics in acquisitions involved unethical actions related to the possible misuse of the acquisitions budget. In the early and middle twentieth century the amounts of money involved in most acquisitions operations seemed very small, leading to the belief that any profits would be insufficient to reward unethical behavior. For many years, most librarians and booksellers generally operated in a manner that did not involve formal legal documents even though the process of acquiring materials for an institution has always had an implied contractual relationship between buyer and seller. Many operations were based on informal agreements and personal relationships between librarians and vendors. Library budgets grew in the mid-twentieth century, society became more litigious, and these informal relations began to disappear. Formal contracts and bids became the norm, and professional ethics became a matter of increasing concern.

In 1984, the Professional Ethics Committee of the American Library Association presented a program about librarian-vendor relations at the ALA's annual conference. Vendors and librarians discussed their relationships with and expectations of each other. Some speakers stated that librarians were, in general, extremely ethical, and that the dinners, trips, and small gifts offered by some vendors were considered normal operating expenses by the business world. Speakers stressed the need for all parties to behave ethically as well as the need for all parties to act in the best interests of their organizations (Tyckoson 1984, 14). Many of the issues raised in the 1984 meeting would be addressed again during the following decade and would be incorporated into the 1994 codes developed by the ALA's Association for Library Collections and Technical Services and by its Acquisitions Section.

In his report of the 1984 meeting, Tyckoson (1984, 15) noted that there was little discussion of the fact that the majority of purchases made by libraries are controlled by only a few people who are responsible for acquisitions and systems purchases, and that therefore the opportunity for ethical abuses was increasing. Acquisitions librarians have control of one of the larger portions of a library's discretionary budget; they work with more businesses and more financial departments than do many other types of librarians, and they have more opportunities to behave unethically (Winters 1999, 340). The increased potential for abuse led to more concern about ethics and more structured business arrangements. Informal agreements between librarians and vendors became very rare; formal contracts became normal business requirements.

Another factor encouraging the development of ethical guidelines for acquisitions librarians has been the increasing prevalence of licensing contracts required to purchase or access electronic resources. Such licensing agreements are complex legal documents that may involve ethical issues of user privacy and corporate confidentiality. The legal requirements and the ethical concerns have become interwoven as librarians and vendors deal with these new contracts in their businesses. The negotiations among librarians, publishers, and vendors often involve issues related to ethical business practices as well.

Librarians are not only the financial stewards of institutional resources but frequently the supervisors of other employees. Supervisory responsibilities require knowledge both of what is legal and of what is right. Personnel policies and regulations have become increasingly complex, and ethical management is crucial in working with employees. Personal values and institutional values are not always identical, and balancing the potential conflicts requires considerable skill.

The responsibility for large budgets for materials and automation, the legal contracts for electronic resources, and the complex requirements of personnel management led the American Library Association and its divisions to explore ethical issues in technical services in greater depth than was possible in its *Code of Ethics.*

ALCTS GUIDELINES

The division of the ALA that is most involved with acquisitions, the Association for Library Collections and Technical Services (ALCTS), began discussing the need for a code of ethics for technical services in the late twentieth century. In 1994, the ALCTS adopted *Guidelines for ALCTS Members to Supplement the American Library Association Code of Ethics.* According to the guidelines, a member

1. strives to develop a collection of materials within collection policies and priorities;
2. strives to provide broad and unbiased access to information;
3. strives to preserve and conserve the materials in the library in accordance with established priorities and programs;
4. develops resource sharing programs to extend and enhance the information sources available to library users;
5. promotes the development and application of standards and professional guidelines;
6. establishes a secure and safe environment for staff and users;
7. fosters and promotes fair, ethical, and legal trade and business practices;
8. maintains equitable treatment and confidentiality in competitive relations and manuscript and grant reviews;
9. supports and abides by any contractual agreements made by the library or its home institution in regard to the provision of or access to information resources, acquisition of services, and financial arrangements. (ALCTS 1994a)

Also in 1994, the Acquisitions Section of the ALCTS presented its *Statement on Principles and Standards of Acquisitions Practice.* In accordance with that statement, a librarian

1. gives first consideration to the objectives and policies of his or her institution;
2. strives to obtain the maximum ultimate value of each dollar of expenditure;

3. grants all competing vendors equal consideration insofar as the established policies of his or her library permit, and regards each transaction on its own merits;

4. subscribes to and works for honesty, truth, and fairness in buying and selling, and denounces all forms and manifestations of bribery;

5. declines personal gifts and gratuities;

6. uses only by consent original ideas and designs devised by one vendor for competitive purchasing purposes;

7. accords a prompt and courteous reception insofar as conditions permit to all who call on legitimate business missions;

8. fosters and promotes fair, ethical, and legal trade practices;

9. avoids sharp practice;

10. strives consistently for knowledge of the publishing and book-selling industry;

11. strives to establish practical and efficient methods for the conduct of his/her office;

12. counsels and assists fellow acquisitions librarians in the performance of their duties, whenever occasion permits. (ALCTS 1994b)

Librarians discussed some of the ALCTS Acquisitions Section's standards at the Feather River Conference (Devlin and Nissley 1995, 59–62) and at the American Library Association annual conference (German 1995, 120–21). While some of the guidelines appear quite clear, others have led to considerable discussion. An analysis of these guidelines follows.

Statement 1, that a librarian gives first consideration to the objectives and policies of the institution, and statement 2, that a librarian strives to obtain the maximum ultimate value of all expenditures, must be balanced by statement 9, that the librarian should avoid sharp business practices. Librarians must be aware of the institutional mission and carry out their responsibilities in a manner that supports institutional policies. While negotiating for materials, librarians have an obligation to be careful stewards, gaining the best price possible. Librarians should not, however, try to negotiate a price that makes it impossible for a vendor to make a profit. The role of the librarian is neither to give the vendor an unreasonable profit nor to drive the vendor out of business. Librarians and vendors are in a business relationship, and librarians should not help vendors profit at the expense of their organization (Johnson 1994, 3). Librarians are behaving unethically when they mislead a vendor by promising a large volume of purchasing in order to receive a substantial discount but then send only a small number of orders, when they mislead the vendor by promising a wide range of types of orders but send only orders for materials that are difficult to obtain or have low discounts, or when they deliberately delay payments.

Librarians can find balancing the various guidelines difficult. For example, some serials publishers have low subscription rates for individuals and much higher rates for institutions. If librarians attempt to save money for their institution by asking individuals to subscribe to journals on behalf of the library, they may be acting in the best interests of their institution while violating their obligation to avoid sharp business practices. Even if librarians consider the differential pricing or the institutional prices to be immorally high, attempting to circumvent the set pricing is equally questionable.

Ethics come into play when libraries are selecting vendors for major portions of their accounts. Statement 3 requires that all competing vendors receive equal consideration. The process of selecting vendors must be as fair as possible. Showing favoritism by deciding in advance which company will be awarded the contract or by providing only one company with information that would give that company an advantage in the competition is unethical. Selection of vendors requires that librarians educate themselves about the process and that all vendors receive accurate information. Librarians must learn as much as possible about the policies of their institution, about the companies who are submitting proposals for the library's account, and about the businesses of publishing and vending. Many institutions have specific requirements for requests for proposals; librarians must work closely with the departments that are responsible for coordinating the bid process. The requirements for the selection and the process by which the selection will be made need to be decided and shared with all vendors at the beginning of the process. Please see chapter 4, "Domestic and Foreign Vendor Selection and Evaluation," for more information about the RFP process.

Statements 4 and 5 address issues of honesty, fairness, gifts, gratuities, and bribery. Many vendors host parties at conferences and take librarians to dinners; some pay for librarians to visit the company offices. While such cases do not involve bribery, they may involve efforts to influence librarians' opinions about the companies. If librarians allow their professional decisions to be influenced by dinners, they have allowed their ethics to be compromised (Boissonnas 1987, 151). If a vendor feels that a donation to a library's endowment fund is required in order to acquire a library's business, the library is behaving unethically (Bullard 1984, 254). Librarians who reject materials for the library's collection because of their personal beliefs or who accept materials because they are unwilling to deal with upset users are being unprofessional and unethical.

Statements 6 and 7 address librarians' behavior toward vendors. Librarians should not reveal confidential information, whether about a vendor to a competitor or about another library to a vendor. During an RFP process, vendors may include a request that some of the information is to be shared only within the RFP committee or task force and the institution. Such requests should be honored. Revealing confidential information, regardless of the source, is unethical.

Vendors visiting libraries frequently travel long distances and often have tight schedules. Librarians should receive them promptly and professionally. While an occasional emergency may make it impossible to keep the appointment, this should be a rare exception, and the librarian should attempt to find another colleague to meet with the vendor. The vendor should realize that librarians' schedules are often equally full and should schedule appointments in advance and be on time for meetings.

Statements 8 and 9 address the need for fair, ethical, and legal business practices. Librarians must learn the business policies and practices of their institution. Most organizations have institutional policies and laws about copyright, licensing agreements and contracts, donations of materials, and personnel management. Ethical and legal issues are intertwined in most of the areas, and librarians must be aware of the appropriate behavior and of institutional regulations. When vendors were asked for comments on how libraries violated these practices, their examples included such behavior as deliberately delaying payments, sending a vendor's bibliographic notification forms to another vendor, and deliberately writing a bid that excludes fair competition (Goehner 1991, 79).

Librarians expect that ethical vendors will not promise what they cannot deliver, will not report items as out of print just because they are hard to obtain, and will not ignore the service needs of the libraries.

Statement 10 addresses the need for librarians to learn about the publishing and bookselling industry. This need becomes even more crucial as the information industry changes rapidly. *Library Journal, American Libraries,* and *Publishers Weekly,* in their print or digital versions, are major resources for news and developments in the industry. Discussion lists such as ACQNET-L, LIBLICENSE-L, COLLDV-L, and SERIALST-L frequently provide the latest news about developments in the field; please see the appendix for information about subscribing to these lists.

In addition to educating themselves, acquisitions librarians frequently find they must educate others in their organizations about acquisitions, publishing, and management of resources (Baker 1992, 4). The head of an institution's purchasing department may know nothing about serials vendors; the acquisitions librarian must be prepared to provide sufficient background information when needed. Institutional lawyers who do not specialize in intellectual property law may not be aware of such issues as fair use or interlibrary loan rights; librarians may have to inform them about some of these issues before licensing agreements are signed. Development officers may not realize that asking vendors to donate to the library is inappropriate; librarians may have to advise them that this is considered unethical. Acquisitions librarians also need to acquaint their vendors with the business practices of their institution, providing vendors with the names of people responsible for specific activities such as invoice approval, the institution's requirements for invoicing, and the institution's procedures for reviewing and signing contracts (Marsh 1999, 332).

Statement 11 says that librarians must conduct their work efficiently and practically. One of the primary responsibilities of an acquisitions department is to monitor and expend a materials budget promptly and properly, with records that can be audited (Granskog 1999, 319). In addition to learning the policies of their institution, librarians must work with other departments, such as the purchasing office, to ensure the department functions effectively. Both personnel and fiscal resources require careful management. Accurate record keeping is vital so that an unexpected financial audit or a personnel lawsuit could be met with a favorable resolution for the institution.

Statement 12 encourages librarians to assist colleagues in their duties. Opportunities for assistance may occur in everyday work situations, at conferences, or on discussion lists, which often contain requests for information. This statement also relates to statement 10, which discusses the need for librarians to learn and share information about acquisitions and publishing.

ETHICS IN LICENSING AGREEMENTS

As acquisitions librarians have become more involved in licensing agreements and contracts, many ethical and legal issues have developed. Librarians must be alert to the need to protect the privacy of users. Although some agreements state that no data will be collected that will identify any individual user, others do not. The right to privacy is an element of the American Library Association's *Code of Ethics;* librarians should request that privacy clauses be included in licensing agreements.

Some contracts include clauses that require that some of the contractual details remain confidential. Such details usually involve the cost of a product or the discount for a service. Some public institutions must make their budgets public; therefore, those institutions may be prohibited from signing such clauses. Librarians must learn the policies of their organizations and resolve any conflicts that may arise.

INFORMATION ETHICS

In his book *Ethical Challenges in Librarianship,* Robert Hauptman (1988, 94) wrote, "Ethics has never played more than a minimal role in librarianship." Among the first to use the phrase "information ethics" to describe the application of ethics theory to library and information science, Hauptman identified two opposing positions at the core of many ethical dilemmas. One position holds that librarians must not allow personal beliefs to influence their professional activities. In opposition to this view is the position that librarians should not ignore the social implications of their professional behavior. The dichotomy of these positions is illustrated in two experiments in which reference librarians were asked for information about making bombs and about making drugs. None of the librarians refused to help the patrons, although some suspected that the information requested might be used for illegal activities. These experiments and much of the literature on information ethics involves reference, intellectual freedom, and censorship of print and electronic resources. These ethical concerns are beyond the scope of this chapter.

With the expansion of the Internet and the growth of automation in libraries, information ethics has grown to include discussions about the role of technology in areas such as privacy and access. The ethical uses of computers and of technology have become a major concern that is reflected in the number of relevant publications as well as the number of movies, television programs, and novels about the abuse of information and technology. Issues involving legal jurisdictions, Internet filtering, censorship, privacy, and the Patriot Act (which expands the ability of law enforcement to obtain library patron records) will probably be in litigation for the next few years. Some of the many relevant resources include the American Library Association's Office of Intellectual Freedom (http://www.ala.org/alaorg/oif) and the International Center for Information Ethics (http://icie.zkm.de) (both accessed June 1, 2003). Two journals specialize in information ethics: *Journal of Information Ethics* began publication in 1992, and *Ethics and Information Technology* began in 1999.

CONCLUSION

For many years, discussions of ethics in librarianship were either theoretical or related to public service and censorship issues. As acquisitions budgets increased, automation costs grew, and management issues became more complex, the need for ethical standards for technical services personnel became clear. The American Library Association's *Code of Ethics* and its *Library Bill of Rights* and the codes of the other library associations are the ethical foundation for librarians. The Association of Library Collections and Technical Services guidelines form the next level of ethical codes for acquisitions librarians. Even though the principles in these codes are general statements, they can guide acquisitions librarians in their professional relationships with all people in their organizations, with colleagues in other institutions, and with those companies with whom they have business relationships.

Libraries, vendors, and publishers continue to face rapid changes in the information industry. When librarians focus on their core values, including their role of providing all kinds of information to their users, they can see past the short-lived fads and through the trendy jargon. Without institutional and professional values, ethical codes can become just another set of guidelines with no relevance to the behavior of personnel. Librarians must identify their personal and institutional values and incorporate those beliefs into their work. "For professional values to flourish and triumph, it is only necessary for us to integrate them into our lives. We need to call them to consciousness and criticize and question them, to apply them to our problems and quandaries, to involve them as we plan and make decisions, and ultimately to cherish and celebrate them. They are the essence of our calling" (Finks 1989, 356).

REFERENCES

ALA Council actions: Council approves new Code of Ethics. 1995. *American Libraries* 26 (7): 676–77.

American Library Association. 1995. *American Library Association Code of Ethics.* <http://www.ala.org/alaorg/oif/ethics.html> (accessed September 1, 2002).

———. 1996. *Library bill of rights.* <http://www.ala.org/work/freedom/lbr.html> (accessed September 1, 2002).

———. 1999. Librarianship: Core values. Draft statement. Chicago: American Library Association.

American Library Association Council. 2001. 2001 Annual Conference. <http://www.ala.org> (accessed September 1, 2002).

Association for Library Collections and Technical Services (ALCTS). 1994a. *Guidelines for ALCTS members to supplement the American Library Association Code of Ethics.* Chicago: American Library Association.

———. 1994b. *Statement on principles and standards of acquisitions practice.* Chicago: American Library Association.

Baker, Sharon L. 1992. Needed: An ethical code for library administrators. *Journal of Library Administration* 16 (4): 1–17.

Boissonnas, Christian M. 1987. The cost is more than that elegant dinner: Your ethics are at steak. *Library Acquisitions: Practice and Theory* 11: 145–52.

Bullard, Scott R. 1984. Ethics of vendor-library relations. *Library Acquisitions: Practice and Theory* 8: 251–54.

Bushing, Mary C. 1993. Acquisitions ethics: The evolution of models for hard times. *Library Acquisitions: Practice and Theory* 17: 47–52.

Devlin, Mary, and Meta Nissley. 1995. Ethics and good business practices: Case studies. *Library Acquisitions: Practice and Theory* 19: 59–62.

Dole, Wanda V., Jitka M. Hurych, and Wallace C. Koehler. 2000. Values for librarians in the information age: An expanded examination. *Library Management* 21: 285–97.

Finks, Lee W. 1989. Values without shame. *American Libraries* 20: 352–56.

German, Lisa. 1995. Let the sun shine in: Evaluating ethics in publisher/vendor-library relations: A report of the program. *Library Acquisitions: Practice and Theory* 19: 120–21.

Goehner, Donna. 1991. Ethical aspects of the librarian/vendor relationship. In *Ethics and the librarian*, edited by F. W. Lancaster. Urbana-Champaign: University of Illinois Graduate School of Library and Information Science.

Gorman, Michael. 2000. *Our enduring values: Librarianship in the 21st century.* Chicago: American Library Association.

Granskog, Kay. 1999. Basic acquisitions accounting and business practice. In *Understanding the business of library acquisitions.* 2nd ed. Edited by Karen A. Schmidt. Chicago: American Library Association.

Hauptman, Robert. 1988. *Ethical challenges in librarianship.* Phoenix: Oryx Press.

———. 1999. Ethics, information technology, and crisis. In *Ethics and electronic information in the twenty-first century*, edited by Lester J. Pourciau. West Lafayette, IN: Purdue University Press.

Johnson, Peggy. 1994. Ethical considerations in decision making. *Technicalities* 14 (2): 2–4.

Lindsey, Jonathan A., and Ann E. Prentice. 1985. *Professional ethics and librarians.* Phoenix: Oryx Press.

Marsh, Connie. 1999. Payment ethics: Librarians as consumers. In *Understanding the business of library acquisitions.* 2nd ed. Edited by Karen A. Schmidt. Chicago: American Library Association.

Ranganathan, S. R. 1963. *The five laws of library science.* Bombay: Asia Publishing House.

Richards, Rob. 2000. Biz of acq—Stewardship, partnership, self-understanding: An exploration of values in acquisitions work. *Against the Grain* 12 (3): 87–90.

Rothstein, Samuel. 1968. In search of ourselves. *Library Journal* 93: 156–57.

Sager, Donald J. 2001. The search for librarianship's core values. *Public Libraries* 40: 149–53.

Severson, Richard W. 1997. *The principles of information ethics.* Armonk, NY: M. E. Sharpe.

Tyckoson, David. 1984. On the convention circuit: Seduction and the librarian: The ethics of librarian-vendor relations. *Technicalities* 4 (September): 14–15.

Winters, Barbara. 1999. Ethics in acquisitions management. In *Understanding the business of library acquisitions.* 2nd ed. Edited by Karen A. Schmidt. Chicago: American Library Association.

Zipkowitz, Fay. 1996. *Professional ethics in librarianship: A real life casebook.* Jefferson, NC: McFarland & Company.

Appendix

This appendix lists sources of information about conferences, corporate Internet sites, electronic discussion lists, other Internet sites, journals, organizations, and reference tools related to acquisitions. All universal resource locators (URLs) were verified between June 1 and June 15, 2003.

AUTOMATED ACQUISITIONS SYSTEMS

Several companies offer acquisitions systems, either as modules that are part of an integrated library system or as separate systems. This section lists the names and URLs of some of the major ones. For lists of additional companies, visit AcqWeb (http://acqweb.library.vanderbilt.edu/) or Library Technology Guides (http://www.librarytechnology.org).

Brodart Automation. <http://www.brodart.com/automation/>.

Endeavor Information Systems. <http://www.endinfosys.com/>.

EOS International. <http://eosintl.com/>.

epixtech, inc. <http://www.epixtech.com>.

Ex Libris. <http://www.exlibris-usa.com>.

Gaylord Information Systems.
  <http://www.gaylord.com/Automation/>.

Geac. <http://www.geac.com>.

Inmagic, Inc. <http://www.inmagic.com>.

Innovative Interfaces, Inc. <http://www.iii.com>.

New Generation Technologies, Inc. <http://www.librarysoft.com>.

On Point, Inc. <http://www.onpointinc.com>.

SIMA, Inc. <http://www.simainc.com>.

SIRS Mandarin, Inc. <http://www.sirs.com>.

SIRSI Corporation. <http://www.sirsi.com>.

Softlink America, Inc. <http://www.softlinkamerica.com>.

TLC: The Library Corporation. <http://www.tlcdelivers.com/>.

VTLS, Inc. <http://www.vtls.com>.

CONFERENCES AND SEMINARS

The primary conferences of interest to librarians in all areas are those held by the major library associations—such as the American Library Association (ALA), the Special Libraries Association, and the Medical Library Association.

At the ALA conferences, the majority of meetings related to acquisitions are sponsored by the Association for Library Collections and Technical Services (ALCTS) or the Library and Information Technology Association (LITA).

For additional programs and for dates, check the "Datebook" column in *American Libraries* or visit the website of the American Library Association (http://www.ala.org/events/).

Some other conferences are of interest to acquisitions librarians; this list includes the major ones.

Academic Library Advancement and Development Network (ALADN). For issues related to fund-raising and development. The conference is held in the spring. <http://dizzy.library. arizona.edu/aladn/>.

American Society for Information Science and Technology (ASIST). <http://www.asis.org>.

Association of College and Research Librarians (ACRL) National Conference. The conference is held every other year in the spring. <http://www.ala.org/acrl/>.

Book Expo America. Exhibits and seminars for the publishing industry. The conference is held in the summer. <http:// bookexpoamerica.com>.

Charleston Acquisitions Conference. For issues related to book and serials acquisitions. The conference is held in the fall. <http://www.cofc.edu/cdconference/>.

Computers in Libraries Conference. For issues related to technology and libraries. The conference is held in the spring. <http://www.infotoday.com>.

EDUCAUSE. For issues related to information technology, libraries, and technology systems. The conference is held in the fall. <http://www.educause.edu/>.

International Federation of Library Associations (IFLA). The conference is held in the summer. <http://www.ifla.org>.

Internet Librarian Conference. For librarians and information managers. The conference is held in the fall. <http://www.infotoday.com>.

North American Serials Interest Group (NASIG). The conference is held in early summer. <http://www.nasig.org>.

National Online Conference. Focuses on information delivery technology. The conference is held in early summer. <http://www.infotoday.com>.

Oklahoma University Libraries Collection Development Conference. The conference is held in the spring. <http://libraries.ou.edu/general/>.

Out-of-Print and Antiquarian Book Market Seminar. For those interested in out-of-print, antiquarian, and rare books. The conference is held in the summer. <www.bookseminars.com>.

Seminar on the Acquisition of Latin American Library Materials (SALALM). The conference is held in the summer. <http://www.salalm.org>.

Society for Scholarly Publishing. For publishers and others involved in scholarly publishing. The conference is held in the summer. <http://www.sspnet.org>.

Timberline Lodge Acquisitions Institute. Discussions of acquisitions and collection development issues for librarians, vendors, and publishers. The conference is held in early summer. <http://libweb.uoregon.edu/acqdept/institute/home.html>.

CORPORATE AND VENDOR INTERNET SITES

Information about publishing trends and developments, recent and projected pricing trends, and links to Internet resources about publishing and libraries can be found on many vendor and company websites. This general information is available to anyone, not just clients or subscribers. Here are some of the major sites that have useful information for acquisitions personnel.

Archival Products. Information and archival supplies, preservation, and conservation. <http://www.archival.com/>.

Blackwell Book Services. Lists of recommended books; links to Internet resources; analyses of book prices. <http://www.blackwell.com/index.asp>.

Brodart. Lists of award-winning books and links to publishers. <http://www.brodart.com>.

EBSCO. Serials price studies and projections; information about issues related to serials. <http://www-us.ebsco.com>.

Gaylord Brothers. Information about preservation, archival techniques, and library supplies. <http://www.gaylord.com/>.

Harrassowitz. Price analyses and comparisons for electronic journals, for scientific, technical, and medical journals, and for music materials; resource guides for electronic journals. <http://www.harrassowitz.de/>.

Information Today, Inc. Lists of publishers, conferences, and publications. <http://www.infotoday.com>.

R. R. Bowker Books in Print. News and events in the publishing industry; links to publishers and to library suppliers and services. <http://www.booksinprint.com/bip/>.

R. R. Bowker Ulrichs. Information about new serials titles and title changes; links to resources about serials. <http://www.ulrichsweb.com/UlrichsWeb/>.

SwetsBlackwell. Information about new serial titles and serials price increases; links to publishers. <http://www.swetsblackwell.com>.

YBP Library Services (Yankee Book Peddler). Lists of recommended books and of literary prizes; trends of book pricing; information about new, changed, or merged publishers. <http://www.ybp.com>.

ELECTRONIC DISCUSSION LISTS

Electronic discussion lists facilitate informative discussions about topics and provide rapid distribution of news. Most discussion lists in the field of library science have moderators who monitor messages to ensure that the topics relate to the subject of the list.

New discussion lists appear frequently, and addresses do change occasionally. For the most current information, consult the *Directory of Electronic Journals* published by the Association for Research Libraries. Also see the websites AcqWeb (http://acqweb.library.vanderbilt.edu/acqweb/ journals.html) and Library-Oriented Lists and Electronic Serials (http:// www.wrlc.org/home.htm).

Many library and information science organizations such as the American Library Association and the American Society for Information Science and Technology host discussion lists for their members. Some may be intended for the entire membership; others may be directed to a specific interest, such as the list for library administration issues hosted by the Library Administration and Management Association of the American Library Association.

Most lists are managed by electronic software. To subscribe to a list, send the managing system a message that includes the name of the discussion list and your name. For example, to subscribe to ACQNET, a list for the discussion of acquisitions topics, send an email message to list-proc@list.proc.appstate.edu as follows: subscribe acqnet-l Jane Smith. Some lists, such as Backserv, have associated websites that allow you to subscribe to the list directly from the website.

Each entry below is arranged as follows: name of the discussion list, a brief description, email address for messages, email address for subscriptions, and Web address if one is available.

ACQNET-L. For those interested in acquisitions work. <Acqnet-l@ listserv.appstate.edu>. <Listproc@listproc.appstate.edu>. <http://acqweb.library.vanderbilt.edu/acqweb/acqnet.html>.

ARL-Ejournal. For discussion of all aspects of the management of electronic journals. <ARL-EJOURNAL@ARL.ORG>. <LISTPROC@ ARL.ORG>. <http://www.cni.org/Hforums/arl-ejournal/about. html>.

Backserv. For exchanging and replacing back issues of serials. <backserv@lists.swetsblackwell.com>. <http://lists. swetsblackwell.com/mailman/listinfo/backserv/>.

COLLDV-L. For those interested in collection development issues. <colldv-l@usc.edu>. <Listproc@usc.edu>.

DIGITAL-COPYRIGHT. For discussions of topics such as copyright law and policies, especially those that deal with higher education. <Digital-copyright@listserv.umuc.edu>. <listproc@ listserv.umuc.edu>.

DIGLIB. For discussion of issues and technologies related to digital libraries. <diglib@infoserv.inist.fr>. <http://infoserv.inist.fr/ wwsympa.fcgi/info/diglib>.

ERIL. For discussion of practical aspects of handling electronic resources. <ERIL-subscribe@topica.com>. <http://www. topica.com/lists/eril>.

ExLibris. For discussion of issues related to rare books and special collections. <exlibris@library.berkeley.edu>. <Listproc@library.berkeley.edu>. <http://palimpsest.stanford.edu/byform/mailing-lists/exlibris>.

GIFTEX-L. For discussions of gifts and exchanges. <Giftex-l@lsv.uky.edu>. <Listserv@lsv.uky.edu>.

GOVDOC-L. For issues related to government information and the Federal Depository Library program. <Govdoc-l@lists.psu.edu>. <Listserv@lists.psu.edu>.

LIBDEV. For issues related to fund-raising and library development in academic libraries. <Libdev@listserv.arizona.edu>. <Listserv@listserv.arizona.edu>. <http://dizzy.library.arizona.edu/aladn/libdev1.html>.

LIBLICENSE-L. For issues related to licensing electronic resources. <liblicense-l@pantheon.yale.edu>. <Listproc@lists.yale.edu>. <http://www.library.yale.edu/~llicense/index.shtml>.

MEDIA-L. For information about media literacy. <Media-L@listserv.binghamton.edu>. <Listserv@listserv.binghamton.edu>.

Newjour. For new electronic journals announcements. <newjour@ccat.sas.upenn.edu>. <Listproc@ccat.sas.upenn.edu>. <http://gort.ucsd.edu/newjour/>.

Public Access Computer Systems Forum (Pacs-1). For discussion of issues related to online catalogs. <pacs-l@listserv.uh.edu>. <Listserv@listserv.uh.edu>. <http://info.lib.uh.edu/pacsl.html>.

SERIALST-L. For discussion of issues related to serials. <serialst@uvmvm.uvm.edu>. <Listserv@list.uvm.edu>. <http://www.uvm.edu/~bmaclenn/serialst.html>.

VIDEOLIB. For discussion of the acquisition and use of video materials in libraries. <VIDEOLIB@library.berkeley.edu>. <Listproc@library.berkeley.edu>. <http://library.berkeley.edu/MRC/vrtlists.html>.

INTERNET SITES RELATED TO ACQUISITIONS

Many Internet sites publish information related to acquisitions; these are a few of the major ones.

AcqLink. Resources for acquisitions librarians. <http://link.bubl.ac.uk/acqlink/>.

AcqWeb. Information about publishers, associations, journals; news about libraries and acquisitions; links to sites including currency conversion and postal information. <http://acqweb.library.vanderbilt.edu>.

American Library Association (ALA). Information on all aspects of libraries and librarianship. <http://www.ala.org>.

Antiquarian Booksellers' Association of America. Information about dealers, books, and the collecting of rare and antiquarian books. <http://abaa.org>.

Association for Library Collections and Technical Services (ALCTS). Information, guidelines, and bibliographies about collection management and technical services. <http://www.ala.org/alcts/>.

Association of Research Libraries (ARL). Information about issues of concern to research libraries, including management, copyright, licensing, preservation, and scholarly publishing. <http://www.arl.org>.

Association of Subscription Agents and Intermediaries (ASA). Lists of subscription agents; information about subscription services. <http://www.subscription-agents.org>.

Back Issues and Exchange Services. Information about serials back issues and exchange resources. <http://www.uvm.edu/~bmaclenn/backexch.html>.

Berkeley Digital Library SunSITE. Resources for building digital collections and services. <http://sunsite.berkeley.edu/>.

Bookwire. News, statistics, and information about publishing. <http://www.bookwire.com/>.

Catalist. The official catalog of electronic discussion lists that use LISTSERV. <http://www.lsoft.com/lists/listref.html>.

Conservation OnLine (CoOL). An extensive collection of materials about conservation. <http://palimpsest.stanford.edu/>.

Current Cites. An annotated bibliography of selected articles, books, and digital documents about information technology. <http://sunsite.berkeley.edu/currentcites/>.

D-Lib. Information about developing the global digital library; includes *D-Lib Magazine.* <http://www.dlib.org>.

Digital Object Identifier System (DOI). Information about a method of identifying electronic documents. <http://www.doi.org/overview.html>.

Documents Data Miner. Information about U.S. depository documents and depository libraries. <http://govdoc.wichita.edu/ddm>.

E-Journals. Links to electronic journals. <http://www.e-journals.org>.

Electronic Books in Libraries. Information and news about electronic books. <http://www.lib.rochester.edu/main/ebooks/index.htm>.

Federal Depository Library Program (FDLP Desktop). <http://www.access.gpo.gov/su_docs/fdlp/>.

Friends of Libraries U.S.A. Information about Friends groups, fund-raising, book sales, and other activities. <http://www.folusa.com>.

GiftXWeb. Information about gifts and exchange resources. <http://hubcap.clemson.edu/~johnsos/G&E/GEHome.html>.

International Center for Information Ethics (ICIE). Resources about information ethics. <http://icie.zkm.de/>.

Libdex. A directory of libraries, online catalogs, and publishers. <http://www.libdex.com>.

LIBLICENSE. Information about licensing digital information. <http://www.library.yale.edu/~llicense/index.shtml>.

Library and Information Technology Association (LITA), American Library Association. <http://www.lita.org>.

Northeast Document Conservation Center (NEDCC). Information about conservation and preservation. <http://www.nedcc.org>.

Planet eBook. Information about electronic books. <http://www.planetebook.com/>.

PubList.com. Information about magazines, journals, newsletters, and other periodicals. <http://www.publist.com/>.

Regional Alliance for Preservation (RAP). Information and educational resources about conservation and preservation. <http://www.rap-arcc.org>.

Scholarly Electronic Publishing Bibliography. A selective bibliography of materials about electronic publishing. <http://info.lib.uh.edu/sepb/sepb.html>.

Serials in Cyberspace. Resources about serials. <http://www.uvm.edu/~bmaclenn/>.

U.S. Library of Congress. Information about the Library of Congress's collections and projects; legislation; copyright; and preservation. <http://lcweb.loc.gov/>.

U.S. National Park Service: Museum Management Program.
Information about conservation and preservation. <http://www.
cr.nps.gov/museum/>.

JOURNALS RELATED TO ACQUISITIONS

Many library science serials publish information related to acquisitions;
this is a selected list of titles that are relevant to the field. When a journal
is available electronically, that is noted. Just as with print journals, some
electronic journals are free, some are restricted to members of an organization, and some require a paid subscription in order to access the contents. The URL is either the address of the electronic edition of the journal
or the publisher of the journal.

Abbey Newsletter. Information about preservation, conservation,
binding, and binding standards. ISSN: 0276-8291. Academy
Book Bindery. Partial contents online. <http://palimpsest.
stanford.edu/byorg/abbey/an/index.html>.

Acquisitions Librarian. Articles related to acquisitions. ISSN:
0896-3576. Haworth Press. Table of contents and abstracts
online. <http://www.haworthpressinc.com>.

Advances in Librarianship. Articles about issues in librarianship.
ISSN: 0065-2850. Academic Press. <http://www.elsevier.com>.

Advances in Library Administration and Organization.
Research articles about library administration and management.
JAI Press. Table of contents online. <http://www.elsevier.com>.

Advances in Serials Management. Research articles about
serials issues. JAI Press. Table of contents online. <http://www.
elsevier.com>.

Against the Grain. Articles related to acquisitions and publishing. ISSN: 1043-2094. Table of contents and sample articles
online. Katrina Strauch. <http://www.against-the-grain.com/>.

ALCTS Newsletter Online. The newsletter of the American Library
Association's Association for Library Collections and Technical
Services. ISSN: 1523-018X. Full text online. <http://www.ala.
org>.

American Libraries. Articles and news about libraries. ISSN:
0002-9769. American Library Association. Partial contents
online. <http://www.ala.org/alonline>.

Annual Review of Information Science and Technology.
Articles about information science. ISSN: 0066-4200. American

Society of Information Science and Technology and Learned Information, Inc. <http://www.asis.org/Publications/ARIST/arist.html> .

Antiquarian Book Monthly. The magazine for antiquarian and rare book collectors. ISSN: 0306-7475. Countrywide Editions, Ltd.

Ariadne. A newsletter about Internet issues for U.K. librarians. ISSN: 1361-3200. Full text online. Joint Information Systems Committee. <http://www.ariadne.ac.uk>.

ARL Newsletter. Newsletter of the Association of Research Libraries; contains news about publishing and member libraries. ISSN: 1050-6098. Full text online. <http://www.arl.org/newsltr/index.html>.

ASIST Bulletin. Published by the American Society for Information Science and Technology. News and articles about information science. ISSN: 0095-4403. Full text online. <http://www.asis.org/Bulletin/>.

Biblio Tech Review. Covers developments in the library automation industry. ISSN: 1463-7146. Biblio Tech, Ltd. Full text online. <http://www.biblio-tech.com>.

Book Collector. Articles about collecting and collectors. ISSN: 0006-7237. Collector, Ltd.

Booklist. Reviews of new materials. ISSN: 0006-7385. American Library Association. Selected contents online. <http://www.ala.org/booklist/index.html>.

Bookseller. Articles about U.K. bookselling and publishing. ISSN: 0006-7539. The Bookseller. Partial contents online. <http://www.thebookseller.com>.

The Bottom Line: Managing Library Finances. Articles on financial management in libraries. ISSN: 0888-045X. MCB University Press. Full text online. <http://www.emeraldinsight.com/bl.htm>.

Bowker Annual: Library and Book Trade Almanac. Information about libraries and publishing. ISSN: 0068-0540. Information Today, Inc. <http://www.infotoday.com>.

Charleston Advisor. News and reviews concerning electronic resources and publishing. ISSN: 1525-4011. Charleston Co. Partial contents online. <http://www.charlestonco.com/>.

Choice. Reviews of books for college and research libraries, published by the American Library Association's Association of College and Research Libraries. ISSN: 0009-4978. Full text online. <http://www.ala.org>.

Chronicle of Higher Education. Articles, reviews, and information related to higher education. ISSN: 0009-5982. Full text online. <http://chronicle.com>.

Collection Building. Articles about collection management issues. ISSN: 0160-4953. MCB University Press. Full text online. <http://www.emeraldinsight.com/cb.htm>.

Collection Management. Articles about collection management issues. ISSN: 0146-2679. Table of contents and abstracts online. Haworth Press. <http://www.haworthpressinc.com>.

College and Research Libraries. Articles about trends and issues in academic and research libraries. American Library Association's College and Research Libraries Division. ISSN: 0010-0870. Table of contents and abstracts online. <http://www.ala.org>.

College and Research Libraries News. News about trends and developments in academic and research libraries, published by the American Library Association's College and Research Libraries Division. ISSN: 0099-0086. Partial contents online. <http://www.ala.org>.

Computers in Libraries. Articles about technology and libraries. ISSN: 1041-7915. Table of contents and partial contents online. Information Today, Inc. <http://www.infotoday.com/cilmag/ ciltop.htm>.

Cultivate Interactive. Articles about digital projects, intellectual property rights, libraries, and museums. ISSN: 1471-3225. European Commission. Digital Heritage and Cultural Content Programme. <http://www.cultivate-int.org>.

Current Awareness Application of New Technologies in Libraries. Bibliography of articles about technology and libraries. K. U. Leuven Central Library. Full text online. <http://lib.ua.ac.be/WGLIB/ATTEND/index.html>.

D-Lib Magazine. An electronic magazine about innovation and research in digital libraries. ISSN: 1082-9873. Digital Library Forum and Corporation for National Research Projects Agency. Full text online. <http://www.dlib.org>.

Ethics and Information Technology. Articles about information ethics. ISSN: 1388-1957. Kluwer Academic Publishers. Full text online. <http://www.kluweronline.com>.

First Monday. A peer-reviewed journal devoted to the Internet. ISSN: 1396-0466. First Monday and the University of Illinois at Chicago. Full text online. <http://www.firstmonday.org>.

Firsts: The Book Collector's Magazine. Articles about book collecting. ISSN: 1066-5471. Firsts Magazine.

Free Online Scholarship Newsletter. News and discussion about the migration of print scholarship to the Internet and efforts to make information available free of charge. <http://www.earlham.edu/~peters/fos/>.

Information Outlook. Articles about special libraries. ISSN: 1091-0808. Full text online. Special Libraries Association. <http://www.sla.org/pubs/serial/io/>.

Information Technology and Libraries. Articles about libraries and technology. ISSN: 0730-9295. Library and Information Technology Association, American Library Association. Table of contents, abstracts, and partial contents online. <http://www.ala.org>.

Information Today. News about electronic information services. ISSN: 8755-6286. Partial contents online. Leaned Information, Inc. <http://www.infotoday.com/it/itnew.htm>.

International Federation of Library Associations (IFLA) Journal. Articles about libraries and librarianship. ISSN: 0340-0352. Table of contents and abstracts online. <http://www.ifla.org/V/iflaj/index.htm>.

International Information and Library Review. Articles about information science and libraries. ISSN: 1057-2317. Academic Press. Full text online. <http://www.elsevier.com>.

Journal of Academic Librarianship. Articles about academic librarianship and scholarly publishing. ISSN: 0099-1333. Elsevier Science, Inc. Full text online. <http://www.elsevier.com>.

Journal of Digital Information. For people working in the field of digital information. ISSN: 1361-1506. British Computer Society. Full text online. <http://jodi.ecs.soton.ac.uk/>.

Journal of Electronic Publishing. Articles about electronic publishing and scholarly publishing. ISSN: 1080-2711. University of Michigan Press. Full text online. <http://www.press.umich.edu/jep/>.

Journal of Information Ethics. Articles about ethics in information science. ISSN: 1061-9321. McFarland & Company, Inc. Table of contents online. <http://www.mcfarlandpub.com>.

Journal of Librarianship and Information Science. Articles about librarianship. ISSN: 0961-0006. R. R. Bowker. Full text online. <http://www.bowker.com>.

Journal of Library Administration. Articles about administration and management. ISSN: 0193-0826. Haworth Press. Table of contents and abstracts online. <http://www.haworthpressinc.com>.

Journal of Scholarly Publishing. Articles about scholarly publishing and publishers. ISSN: 1198-9742. University of Toronto Press. Table of contents and abstracts online. <http://www.utpjournals.com>.

Journal of the American Institute for Conservation. Articles about conservation of materials. ISSN: 0197-1360. Full text of archival articles online. <http://aic.stanford.edu/jaic/index.html>.

Journal of the American Society for Information Science and Technology. Articles about issues and developments related to information science. ISSN: 1532-2882. Full text online. <http://www.asis.org/Publications/JASIS/jasisl.html>.

Learned Publishing. The journal of the Association of Learned and Professional Society Publishers. News and articles concerning all aspects of academic and professional publishing. ISSN: 0953-1513. Full text online. <http://www.alpsp.org/journal.htm>.

Librarian's eBook Newsletter. News about electronic books. Full text online. <http://www.lib.rochester.edu/main/ebooks/archive.htm>.

Library Administration and Management. Articles about management. ISSN: 0888-4463. Library Administration and Management Association, American Library Association. Table of contents online. <http://www.ala.org>.

Library Collections, Acquisitions, and Technical Services. Articles and conference reports related to collection management, acquisitions, and technical services. ISSN: 1464-9055 Elsevier Science, Inc. Full text online. <http://www.elsevier.com>.

Library Hi-Tech. Articles about technology and libraries. ISSN: 0737-8831. Pierian Press. Full text online. <http://www.emeraldinsight.com/lht.htm>.

Library Issues: Briefings for Faculty and Administrators. Issues relating to academic libraries. ISSN: 0734-3035. Mountainside Publishing Co., Inc. Full text online. <http://www.libraryissues.com>.

Library Journal. News, articles, and reviews. ISSN: 0363-0277. Library Journal. Partial contents online. <http://libraryjournal.reviewsnews.com/>.

Library Philosophy and Practice. Articles that show the connection between library practice and the philosophy and theory behind it. ISSN: 1522-0222. Full text online. <http://www.uidaho.edu/~mbolin/lp&p.htm>.

Library Resources and Technical Services. Articles about technical services issues and trends, published by the Association for Library Collections and Technical Services. ISSN: 0024-2527. Table of contents online. <http://www.ala.org>.

Library Technology Reports. Information about library systems and technology. ISSN: 0024-2586. Library Technology Reports, American Library Association. Full text online. <http://www.techsource.ala.org>.

Library Trends. Articles about all aspects of libraries and library science. ISSN: 0024-2594. University of Illinois Press. Table of contents and abstracts online. <http://www.lis.uiuc.edu/puboff/catalog/trends/>.

LIBRES: Library and Information Science Research. Research about libraries and information science. ISSN: 1058-6768. Full text online. <http://libres.curtin.edu.au>.

Libri. Articles about libraries and information science. ISSN: 0024-2667. K. G. Saur Verlag. Table of contents online. <http://www.saur.de/home.htm>.

Logos: The Journal of the World Book Community. Articles about issues related to publishing. ISSN: 0957-9656. Whurr Publishers, Ltd. Selected articles online. <http://www.osi.hu/cpd/logos.html>.

NASIG Newsletter. News about NASIG activities and membership. ISSN: 0892-1733. Full text online. <http://www.nasig.org>.

New Library Scene. News and articles about binding and conservation. ISSN: 0735-8571. Library Binding Institute. <http://www.lbibinders.org>.

One-Person Library. Articles about libraries operated with one staff member. ISSN: 0748-8831. OPL Resources. Table of contents and index online. <http://www.ibi-opl.com/newsletter/opl.html>.

Portal: Libraries and the Academy. Articles about academic librarianship and scholarly publishing. ISSN: 1531-2540 (print); 1530-7131 (electronic). Johns Hopkins University Press. Full text online. <www.press.jhu.edu/press/journals/pla>.

Publishers Weekly. News about publishing and reviews. ISSN: 0000-0019. Publishers Weekly. Partial contents online. <http://publishersweekly.reviewsnews.com/>.

Publishing Research Quarterly. Articles about publishing and scholarly communication. ISSN: 1053-8801. Transaction Periodicals Consortium. Full text online. <http://www.transactionpub.com/>.

Resource Sharing and Information Networks. Articles about networking and interlibrary cooperation. ISSN: 0737-7797. Haworth Press. Table of contents and abstracts online. <http://www.haworthpressinc.com>.

Serials: The Journal for the Serials Community. Articles about serials. ISSN: 0953-0460. United Kingdom Serials Group. Full text online. <http://www.uksg.org>.

Serials Librarian. Articles about serials. ISSN: 0361-526X. Haworth Press. Table of contents and abstracts online. <http://www.haworthpressinc.com>.

Serials Review. Articles about serials. ISSN: 0098-7913. Elsevier Science, Inc. Full text online. <http://www.elsevier.com>.

Taking Stock: Libraries and the Book Trade. Articles about publishing and libraries. ISSN: 0966-6745. National Acquisitions Group.

Technical Services Quarterly. Articles about technical services. ISSN: 0731-7131. Haworth Press. Table of contents and abstracts online. <http://www.haworthpressinc.com>.

Technicalities. Articles about technical services. ISSN: 0272-0884. Trozzolo Resources, Inc. Full text online through Proquest. <http://www.trozzolo.com>.

ORGANIZATIONS

Many organizations and associations work in areas related to librarianship. The following are some of the major ones. For additional groups, such as state and regional associations, please consult the lists on AcqWeb (http://acqweb.library.vanderbilt.edu/).

Academic Library Advancement and Development Network (ALADN). Explores issues involving library fund-raising and development. <http://dizzy.library.arizona.edu/aladn/welcome.html>.

American Association of Law Libraries. Promotes and enhances the status of law libraries and librarians. <http://www.aallnet.org>.

American Association of University Presses (AAUP). An association of nonprofit scholarly publishers that sponsors programs and provides information. <http://aaupnet.org>.

American Institute for Conservation of Historic and Artistic Works. An organization of conservation professionals whose purpose is to advance the practice and promote the importance of preservation of cultural property. <http://aic.stanford.edu>.

American Library Association (ALA). Provides leadership for the development, promotion, and improvement of library services and librarianship. <http://www.ala.org>.

American Society for Information Science and Technology (ASIST). Its purpose is to advance information science and to encourage information professionalism through education and advocacy. <http://www.asis.org>.

Antiquarian Booksellers' Association of America. An association of rare and antiquarian booksellers; its mission is to promote ethical standards and professionalism in the antiquarian book trade. <http://abaa.org>.

Aslib: The Association for Information Management. An association of companies and organizations concerned with managing information resources efficiently. <http://www.aslib.co.uk/>.

Association of American Publishers (AAP). The main trade association of American publishers; its purposes are to promote reading and provide support for its members. <http://www.publishers.org>.

Association of Learned and Professional Society Publishers (ALPSP). Represents not-for-profit publishers, providing information, advice, and professional development activities. <http://www.alpsp.org>.

Association of Research Libraries (ARL). An association of major North American research libraries; it provides information and educational programs. <http://www.arl.org>.

Association of Subscription Agents and Intermediaries (ASA). Its purpose is to promote high standards of service for libraries and publishers. <http://www.subscription-agents.org>.

Book Industry Communication (BIC). Develops and promotes standards for electronic commerce and communication in the book and serials industry. <http://www.bic.org.uk/>.

Book Industry Study Group. Gathers, analyzes, and disseminates information about the publishing industry. <http://www.bisg.org>.

Canadian Library Association (CLA). Provides services to those involved in library or information science in Canada. <http://www.cla.ca>.

Chartered Institute of Library and Information Professionals (CILIP). The British association for librarians and information professionals. <http://www.cilip.org.uk/>.

Coalition for Networked Information (CNI). For those interested in issues related to networked information technologies and scholarly communication. <http://www.cni.org>.

Council on Library and Information Resources (CLIR). Promotes preservation of and access to information. <http://www.clir.org>.

Electronic Frontier Foundation. Tracks copyright, intellectual property, and intellectual freedom issues. <http://www.eff.org>.

Friends of Libraries U.S.A. Provides information for and about Friends groups. <http://www.folusa.com>.

International Coalition of Library Consortia (ICOLC). A group of library consortia, mainly of higher education institutions, that discusses issues of common interest. <http://www.library.yale.edu/consortia>.

International Federation of Library Associations (IFLA). An international association that promotes library services. <http://www.ifla.org>.

International Organization for Standardization (ISO). Promotes development of international standards related to the exchange of goods and services. <http://www.iso.ch/>.

Library Binding Institute. Creates and promotes standards related to binding. <http://www.lbibinders.org>.

Medical Library Association (MLA). Provides education and advocacy for health information professionals. <http://www.mlanet.org>.

National Information Standards Organization (NISO). Develops and promotes technical standards used in information services. <http://www.niso.org>.

North American Serials Interest Group (NASIG). Provides educational and information services for information professionals interested in serials. <http://www.nasig.org>.

Northeast Document Conservation Center (NEDCC). A regional center for preservation and conservation activities and education. <http://www.nedcc.org>.

Regional Alliance for Preservation (RAP). An alliance of regional preservation centers. <http://www.rap-arcc.org>.

Research Libraries Group. An alliance of major North American research libraries; it provides information and educational programs. <http://www.rlg.org>.

Seminar on the Acquisition of Latin American Library Materials (SALALM). Promotes dissemination of Latin American publications and librarianship. <http://www.salalm.org>.

Special Libraries Association (SLA). Provides educational services and advocacy for those working in all types of special libraries. <http://www.sla.org>.

Society for Scholarly Publishing (SSP). Advances scholarly publishing and the professional development of its members. <http://www.sspnet.org>.

Society of American Archivists (SAA). Provides educational programs and services for archivists. <http://www.archivists.org>.

United Kingdom Serials Group (UKSG). Encourages the exchange and promotion of ideas about serials. <http://www.uksg.org>.

REFERENCE TOOLS

Acquisitions librarians find many reference tools useful when searching for addresses. Here are some relevant sources.

American Book Trade Directory. Information about dealers, importers, and appraisers. Information Today, Inc. <http://www.infotoday.com>.

American Library Directory. Libraries in the United States and Canada. Information Today, Inc. <http://www.infotoday.com>.

AV Market Place. Information about audiovisual dealers and producers. Information Today, Inc. <http://www.infotoday.com>.

Books in Print. Print and online versions. The online version includes audio and video materials. R.R. Bowker. <http://www.bowker.com/>.

Bowker Annual: Library and Book Trade Almanac. Information about libraries and publishing including statistics, agencies, and organizations. Information Today, Inc. <http://www.infotoday.com>.

Directory of British Associations and Associations in Ireland. Print and CD-ROM versions. CBD Research, Ltd. <http://www.cbdresearch.com/>.

Directory of Corporate Affiliations. Print and online versions. National Register Publishing Co. <http://www.nationalregisterpub.com>.

Directory of Publications and Broadcast Media. Information about newspapers, periodicals, and media. Print and online versions. Gale Group. <http://www.galegroup.com/>.

Directory of Scholarly Electronic Journals and Academic Discussion Lists. Association of Research Libraries. <http://www.arl.org>.

Directory of Special Libraries and Information Centers. Gale Group. <http://www.galegroup.com/>.

Editor and Publisher International Year Book. Information about newspapers. Print and CD-ROM versions. Editor and Publisher. <http://www.editorandpublisher.com>.

Encyclopedia of Associations. Print and online versions. Gale Group. <http://www.galegroup.com/>.

Europa Directory of International Organizations. Europa Publications. <http://www.europapublications.co.uk/>.

Europa World Year Book. Information about associations, governments, publications, and universities. Europa Publications. <http://www.europapublications.co.uk/>.

Information Industry Directory. Information about CD-ROM and online publishers, associations, and companies. Gale Group. <http://www.galegroup.com/>.

International Directory of Little Magazines and Small Presses. Print and CD-ROM versions. The CD-ROM version also includes the *Small Press Record of Books in Print, The Directory of Poetry Publishers,* and other resources. Dustbooks. <http://www.dustbooks.com>.

International Literary Market Place. Information about publishers, dealers, manufacturers, and associations. Print and online versions. Information Today, Inc. <http://www.infotoday.com>.

Literary Market Place. Information about North American publishers, dealers, manufacturers, and associations. Print and online versions. Information Today, Inc. <http://www.infotoday.com>.

Magazines for Libraries. Recommended magazines for libraries. R. R. Bowker. <http://www.bowker.com/>.

Museums of the World. Print and CD-ROM versions. K. G. Saur. <http://www.galegroup.com/>.

Museums Yearbook. Information about U.K. museums. Museums Association. <http://www.museumsassociation.org>.

National Directory of Magazines. Print and online versions. Oxbridge Communications, Inc. <http://www.mediafinder.com>.

Official Museum Directory. Information about U.S. museums. Print and online versions. National Register Publishing. <http://www.omd-online.com/>.

Oxbridge Directory of Newsletters. Print and online versions. Oxbridge Communications, Inc. <http://www.mediafinder.com>.

Publishers Directory. Information about U.S. and Canadian publishers. Gale Group. <http://www.galegroup.com/>.

Publishers' International ISBN Directory. Print and CD-ROM versions. K. G. Saur. <http://www.galegroup.com/>.

Research Centers Directory. Gale Group. <http://www.galegroup.com/>.

Serials Directory. Print and online versions. EBSCO Industries, Inc. <http://www-us.ebsco.com/>.

Standard Periodical Directory. Print and online versions. Oxbridge Communications, Inc. <http://www.mediafinder.com>.

Ulrich's Periodicals Directory. Print and online versions. R. R. Bowker. <http://www.bowker.com/>.

Ward's Business Directory of U.S. Private and Public Companies. Print and online versions. Information Access Co. <http://www.galegroup.com/>.

Working Press of the Nation. Information about newspapers, magazines, and broadcast media. R. R. Bowker. <http://www.bowker.com/>.

World Guide to Libraries. Print and CD-ROM versions. K. G. Saur. <http://www.galegroup.com/>.

World of Learning. Information about associations, universities, and publications. Europa Publications. <http://www.europapublications.co.uk/>.

Yearbook of International Organizations. Print and CD-ROM versions. K. G. Saur. <http://www.galegroup.com/>.

Glossary

Many definitions herein are reprinted from *The RFP Process: Effective Management of the Acquisition of Library Materials* (Frances C. Wilkinson and Connie Capers Thorson, Libraries Unlimited, 1998) with the permission of Libraries Unlimited, Inc. Others were composed or revised by the book's authors. Still others are attributed to their source by means of a citation included in the definition. Definitions in this glossary are not meant to serve as all-inclusive definitions, but rather the terms and phrases are defined in the context of the acquisitions process. Universal resource locators (URLs) were verified and accurate as of June 2, 2003.

adhesive binding. A method of binding in which pages are held together with glue rather than sewn together.

administrative services. Offices, often found in large libraries, that handle both accounting and personnel. Members of these operations have knowledge of institutional regulations and policies.

agent. A person or company retained by many publishers to represent their business interests to libraries and other clients. *See also* **dealer, jobber,** and **vendor.**

aggregator. A company providing electronic databases that include both indexing and full-text content that may have been originally published in a wide range of sources.

alkaline paper. Paper with little or no acid content and intended to last indefinitely.

alliance. A group of libraries or other entities that work together for a common goal or interest. Such a group can often negotiate **contracts**

for its members for various library services at greatly reduced prices. Also known as **consortium.**

ANSI ASC X12. An acronym for American National Standards Institute, Accredited Standards Committee X12. ASC develops standards in telecommunications and international trade. X12, a subcommittee of ASC, is charged with developing and maintaining electronic data interchange **(EDI)** standards. This standard structure for electronic communication specifies a hierarchical structure of transaction sets to facilitate electronic commerce data and business transaction exchange. Each transaction set is a different kind of document (e.g., purchase orders, invoicing, dates, times, etc.). (See http://www. x12.org.)

approval plan. Approval plans provide books matched to a preapproved profile of subjects desired by the library or institution. Librarians and other personnel physically review copies of the books and make their selections. Books not selected are returned to the **vendor.** Libraries receive shipments of approval books at predetermined intervals, generally weekly. Many approval plans also provide notification, either by print forms or electronically, for other books that the librarians may want to consider for purchase.

ARL. *See* **Association of Research Libraries.**

ASCII. American Standard Code for Information Interchange. This text file comes from the ASCII code, which is a specification that defines how various characters, numbers, spaces, and symbols are represented as computer data.

Association of Research Libraries (ARL). ARL is an organization consisting of more than 120 of the largest research and academic libraries in the United States and Canada. It provides leadership within the educational community in areas such as copyright, intellectual property, scholarly publishing, and access to international research resources. It operates as a forum for the exchange of ideas and action, as well as provides information via its statistics and measurement programs. (See http://www.arl.org for more information.)

authentication. A security technique in which computer systems authenticate the identity of the user so that unauthorized personnel cannot access systems to perform functions such as order materials or add unwanted material to a library database. **Password** or user ID access or **IP address** access is commonly used on the **World Wide Web** as well. *See also* **levels of access.**

authority records. Records in a bibliographic database that verify the accuracy of a personal or corporate name, the uniform title of a work, subject headings, and other important cataloging information. These records ensure that an author's name, for example, is always listed the same way in the card or online catalog and record retrieval is consistent and comprehensive.

automated fund accounting. An automated system that uses an order record to track fund accounting, which allows the library's system to make an intelligible record of the funds spent or to be spent for any item. The aggregate of this information is the fund-accounting record. Many integrated library systems offer elaborate fund-accounting subsystems in addition to the online catalog or inventory subsystems. The entire fund-accounting process is greatly enhanced by automation. See also **fund codes.**

bar code. A machine-readable code that appears as a pattern of vertical lines or stripes printed on books, **serials,** or media to identify them. It is used in libraries to check in or transfer titles, add **vendor** numbers to order records, or facilitate patron checkout.

BASIC. Book and Serials Industry Communications. A group of the **Book Industry Study Group** that develops **EDI** and other standards for the book and serials industries. In 1998, **BISAC** (Book Industry Systems Advisory Committee) and **SISAC** (Serials Industry Systems Advisory Committee) merged to form BASIC. The BISAC and SISAC names continue to be used when referring to the data interchange standards created by those groups. (See http://www.bisg.org for more information.)

bibliographic data. The information found in the cataloging record describing a book, **serial,** or other piece of library material that pertains to the publication of the piece. Such data provide the basis for the card or online cataloging record.

bibliographic form. Information available from most approval **vendor**s containing bibliographic and other data for books not intended to be supplied automatically as part of the **approval plan**'s profile. These data can be supplied on printed paper or in an electronic format.

bibliographic utilities. Entities such as **OCLC** and **RLIN** are the major providers of shared bibliographic or cataloging records to libraries for their online public catalogs.

BISAC. See **BASIC.**

blanket order plan. A **vendor** plan that does not provide for the return of unwanted titles by the library. The library must keep every title selected for and sent to it. Blanket order plans are designed to encompass numerous broad subject or geographical areas.

boilerplate. Standardized wording used by the library or purchasing office to provide the **vendor** with clear information regarding the type (**approval plans, firm orders, standing orders,** serials subscriptions) and format (print, electronic, **microform**) of materials that the **RFP** covers, the services the RFP seeks from the vendor, the estimated dollar value of the contract, the time frame in which the vendor has to respond, the **format** in which it should respond, a description of the library and its parent organization, the size and strength of the library collections, the state of library automation, contact names, and the criteria to be used to evaluate the vendor's proposal.

Book Industry Study Group. An organization representing all segments of the publishing industry. It collects and distributes information and statistics, establishes technical standards, and develops educational programs for the industry. *See also* **BASIC.**

bookseller. A person or company that sells books. Booksellers are known by various names, including **jobber, vendor,** and **agent.** The bookseller has a long and distinguished history; booksellers range in size from the corner bookstore to a large corporation with offices around the world.

Cataloging-in-Publication information. *See* **CIP.**

cataloging records. The permanent record for any publication, regardless of **format.** It includes information about the author or authors, the title, the publisher, the physical description, the edition, the subjects addressed in the publication, and any other facts perceived as important for a specific item.

CD-ROM. Compact disc read-only memory. A computer-based storage system.

cessation. The demise of a publication. A **vendor** of periodical materials should notify its customers when titles have ceased publication, so that the library may adjust its records accordingly.

CIP. Cataloging-in-Publication information. Publishers provide specified information to the Library of Congress when supplying the details required for the registration of copyright. The Library of Congress uses the information to develop a preliminary cataloging record for the title (regardless of **format**), which is then returned to the publisher. The CIP gives the **vendor,** library, or reader information about the probable cataloging and classification information for the title and is usually the first cataloging record provided to and by a bibliographic utility. It is often printed on the verso of the title page of a book.

claim. A report generated by the library and sent to the **vendor** or publisher when an item ordered is not received by the library. Some **ILS**s provide claims after a specified time has passed.

claim reports. Documentation relating to claims. There are two kinds: reports supplied by the **ILS** (recording the claims generated) and reports supplied by the **vendor** (responding to specific claims).

classification systems. Systems such as the Dewey decimal system or the Library of Congress system that streamline the arrangement of library materials. An item's classification is normally within a subject area denoted by a regularized combination of Roman letters and Arabic numerals. These classifications provide what are commonly known as call numbers. Such numbers are also used to provide information about the location of the material within the library.

CLIR. Council on Library and Information Resources. An organization that addresses issues related to **preservation,** resources for scholarship, digital libraries, the economics of information, leadership, and international developments in the field of information. (See http://www.clir.org for more information.)

codes. The mechanism in an **ILS** that accommodates bibliographic, order, check-in, and item record functions. Although this information is generally masked in the public record, it is available to library staff who use the coded information in a variety of ways. For example, there can be codes for frequency of publication, for **vendor**s, for languages of publication, for title changes, for funds, for locations, for reports on delayed publications, or for whether the prices invoiced are firm or subject to additional charges later. Codes are often the mechanism provided by the system to generate **management reports.**

collection development officer. A librarian who directs the efforts of a group of colleagues in managing and building the many diverse collections for the library. Most often found in large research, academic, and public libraries.

collection development policy statement. A policy statement describing the library's collecting philosophy and defining the relative importance of specific subjects. The statement for a specific subject may include information on the existing level of the collection as well as plans for future changes. The level is defined by the depth and strength of the collection; for example, a research-level collection would support doctoral and advanced independent research in a given subject.

comes-with title. A title that comes at no additional charge as a result of purchasing another title. For example, some publishers, particularly societies and associations, will supply a newsletter or other publication with a subscription to a journal.

competitive procurement process. An often state-mandated process, that affords **vendor**s an equal opportunity to submit proposals or bids stating their ability to supply goods or services—for example, books, **serials,** media, and equipment. In this process the rules and requirements are the same for all vendors, with no vendor being given special advantage. Competitive procurement is most often accomplished via the **RFP, RFQ, RFI,** or bid process.

computer-based services. Computerized services provided to the library by the **vendor.** They may include various system interfaces and capabilities, as well as other electronic services such as electronic tagging, ordering, claiming, **management reports,** vendor inventory, and usage statistics. *See also* **vendor's host system.**

conservation. Repairing or treating materials in order to maintain or restore the physical item. *See also* **preservation.**

consolidated approval plan. A plan in which the library consolidates all **approval plans** and book acquisitions with one **vendor.** This has the advantage of requiring only one profile, one set of vendor procedures, and one systems configuration to consider. Generally the **discount** offered is greater for larger accounts.

consortium. A group of libraries or other entities that work together for a common goal or interest. Many libraries are entering into consortium arrangements with other libraries to procure more advantageous pricing arrangements and other negotiated items.

contract. A legal, written agreement between the library or institution and the publisher or **vendor** clearly stating the requirements and specifications of the agreement. The person or persons authorized to sign contracts (librarian, purchasing officer, or institution attorney) will vary among institutions; check before signing any contract. For libraries using the **RFP** process, the contract may consist of a copy of the RFP and the vendor's proposal along with the award letter and conditions of the award.

contract compliance. The specification that both the library and the publisher or **vendor** must act in accordance with the terms of the contract. Noncompliance is usually grounds for canceling the contract.

conversion fee. The fee that some foreign **vendor**s charge to libraries that pay in U.S. dollars to convert the payments into the currency of the vendor's country. Most vendors, however, have banks in the United States so those libraries can make payment in dollars without penalty.

copublished material. An item that is published jointly by more than one entity. Art exhibition catalogs are examples of materials that are often copublished. Many small museums and galleries copublish the catalogs of their exhibitions because they cannot bear the costs alone. Such copublishing can be a problem if the **vendor** does not have adequate ways of guarding against **duplication.**

copy cataloging. The process of cataloging materials by taking existing records from resources such as **OCLC**'s **WorldCat** or **RLIN** and using them in the library's system with no, or minimal, changes to the record. Most items with acceptable records are English language materials published within the past decade by major publishers.

copyright holder. The individual publisher or developer who legally has the right to publish, reprint, or reproduce copyrighted material. The holder may or may not be the **vendor** of the material. Most states allow for the purchase of materials from the copyright holder without bid, regardless of the cost of the item.

copyright royalties. A sum paid to a copyright holder. Royalties must be paid to publishers for more than the minimal use of copyrighted material, regardless of format. Nonpayment can result in prosecution.

cost projections. Forecasts, estimates, or best guesses made by **vendor**s using information on current trends and gathered from publishers and other sources to determine the rate of inflation for various categories of materials. Libraries find cost projections supplied by vendors, particularly periodicals vendors, very useful because the projections help them allocate their budgets.

Council on Library and Information Resources. *See* **CLIR.**

country of origin. The country where an item is published. When determining if and how to divide its business, a library may prefer to purchase materials from a **vendor** in the country of origin.

coverage. The types of materials supplied by **vendor**s may include specific **formats,** publishers, geographic areas, subjects, or languages.

credit. A surplus assigned to a library's account when a payment has been made and the item is not supplied, when an item is defective, or when a **prepayment** discount is given.

critical-thinking skills. Those skills necessary to interpret, understand, use, analyze, and evaluate information, answers, reports, articles, and books.

customer service. Assistance provided to the library by the **vendor.** Such service includes a customer service representative, or representatives, to answer questions about orders, invoices, and **computer-based services; a sales representative** who visits the library; and any other service that will make for the efficient acquisition of materials.

customized reports. *See* **management reports.**

data integrity and privacy on the Internet. *See* **authentication; encryption.** *See also* **levels of access.**

deacidification. A process that neutralizes the acid content in paper to prevent further deterioration of the paper.

dealer. A **vendor** of library materials. *See also* **agent** or **jobber.**

debarment. The exclusion of a **vendor** from consideration for a contract for a valid reason.

deposit account. A sum of money kept in an account with the publisher or **vendor** for the library. This practice may result in a larger **discount** or deposit credit to the library.

Digital Library Federation. A **consortium** of libraries and related agencies providing leadership in the use of electronic information technologies. (See http://www.diglib.org for more information.)

digital object identifier. A system for identifying, exchanging, and locating digital items such as articles or **serials** issues. The unique number assigned to each item; it functions as a permanent electronic link. (See http://www.doi.org for more information.)

discount or discount rate. A reduction in the list price of materials. Most approval and many **vendor**s of **STO**s as well as many publishers will offer libraries substantial discounts. Although these discounts depend on the discounts offered to the vendors by publishers, such discounts are often established at a set rate for the library's purchases if the range of materials to be bought is fairly broad. Publishers and **regional library networks** may offer discounts on electronic resources to members of a **consortium**.

discussion list. A mailing list of **email** addresses for individuals who have subscribed to it. Generally devoted to a particular topic or subject area (e.g., ACQNET for acquisitions, or SERIALST for serials), such lists are used to discuss information and problems. Any message sent to the list will be sent to everyone in the group either automatically or through a moderator.

dispatch data. An **EDI** message from the publisher. It verifies the date of shipment of materials from the publisher and serves as the manifest notice of the shipment of goods. Libraries can use dispatch data to determine if a title was recently shipped and thus prevent the library from claiming it prematurely.

domain name. An alphabetic representation of an **Internet** site's **IP address** number (e.g., http://www.ala.org).

domestic approval plan. An **approval plan** for materials published in the United States. In some cases, domestic approval plans may cover Canadian materials.

domestic serial. A **serial** published in the United States or, in some cases, in Canada.

download. To transfer data from one system to another. For libraries, to download a record is to transfer that record from a **bibliographic utility** or other source to a local database or online catalog system. Downloading a record or other information can also be accomplished from a **vendor**'s online system.

Dublin Core. A way of describing electronic resources using standards agreed upon in a 1995 meeting held in Dublin, Ohio. (See http://dublincore.org for more information.)

duplication. The receipt of more copies of a title than the library ordered. Most academic libraries do not buy duplicates; however, public libraries frequently do. **Vendor**s of **approval plan**s must be able to exclude a library's **STO**s from titles supplied on the approval plan, as well as materials simultaneously published in the United States and England or the Netherlands.

EDI. Electronic data interchange. The computer-to-computer exchange of business messages in standard format transactions without the use of human intervention.

EDI translation software. Commercially available software packages ranging from personal computer stand-alone versions to mainframe versions that allow coded **EDI** messages to be converted to and from a native system, on the library's, **vendor**'s, or publisher's systems. These translation programs are used by some **ILS**s.

EDIFACT. *See* **UN-EDIFACT**.

electronic invoices. Electronically generated invoices processed on the library's **integrated library system. Vendor** data used in the process can be received over the **Internet,** on diskette, over phone lines, or on tape.

electronic journals. Journals that are published, distributed, and accessed electronically in addition to or instead of in paper form.

electronic ordering. Requests for materials sent directly to the **vendor**'s online system via the **Internet** as **email,** coded **EDI** messages, or **FTP** files. Electronic ordering eliminates the need for generating and sending paper purchase orders. Many **ILS**s provide electronic mail interchange for sending electronic orders.

email. Electronic mail messages distributed from one computer system to one or more persons using the **Internet.** Most **vendor**s and libraries are communicating via electronic mail.

encryption. The process of encoding, or locking, information before transmission to provide data security. Encryption files must be unencrypted or unlocked before the receiver can read the message. A **password** or user ID is required to access the information. *See also* **authentication** and **levels of access.**

ephemera. Printed materials that are intended to have short-lived interest or usefulness. These materials may be collected to support a research library's comprehensive collection.

extensible markup language. *See* **XML.**

fair use. The right to make a copy of a portion of a cataloged work for personal use or for **interlibrary loan** without permission of the copyright owner.

file transfer protocol. *See* **FTP.**

firewall. Single or multiple security devices that reside in computers or partitioned sections of a computer that deny access to unauthorized users. Firewalls are generally used to separate the public or external sections from the private or internal sections of a library or company's computer. Users must have a **password** or user ID or authorized **IP address** to pass through a firewall to reach the desired data.

firm order. A book ordered on a **title-by-title selection** basis, whether from a publisher, book **dealer,** or **vendor.** It is normally not returnable.

format. The physical rendition of information (e.g., book, microfilm, videotape, electronic).

frequency change. A change in the publication interval. A title, generally a **serial** title, is produced at certain intervals or frequencies (e.g., weekly, monthly, quarterly, annually); a frequency change means the title is now produced at an interval that is different from its previous interval.

FTP. File transfer protocol. Allows the transfer of files from one computer to another. The user can either transfer files electronically from remote computers back to the user's computer or can transfer files from the user's computer to a remote computer. For example, the library can transfer files for its current shipment of approval books electronically from the **vendor**'s computer back to the library's computer to create bibliographic and order records for those books in its **ILS.**

fulfillment agency. A company hired by publishers to handle mailing of **serials** issues to subscribers, either individuals, libraries, or other entities.

fulfillment rate. The time period that the **vendor** takes to fill orders and the number of orders filled. Many electronic systems generate this information on a regular basis.

full text. The complete content of an item that is available in electronic format. It may be an individual article or the complete contents of a journal issue or book.

fund codes. Codes used in **ILS**s to represent accounts of money devoted to different purchasing areas (e.g., broad areas such as science or humanities or narrower areas such as psychology or dance). Fund codes define the specific budget line an item will be charged against in an ILS. They can also be supplied to **vendor**s to add to the electronically downloaded or invoiced records. In addition, they are used to produce **management reports** by fund.

gateway. A means to connect computer networks, allowing the transfer of data between them. It also allows users on one network access to another network. *See also* **portal.**

general terms and conditions. Stipulations in a **contract** used to define those issues that affect the award, fulfillment, and possible longevity of the contract. Such provisions may include but are not limited to information regarding acceptance and rejection of goods and services, addresses for notices, assignment of the contract, multiple awards, cancellation, changes and alterations after the award, conflict-of-interest clauses, discounts, governing law, indemnification and insurance, inspections, patent and copyright indemnity, penalties, proposed negotiation rules, termination and delays, warranties, and equal opportunity and affirmative action statements.

gifts and exchange. A department, section, or area in a library that is responsible for receiving (often unsolicited) gifts from a variety of sources and exchanging materials (usually periodicals) with other libraries both nationally and internationally.

global change. An operation in **integrated library systems** (generally requiring one or very few keystrokes) that affects a specified field in all records that contain that field, substituting one field or code for another.

hot-button issues. Issues that are of immediate but perhaps fleeting interest.

HTML. Hypertext markup language. HTML is the language that defines how to code a document for use in **World Wide Web** applications and is the programming source code behind the Web browser display of a document. HTML is a subset of SGML (standard generalized markup language). *See also* **SGML** and **XML.**

hypertext or hyperlink. Links between **World Wide Web** resources are known as hyperlinks, and the documents that contain the links are known as hypertext documents. World Wide Web documents have **HTML** commands embedded in them that connect the link with the text. Hyperlinks or icons can be clicked on to lead to other **webpage**s or to other sections of the same webpage to facilitate nonlinear review or connections between content.

ICOLC. International Coalition of Library Consortia. An organization that facilitates discussion among library consortia on electronic information resources and issues. (See http://www.library.yale.edu/consortia/ for more information.)

ILS. Integrated library system. An integrated library system is one in which components or modules work together to perform library functions, such as ordering, receiving, claiming, cataloging, **online public access catalog,** circulation, reserves, **interlibrary loan,** and **World Wide Web** and database access, providing on-site as well as remote use to patrons and library staff. ILSs are also sometimes referred to as library management systems.

information broker. A person or company that sells information.

information provider. *See* **information broker.**

integrated library system. *See* **ILS.**

interdisciplinary materials. Materials involving two or more academic, scientific, or artistic areas of learning or disciplines.

interlibrary loan. A process in which libraries lend materials to other libraries, or borrow materials from other libraries, at the request of their patrons.

International Coalition of Library Consortia. *See* **ICOLC.**

Internet. A global network of linked computer networks; the series of interconnected networks that include local area, regional, national, and international backbone networks. The U.S. Department of Defense created the Internet for military purposes. It now serves a broader global community including educational institutions, government agencies, commercial organizations, and individuals.

invoice data element. A unit of information displayed on or pertaining to an invoice. It may include information displayed on the invoice such as library bill-to or ship-to addresses, title, library-generated purchase order number, **ISBN** or **ISSN, fund code,** and **discount** or service charge for books and **serials.** In addition, for serials, frequency of publication and notice of cessation or title change may also be displayed on the invoice. Elements pertaining to the invoice include format of the invoice or number of paper copies desired.

IP address. Internet protocol address. A unique identifier composed of four sets of numbers separated by periods that indicates how to reach an Internet computer (e.g., IP number = 192.35.222.222). IP addresses are used to determine the path to a computer's physical location via interconnected wide area networks and local area networks.

ISBN. International Standard Book Number. Established in 1969, it is a unique ten-digit number assigned to a nonserial publication. It can be used for ordering, invoicing, and searching for a title in an electronic database.

ISSN. International Standard Serial Number. A unique eight-digit number assigned to a **serial** publication. It can be used for ordering, invoicing, and searching for a title in an electronic database.

JavaScript. A scripting language for **World Wide Web** pages. Scripts written with JavaScript can be embedded in **HTML** documents that function independent of operating system platforms (Windows, Mac, Unix). JavaScript is intended to provide a quicker and simpler language for enhancing **webpage**s and servers. JavaScripts can perform an action, such as play an audio file or execute a program displaying information when a user opens or exits a page.

jobber. A person or company also referred to as a wholesaler or a subcontractor of a good or service, or one who deals with something for profit; may be used interchangeably with **vendor.**

levels of access. Password levels, determined by the system administrators, that can provide or deny access and show reduced or enhanced information to an individual user in an **integrated library system** or other electronic system. For example, while bibliographers may need to have access to order information, they probably do not need access to the program that actually places an order. *See also* **authentication.**

library-generated purchase order number. A unique number (usually ending in a check digit—a randomly assigned number) generated by an **integrated library system** or other electronic ordering system.

licensing agreement. A written contract between the library or institution and the entity authorizing access to certain digital information and electronic materials that sets forth specific terms, rules, and regulations for the use of the particular database or product. *See also* **contract** and **general terms and conditions.**

long-range plan. A formulated, systematic plan for predicting future trends and directing future activities to achieve expected results for an organization for periods longer than one year. *See also* **strategic planning.**

machine-readable cataloging. *See* **MARC.**

management reports. Reports are made to order or modified according to individual library requirements. They include reports about current expenditures, historical expenditures (e.g., the last three years), fulfillment time, and number of titles supplied in a given subject. Reports can often be generated on-site via access to **computer-based services** provided by the **vendor.**

MARC. Machine-readable cataloging. It provides a standard for file, record, and data structure for transfer of bibliographic information.

mass-market paperbacks. Books with paper covers, usually about 6 3/4 inches by 4 1/4 inches, generally printed on acidic paper and not intended for extended library use. *See also* **trade paperback books.**

master copy. The original document that is kept as the archival copy and used only to create copies that are intended for circulation.

membership. A library may become an institutional member of an association, society, group, or organization either to support the goals of the group or to obtain its published materials. Memberships may be the only way to acquire the publication of some groups.

metadata. Data about data; records describing items using standards such as the **Dublin Core** or **MARC** records.

microform. The photographic images of a document reproduced on film or paper. Microfiche and microfilm are common types of microform. Although some materials are produced only in these **formats,** they are also particularly popular and useful formats for materials no longer in print or materials that need to be preserved, such as periodicals or newspapers. They generally require far less storage space than paper documents.

midlist books. In publishing, books that are expected to sell a moderate amount of copies as compared to books that are expected to be best-sellers. These books rarely receive major publicity and have relatively small **print runs.**

mix. The mix is the percentage of titles that fall into a given subject category (e.g., science, humanities, social sciences, or art) for **serials** or **approval plans.** The **vendor** receives varying levels of **discount** or no discount at all from publishers, with some subject areas tending to generate higher discounts than others do. The discount rate that the vendor receives from the publisher affects the discount the library receives from the vendor for books or the service charge that the library pays to the vendor for serials.

monograph. "A nonserial item (i.e., an item either complete in one part or complete, or intended to be completed, in a finite number of separate parts)" (Michael Gorman and Paul Winkler, editors, *Anglo-American Cataloging Rules,* 2nd ed., 1988 revised, American Library Association).

monographic series. "A group of separate items related to one another by the fact that each item bears, in addition to its own title proper, a collective title applying to the group as a whole. The individual items may or may not be numbered" (Michael Gorman and Paul Winkler, editors, *Anglo-American Cataloging Rules*, 2nd ed., 1988 revised, American Library Association).

monographs in publishers' series. Volumes published in a series that have only a very broad subject in common. Created as a marketing device by publishers.

music score. "A series of staves on which all the different instrumental and/or vocal parts of a musical work are written, one under the other in vertical alignment, so that the parts may be read simultaneously" (Michael Gorman and Paul Winkler, editors, *Anglo-American Cataloging Rules*, 2nd ed., 1988 revised, American Library Association).

news alerting service. *See* **push or pull World Wide Web technologies.**

NGO. Nongovernmental organization. Organizations, such as Amnesty International or UNESCO, that are not part of any national group.

nonprint media. Formats such as audiovisual, **microform,** or software media; materials not printed on paper.

nonreturnable. Materials that cannot be sent back to the **vendor** or publisher from which they were obtained by the library for a refund, exchange, or **credit.** Some publishers, particularly small ones or professional organizations, will sell to a vendor only when there is an agreement that no titles can be returned.

nonsubject parameters. Characteristics in a library's **approval plan** profile that do not relate to the subject of the books. They may include characteristics such as **format,** academic level, price, and publisher. Applied in combination with the **subject parameters,** they determine which books are to be sent to the library and which are to be excluded.

numbered series. "A separately numbered sequence of volumes within a series or serial" (Michael Gorman and Paul Winkler, editors, *Anglo-American Cataloging Rules*, 2nd ed., 1988 revised, American Library Association).

OCLC. Online Computer Library Center, Inc. OCLC is a **bibliographic utility** based in Dublin, Ohio. It provides bibliographic, database, and other library services to libraries throughout the world, often through **regional library network**s also referred to as regional intermediary vendors.

Online Computer Library Center, Inc. *See* **OCLC.**

online public access catalog. *See* **OPAC.**

OPAC. Online public access catalog. Online records of the holding of a library or group of libraries. It may also include information about library services.

open archive. An electronic database containing full-text articles, **preprint**s, or documents, usually available without fees or restrictions on access.

out-of-print materials. Items no longer available from the publisher or from **vendor**s, and for which there are no plans to print more copies.

out-of-print searching. A service in which a **vendor** attempts to locate and secure for the library books, **serials,** and media that are no longer in print.

out-of-stock materials. Items no longer available from the publisher or from **vendor**s but which might be reprinted.

outsourcing. The contracting out of certain library functions to a private enterprise. Using a **vendor** to obtain cataloged, shelf-ready books is a form of outsourcing.

packages. Combinations of publications, possibly including journals, conference proceedings, or books, sold by the publisher as a group. Some packages include electronic versions in addition to, or instead of, the printed versions.

password. A code required to access a computer system or electronic resource.

periodical. *See* **serial.**

portal. A method of providing access to a wide range of electronic information that is transparent to the user. It allows the user to have direct access to resources without having to log in to each different source. The content is dynamic; the search engines gather information continuously. A portal may be personalized by individual users.

prepayment. A payment made for a specific book, **serial,** electronic resource, or other material prior to its being supplied to the library. This practice is especially common for **nonreturnable** or expensive materials. Many publishers require prepayment for selected titles, while most **vendor**s do not require prepayment.

prepayment credit. A percentage of the total library expenditure prepaid to periodical **vendor**s who offer libraries a prepayment discount for early payment of the annual renewal invoice.

preprint. A preliminary version of research, a conference presentation, and so on made available prior to its formal publication.

preservation. The slowing or preventing of deterioration of materials by a number of methods including **conservation,** binding, microfilming, or scanning.

print run. The number of copies of a book that are printed by the publisher.

procurement code. A set of legal rules or statutes for acquiring goods or services.

professional association or society. A group or body of individuals united by a common interest, principle, or purpose pertaining to a specific profession. Such a group may publish important materials of special interest to its members. It often makes its materials available to libraries only through institutional membership in the organization. *See also* **membership.**

profile. The document that tells a **vendor** what materials to supply or not to supply on an **approval plan** or **blanket order plan.** It contains instructions not only on what subjects are to be included and excluded but also on such **nonsubject parameters** as **format,** cost, publisher, language, and **country of origin.** The library and the vendor must work together closely to create the profile, as it is the instrument that determines the success or failure of any plan. The profile must be monitored continuously and modified as needed for the plan to function optimally.

property stamping. The act of stamping a book or **serial** (generally using a rubber stamp and inkpad) with the name of the library and other pertinent information to indicate the library's ownership of the material. This service can be provided as part of a **vendor**'s **shelf-ready materials** service, as a **value-added service,** for an additional fee. A label or tag identification can be used instead of a property stamp.

purchase order number. A unique number assigned by the library to identify an order. This number may be assigned automatically by the library's **ILS** or manually if the library's acquisition system is not electronic.

purchasing department. The department in an institution charged with overseeing the purchase of materials. The purchasing department does not usually involve itself in the purchase of specific books and serials for the library because of that process's highly specialized nature, but it will generally oversee the **RFP** process to ensure that all phases follow competitive procurement regulations and process the contract award documents. It may also be the department that reviews, negotiates, and signs **contracts** for electronic resources.

push or pull World Wide Web technologies. Mechanisms that allow the user to either receive or get desired information. Push technology sends data from the **World Wide Web** to the user without further user intervention; the user requests this specified type of data once and updates are sent automatically as they become available. Pull technology is used by the user to access World Wide Web information directly. For example, a user signs up for a **news alerting service** and receives automatic messages on specific topics (push); a user goes to a company's World Wide Web site to find and read the press release section (pull).

rapid update. A function, available on most **ILS**s, that allows the operator to quickly change a data element in fixed-length fields or an information string in variable-length fields, in one record after the other, making the same change to each record.

realia. Three-dimensional objects such as artifacts, models, relics, and dioramas. Usually acquired for special collections or for school and classroom use.

reformat. To transfer information from one **format** to another as in microfilming or digitizing.

regional and local publications. Materials published by small local and regional publishers, which are often issued in very small print runs. Most large **vendors** of **approval plan**s are not able to supply such materials; libraries should arrange with local vendors to acquire these items.

regional intermediary vendor. *See* **regional library network.**

regional library network. Any nonprofit, multistate organization that promotes, develops, and supports programs related to access to information services for its library members, such as Amigos and SOLINET. Also referred to as regional intermediary **vendor**s.

request for information. *See* **RFI.**

request for proposal. *See* **RFP.**

request for quotation. *See* **RFQ.**

Research Libraries Group. *See* **RLG.**

Research Libraries Information Network. *See* **RLIN.**

RFI. Request for information. The RFI asks for general information from the **vendor** regarding its available services. It does not state library requirements or desired elements. RFIs are often valuable tools for a library that is trying to determine what it requires prior to writing the **RFP.**

RFP. Request for proposal. The RFP can be viewed as a process as well as a document. As a process, it provides a clear, impartial method for a library to state its needs, evaluate **vendor** proposals, and justify its vendor selection and contract award, based on objective decisions regarding those proposals rather than solely on emotional reactions either for or against a particular vendor. As a document, it can be used to monitor vendor compliance and performance. In the document, the library's requirements and desired elements for vendor services are clearly articulated as are the steps to be followed for vendors that wish to submit proposals to handle the library's account or accounts.

RFQ. Request for quote or quotation. When using an RFQ, awards are based on the lowest-price bid for a good or service. No other factors are taken into consideration in a true RFQ, although in some modified versions of the RFQ they may be considered to a lesser degree. This process is best suited to the purchase of goods rather than services.

Richard Abel. The **bookseller** usually credited with the development of **approval plan**s.

RLG. Research Libraries Group. Established in 1974, it is an alliance of universities, libraries, societies, and other groups with research collections. In addition to addressing collaborative approaches to sharing access to these resources, it also develops and provides access to information databases. RLG developed the RLG union catalog that includes data describing books, periodicals, media, maps, posters, manuscripts, and other materials. (See http://www.rlg.org for more information.)

RLIN. Research Libraries Information Network. An online catalog and bibliographic utility of the Research Libraries Group.

routing slips. Slips used to send or route specific publications to departments or groups of individuals upon arrival and processing in the library.

rush orders. Orders that are placed with a **vendor** or publisher with the understanding that they will be supplied to the library on a priority basis.

sales representative. An **agent** for the **vendor,** representing its products and services to libraries. The sales representative visits the library one or more times per year as needed to consult about the library's needs, check on the library's satisfaction with the vendor's service, discuss trends in the marketplace, and apprise the library of new developments or services available through the vendor.

sample issue request. A request by the library to the publisher or **vendor** to supply a free issue of a **serial.** The library uses the sample issue to decide whether to add the title to its collection.

security strips. Magnetic strips placed in the spine of a book, placed between the pages of a **serial,** or affixed to **nonprint media.** The strips are then sensitized so that an alarm will sound if someone attempts to take the materials out of the building or area without checking them out and properly desensitizing them. The alarm system that reads the magnetic strip is located in detection panels that are positioned at library exits.

selectors or bibliographers. Generally found in academic or large public libraries, a librarian who is assigned to determine which materials to purchase for a particular subject area or areas. He or she monitors a budget allocation, **approval plan**s, and periodical expenditures for the assigned areas. A selector or bibliographer may also be responsible for working closely with academic departments or other constituents and for managing and evaluating the collections in their areas.

serial. "A publication in any medium issued in successive parts bearing numerical or chronological designations and intended to continue indefinitely. Serials include periodicals, newspapers, annuals (reports, yearbooks, etc.); the journals, memoirs, proceedings, transactions, etc., of societies; and numbered monographic series" (Michael Gorman and Paul Winkler, editors, *Anglo-American Cataloging Rules,* 2nd ed., 1988 revised, American Library Association).

serials check-in. A control system that records the receipt of **serials** (periodicals and other continuing publications). Serials check-in may be manual, using cards to record data, often housed in a Kardex™

file system, or automated, using a sophisticated database program in an in-house system, or a serials control module in an **ILS.**

serials holdings (statements or data) standard. The standard for serials holdings that sets the rules for creating consistent records of the serials located at a particular institution. It outlines the data elements, prescribed punctuation, and specification for displaying the data. According to the standard, serials holdings statements can be prepared at four levels of increasing specificity. The volumes or years of a **serial** a library owns are accessible to patrons and staff in the holdings data, which state volumes, issues, and years owned, as well as location.

serials price increase. The amount or percentage that the price of a **serial** or category of serials has increased from one year or period to another. Because the cost of serials has grown at such a rapid rate, many libraries, especially large academic and research libraries, have experienced difficulty subscribing to all the titles needed by their patrons. Prices have increased faster than the consumer price index over the past decade and a half, with serials inflation generally around 10 percent per year. Even with moderate serials cancellation projects, serials expenditures continue to erode materials budgets. Total annual serials expenditures vary with the type and size of the library but generally range from a few hundred dollars for school and small public libraries to millions of dollars for medium to large academic and research libraries.

serials vendor. *See* **subscription service.**

service charge. A charge above the cost of the titles managed by the **vendor** for the assistance or service provided to the library. The amount of the service charge generally depends on the size and **mix** of the library's account. Service charges are usually associated with **serials** accounts due to limited or no publisher **discounts,** especially in the humanities and social sciences.

service representative. The person at the **vendor**'s office who is assigned to assist the library with all areas of its account, ranging from answering simple questions to solving complex problems.

set. A group of materials expected to have a specific number of volumes usually determined in advance. The set may be published all at once or as a series of volumes over a period of years. Publication ceases when the set is complete or discontinued.

SGML. Standard generalized markup language. An extensive international set of rules for document tagging that indicates the nature of the content and display of electronic publications. *See also* **HTML** and **XML.**

shelf-ready materials. Journals and books that are supplied by a **vendor,** already processed and ready to be shelved by the library, for an added charge. They are cataloged, have spine labels with call numbers, are marked with the library's property stamp, and are ready for circulating. Various other services, such as affixing **security strips** and **serials check-in** from a remote site, may be available; services vary by vendor.

SICI. Serials Item Contribution Identifier. Developed by **SISAC,** it includes the **ISSN** and other identifying information and can be used for **interlibrary loan, serials check-in,** and serials claiming as a unique identifier. It can be used to identify individual articles for abstracting and indexing services or to identify **serials** issues for ordering and claiming.

simultaneous publications. Books that are published at the same time in two or more countries—for example, in the United States and the United Kingdom. **Vendor**s of **approval plan**s providing both domestic and foreign publications need mechanisms to avoid supplying the book twice.

single-purchase serial. A **serial** purchased as a single issue or volume, often to fill in a gap in the library's collection. An issue devoted to a special topic may also be acquired as a single purchase.

SISAC. *See* **BASIC.**

site licenses. *See* **licensing agreement.**

societies, associations, research institutes. *See* **professional association or society.**

sole source. The only source that can supply an item or a service.

split a contract. To award segments of a **contract** to two or more **vendor**s.

standard. A measure that serves as a nationally or internationally agreed upon basis or example to conform to, ensuring consistency. There are many standards within the library field such as **ISBN** and **ISSN.**

standard generalized markup language. *See* **SGML.**

standing order. *See* **STO.**

statement of financial solvency. A statement supplied on behalf of a **vendor** by a reputable financial institution or auditor attesting to its financial strength and indicating its capacity to meet its liabilities. This document provides important information to a library that is deciding which vendor to do business with.

STM publishers. Companies that publish scientific, technical, and medical materials.

STO. Standing order. An instruction to a **vendor** to regularly supply a specified title. Standing orders are generally placed for nonperiodical **serial**s such as annuals, yearbooks, and series. These titles are not generally paid for until the library receives them. Some libraries, however, opt to prepay for them as part of their serials renewals, even though the price may be an estimate.

strategic planning. A formulated, detailed plan in which an organization identifies and develops its long-range goals and selects activities for achieving them. *See also* **long-range planning.**

SUB. An abbreviation for subscription. Subscriptions are a regular method of procurement for publications such as periodicals, journals, popular magazines, newspapers, abstracts, and indexes generally issued more than once a year. These are generally paid for in advance of receipt by the library.

subject parameters. The part of the **approval plan** profile that specifies which subjects should be sent to the library as books, which should be provided as bibliographic notifications on forms or slips or electronically, and which should not be sent at all. They are used in combination with **nonsubject parameters** to form the library's total approval profile.

subscription. See **SUB.**

subscription agency. See **subscription service.**

subscription agent. See **subscription service.**

subscription service. A commercial **agency** that processes **serial**s orders for all types of libraries. It provides a variety of services for the librarian including placing orders with the publisher, processing renewals, consolidating many publisher invoices into one or several **vendor**-generated invoices, processing **claim**s, and providing a variety of specialized customer and **computer-based services.** Vendors maintain detailed records and **management reports** for titles that the library has on order with them.

suspended publication. A publication that is temporarily not produced. Reasons for this vary but might involve financial exigency, natural disaster, war, or other similar difficulties.

table of contents notes. The 505 field of the **MARC** record into which a cataloging agency can input table of contents information. Many approval **vendor**s who provide cataloging as part of their service offer this **valued-added service.** Libraries that acquire records with tables of contents have the ability to index this field in their local online systems, thus enabling patrons to search for words appearing in the table of contents.

TCP/IP. Transmission control protocol/**Internet** protocol. The set of protocols on the Internet that allows **Telnet** sessions, **file transfer protocol, email,** and other services. These protocols are used to organize computers and communication devices into a network. Specifically, the IP transmits the data from one place to another, and the TCP manages the flow and ensures that the data are transmitted correctly.

technical report literature. Documents issued by scientific laboratories, departments, or government agencies dealing with technical information. These are generally obtained from the issuing body. Many defense laboratories have electronic collections of their reports (some retroactive to the 1970s). The National Technical Information Service (NTIS) is the central source for U.S. government scientific, technical, engineering, and business reports. (See http://www.ntis.gov for more information.)

Telnet. The communications layer of the **TCP/IP** suite that allows users, programmers, and system administrators remote access to a server or computer, enabling a variety of communications to occur.

title-by-title selection. Book or **serial** titles that are selected one at a time instead of being received through **approval plans, bibliographic forms** or slips or electronic notifications, **STO**s, or **SUB**s. These titles may be ordered on the basis of selector or bibliographer decisions or patron requests. *See also* **firm orders.**

title change. The action of a publisher of a **serial** to change the title of that serial from one name to another. It is imperative that a **vendor** have mechanisms in place to notify libraries of such changes so that receipt can continue without interruption.

trade paperback books. Books with paper covers that are generally printed on nonacidic paper and intended to withstand numerous library circulations. They may be original or reprinted works. *See also* **mass-market paperbacks.**

transfer assistance allowance. A onetime allowance granted by the **vendor** to the library, usually in the form of a credit percentage or a reduced **service charge,** to defray the cost to the library of transferring its titles to one vendor from another vendor.

transfer process. The transfer of titles in a given category (e.g., **domestic serial**s, European periodicals) from one or more **vendor**s to one or more vendors, requiring careful planning. Also known as the transition process.

transition process. *See* **transfer process.**

translation software. *See* **EDI translation software.**

transmission control protocol/Internet protocol. *See* **TCP/IP.**

trial electronic resources request. A request by the library of the publisher or **vendor** to supply free access to an electronic resource for a limited period. The library generally uses such a trial to decide whether to add an electronic resource to its collection.

UN-EDIFACT. United Nations, Electronic Data Interchange for Administration, Commerce, and Transport. It has developed into an international level of book and serial **EDI** messages for the entire business cycle. EDIFACT is being implemented in many **integrated library systems** in Europe and the United States. (See http://www.unece.org/trade/untdid/welcome.htm for more information.)

university press. A press representing the publishing arm of the university to which it is attached. University presses range in size from large, publishing more than two hundred books a year, to small, producing very small **print runs.** Supported and controlled by their universities, they are known for publishing scholarly research for specialized audiences, but they may publish some trade books intended for general readership, as well as scholarly journals. Their publishing programs often reflect local research specialties or regional interests. Although many presses, especially smaller ones, exist primarily on subsidies from their universities, others make a profit.

URL. Uniform resource locator. The address that represents a **Web server** and its documents. It is usually preceded by "http://" for websites and often, but not always, includes "www." For example, the URL for the American Library Association is http://www.ala.org.

user ID. *See* **password.**

value-added network. *See* **VAN.**

value-added service. A service offered by a **vendor** that enhances a basic product thus adding value to it, such as adding **table of contents notes** to a cataloging record.

VAN. Value-added network. A special network that provides a communications infrastructure through which messages travel to mailboxes for storage until they are picked up. VANs ensure the security of the communication and track the transmissions and receipt of the messages, as well as ensure that the messages meet **standards** such as **X12,** thus adding value to the network.

vanity publisher. A publisher that requires authors to pay for some or all of the costs of producing their books.

vendor. The seller or provider of materials to libraries, regardless of **format.** May be used interchangeably with **agent, dealer,** and **jobber.**

vendor evaluation project. A plan designed to appraise or judge vendor performance—how well the vendor met the conditions of its **contract** with the library. Such factors as vendor turnaround time for orders, invoices, and **claims** as well as other performance data elements can be quantitatively measured. More subjective, qualitative measures regarding the vendor's service may also be considered in the evaluation.

vendor performance data. Data used in vendor evaluation projects, including such elements as **fulfillment rates** or fulfillment times, rate of returns for approval plans, number of **claims,** and claims response time. Many **ILS**s and other library systems can provide some of these data for the library.

vendor-sponsored instructional program. A program that provides instruction and information for new library customers to acquaint them with the **vendor** and its products and services, and for new or existing customers regarding developments in the marketplace.

vendor's host system (vendor's in-house system). A computer system used internally by the **vendor.** Customers may or may not have access directly to the system via **Telnet** or the **World Wide Web.** Generally, such systems are proprietary systems with interfaces to provide customer access via **Z39.50** or a native mode. *See also* **computer-based services.**

Web browser technologies. Computer programs that allow users to access websites and **webpage**s by converting **HTML** into readable text, images, and sounds. Browsers (e.g., Netscape Navigator, Internet Explorer) can be graphical or text based.

Web server. A service that makes a set of **webpage**s available to users.

webpage. Data (text, graphics, and audio) that are stored on a Web server as a file written in **HTML** and identified by a **URL.** The webpage may refer to other webpages via **hypertext** links. A **vendor**'s webpage outlines its services and other information about the company's background.

WorldCat. An **OCLC** product, available for remote electronic searching, that is made up of international holdings cataloged by OCLC member libraries. It is a searchable bibliographic database of books, **serials,** recordings, manuscripts, and other materials.

World Wide Web. *See* **WWW.**

WWW (W3 or the Web). World Wide Web. Created in 1989, it is a global **hypertext** system that uses the Internet to access and retrieve information. The WWW is navigated by use of a Web browser to access **HTML**-coded documents on **Web server**s around the world.

X12. *See* **ANSI ASC X12.**

XML. Extensible markup language. A subset of **SGML** that is designed for Web documents. It defines the kind of information contained in a document or data source rather than the display of the information, which is defined by **HTML** code.

Z39.50 1988 protocol. The national standard developed by the National Information Standards Organization (NISO) titled "Information Retrieval Service Definition and Protocol Specification for Library Applications." A search-and-retrieval protocol by which one computer can query another computer and transfer resulting records. This protocol provides the framework for **online public access catalog** users to search remote catalogs on the Internet using the commands of their own local systems, bringing a seamless interface between and among systems that would otherwise be incompatible. (See http://www.loc.gov/z3950/agency for more information.)

Index

About the Authors

FRANCES C. WILKINSON is Director, Acquisitions and Serials Department, General Library, and Associate Professor of Librarianship, University of New Mexico, Albuquerque.

LINDA K. LEWIS is Associate Professor of Librarianship, University of New Mexico, Albuquerque.